Theoretical Software Diagnostics

Collected Articles
Fourth Edition

Dmitry Vostokov
Software Diagnostics Institute

OpenTask

Published by OpenTask, Republic of Ireland

OpenTask books are available through booksellers and distributors worldwide. For further information or comments, send requests to press@opentask.com.

A CIP catalog record for this book is available from the British Library.

ISBN-13: 978-1-912636-91-4 (Paperback)

Revision 4.01 (April 2024)

Table of Contents

Table of Contents 3

Preface to the Fourth Edition 11

Preface to the Third Edition 12

Preface to the Second Edition 13

About the Author 14

Threads of Thinking 15

Volume 1: August 2006 – December 2007 16
Volume 2: January 2008 – September 2008 17
Volume 3: October 2008 – June 2009 18
Volume 4: July 2009 – January 2010 19
Volume 5: February 2010 – October 2010 20
Volume 6: November 2010 – October 2011 21
Volumes 7 – 10: November 2011 – May 2017 22
Volumes 11 – 13: June 2017 – July 2020 23
Volumes 14 – 16 and Beyond: August 2020 – Present 24

Volume 1 25

Multiple Exceptions 25
Four Pillars 28
Five Golden Rules 29
Critical Thinking 30
Troubleshooting as Debugging 31
What is a Software Defect? 33
Four Causes of Crash Dumps 35
What is Memory Dump Analysis? 37
Crashes and Hangs Differentiated 38
Memory Dump - A Mathematical Definition 39
Threads as Braided Strings in Abstract Space 41

Volume 2 45

Debugware Patterns 45

Three Main Ideas of Debugging 46
The Hidden Tomb in Pyramid of Software Change 47
Ceteris Paribus in Comparative Troubleshooting 48
Object-Oriented Debugging and Troubleshooting 49
Component-Based Debugging and Troubleshooting 50
Domain-Driven Debugging and Troubleshooting 51
Causal Models 52
PARTS: Problem Solving Power of Thought 53
Memoretics 54
Memiotics 55
Memory Analysis 56

Volume 3 57

Introduction to Software Trace Analysis Patterns 57
Software Narratology: A Definition 58
Software Trace: A Mathematical Definition 59
Geometrical Debugging 60
Riemann Programming Language 62
The Measure of Debugging and Memory Dump Analysis Complexity 63
I'm RARE 64
T&D Labyrinth 65
Efficient vs. Effective: DATA View 67
A Copernican Revolution in Debugging 68
Is Memory Dump Analysis a Science? 69
Universal Memory Dump: A Definition 70
Quantum Memory Dumps 71
On Subjectivity of Software Defects 72
My Dangerous Idea: Parameterized Science 73
Unique Events and Historical Narratives 74
Chemistry of Virtual Memory 75
Graphical Notation for Memory Dumps 77

Volume 4 81

Succession of Patterns 81
Workaround Patterns 82
Metaphorical Bijectionism: A Method of Inquiry 83
Memory Dumps as Posets 86
MemD Category 88
Operating Closure of Memory 91

Fiber Bundle of Memory Space 93
Cubic Memory Representation........ 94
Manifold Memory Space 96
Extending Multithreading to Multibraiding (Adjoint Threading) 98

Volume 5........ 103

Software Behavior Patterns........ 103
Structural Memory Patterns........ 104
General Memory Analysis........ 105
Memory Systems Language........ 106
Notation for Memory and Trace Analysis........ 107
Models of Software Behavior 108
Category Theory and Troubleshooting........ 109
Collective Pointer 110
On Unconscious........ 113
Psychoanalysis of Software Troubleshooting and Debugging........ 114
Archaeological Foundations for Memory Analysis 115
Software Chorography and Chorology: A Definition 116
Basic Software PLOTs 118
The Extended Software Trace........ 120
Presenting a Software Story 121
Two Readings of a Software Trace 122

Volume 6........ 125

Intelligence Analysis Patterns........ 125
A.C.P. Root Cause Analysis Methodology........ 126
Function Activity Theory........ 127
Close and Deconstructive Readings of a Software Trace 128
Analysis, Architectural, Design, Implementation and Usage Debugging Patterns 129
Generative Debugging........ 130
Metadefect Template Library........ 131
Orbifold Memory Space 132
Uses of Memoretics........ 133
Crossdisciplinary Memoretics as Interdisciplinary Science 134
Coarse vs. Fine Grained DNA of Software Behavior 135
The Way of Philip Marlowe: Abductive Reasoning for Troubleshooting and Debugging 136
The New School of Debugging........ 137
A Periodic Table of Software Defects 138

User Interface Problem Analysis Patterns 139

Volume 7 141

Software Anti-Narrative 141
Narremes in Software Narratology 142
Narralog - A Software Trace Modeling Language 143
What is a Software Narrative? 144
Software Narrative Planes 145
Software Narratology Square 147
Software Trace Analysis Patterns Domain Hierarchy 148
Generalized Software Narrative and Trace 149
Unified Computer Diagnostics: Incorporating Hardware Narratology 150
Introducing Software Narratology of Things (Software NT) 151
What are Software Trace and Memory Dump Analysis? A One Sentence Definition 152
Software Problem Description Language 153
Software Problem Description Patterns 154
Software Behavior Pattern Prediction 155
Patterns of Software Diagnostics 156
Highly Effective Diagnostics 157
Network Trace Analysis Patterns 158
Pattern-Based Software Diagnostics 160
Software Diagnostics Discipline 161
Architecture of memCPU 162
Phenomenology of Software Diagnostics: A First Sketch 163
Software Diagnostics Report Schemes 164
Software Diagnostics Training: Two Approaches 165
The Structure of Software Problem Solving Organization 166
Software Disruption Patterns 167
Static Code Analysis Patterns 168
Bridging the Great Divide 169
Elementary Software Diagnostics Patterns 170
Zero Fault Software Diagnostics 171
Agile Software Diagnostics 173
ADDR Pattern Catalog 174
Thinking-Based Software Diagnostics 175
Memory Acquisition Pattern Catalog 176
Trace Acquisition Pattern Catalog 177
Patterns of Software Diagnostics Architecture 178
Detecting and Predicting the Unknown 180
Software Diagnostics as Psychology 181

Software Diagnostics as Literary Criticism 182
Rapid Software Diagnostics Process (RSDP) 183
Right First Time Software Diagnosis 184
Software Diagnosis Codes 185
Vulnerability Analysis Patterns (VAP) 186
Analytic Memory Dump - A Mathematical Definition 188
General Abnormal Patterns of Structure and Behavior 189
Malware Analysis Patterns 190
Software Trace Diagrams (STDiagrams) 191

Volume 8 195

A Pattern Language for Performance Analysis 195
The Timeless Way of Diagnostics 196
Pattern-Oriented Debugging Process 197
Malnarratives 200
Higher-Order Pattern Narratives (Analyzing Diagnostic Analysis)... 202
Special and General Trace and Log Analysis 206
Projective Debugging 209
Pattern! What Pattern? 216
We did not See Anything 219
Coding and Articoding 221
Adjoint Space 223

Volume 9 227

Diagnostics, Forensics, Prognostics: The Copernican Revolution 227
Pattern Repertoire 229
Pattern-Oriented Software Internals: Pattern Paradigms and Software Internals Pattern Stack 231
Software Diagnostics Canvas 235
Software Traces and Logs as Proteins 237
Patterns-Based Root Cause Analysis Methodology 239
Teaching Complex Diagnostic Scenarios with Artificial Debugger (ArtDbg) and Pseudo-Memory Dumps 242
The Scope of Software Diagnostics 244
Diagnostics of Things (DoT) 246
Riemann Root Cause Analysis Language 247
Problem Solving as Code 250
Dia|gram Graphical Diagnostic Analysis Language 251
Iterative Pattern-Oriented Root Cause Analysis 253
Theoretical Software Diagnostics and Education 255

Volume 10 257

Topological Software Trace and Log Analysis 257
Software Diagnostic Space as a General Graph of Software Narratives 258
Software Diagnostics as Archaeology 263
Pattern-Oriented Diagnostic Analysis Process 264
Principles of Pattern-Oriented Software Data Analysis 265
Abstract Debugging Commands (ADC) Initiative 267
Reducing Analysis Pattern Complexity via Elementary Analysis Patterns 268
Categorical Foundations of Software Diagnostics 271
Existential Prognostics: Periodic Table of Diagnostic Patterns 273
Software Codiagnostics 275

Volume 11 277

The Most Important Skill in Software Diagnostics 277
Diagnostic Operads 279
Mathematical Concepts in Software Diagnostics and Software Data Analysis 282
Software Diagnostics Engineering 285
Narrachain 287
Diagnostics-Driven Development 289
Integral Diamathics – Tracing the Road to Root Cause 290
Meso-problem Solving using Meso-patterns 292
Lego Log Analysis 295
Artificial Chemistry Approach to Software Trace and Log Analysis 299

Volume 12 305

Introducing Software Pathology 305
Log's Loxels and Trace Message's Mexels Graphical Representation of Software Traces and Logs 307
Analysis Pattern Duality 313
Application of Trace and Log Analysis Patterns to Image Analysis: Introducing Space-like Narratology 314
Machine Learning Square and Software Diagnostics Institute Roadmap 316

Volume 13 319

Debugging and Category Theory 319
Introducing Diags: Diagnostic Analysis Gestures and Logues.......... 331

Volume 14 333

Introducing Methodology and System of Cloud Analysis Patterns (CAPS) 333
The Fractal Nature of Software Traces and Logs 342
General Architecture of Analysis Pattern Networks 343
Software Narratives under Constraints 348
Literary Theory Terms 349

Volume 15 351

The Dream of Quantum Software Diagnostics 351
Systematic Software Diagnostics.. 352
REPL Streaming (REPLS)... 354
Dia|gram Language and Memory Dump Analysis Patterns 355
Traces and Logs as 2-categories 361
Diagnostics of Artificial Intelligence 363
Proof of Concept Engineering Patterns 364

Volume 16 367

Introducing Lov Language.. 367
Carnot Cycle Metaphor for Trace and Log Analysis......................... 368
Defect Mechanism Patterns (DMP) 369

Debugged! MZ/PE, Volume 2, Issue 1 371

What is an Adjoint Thread? 371

Unpublished 377

Functionalist Trace Analysis 377

Notes 379

[This page is intentionally left blank]

Preface to the Fourth Edition

Two new Memory Dump Analysis Anthology (Diagnomicon) volumes have been released since the publication of the third edition more than three years ago, and another one is almost ready for publication. Ideas from cloud-native computing, visualization, AI, machine learning, and physics have been introduced to theoretical software diagnostics and are reflected in 15 added articles. Previous ideas from narratology, literary theory, and applied categorical thinking were also expanded. We also updated threads of thinking, the list of mathematical concepts, and notes' references.

While editing this edition, the latest version of the popular editor crashed a dozen times.

Preface to the Third Edition

Three new Memory Dump Analysis Anthology volumes have been released since the publication of the second edition more than two and a half years ago. More ideas from mathematics, new visualization, data analysis, and interdisciplinary approaches have been introduced to software diagnostics theory and are reflected in the 10 added articles. We also updated threads of thinking, the list of mathematical concepts, and notes' references.

This reference book is a part of the streaming architecture of pattern-oriented software diagnostics publications:

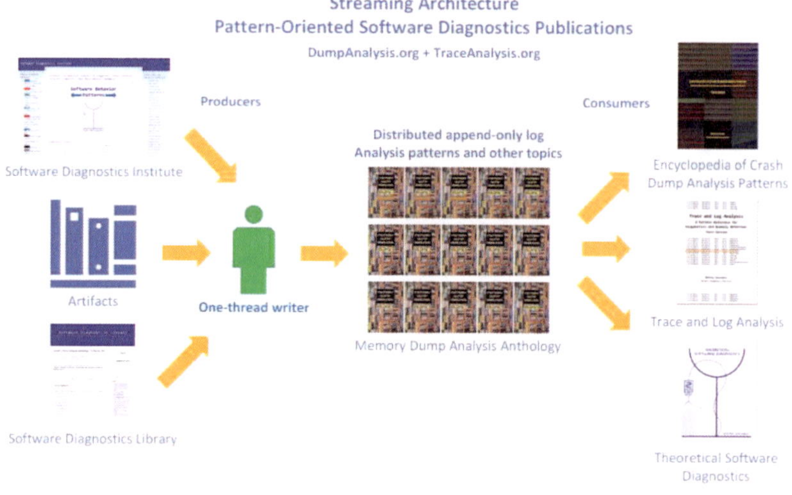

Preface to the Second Edition

This book reprints selected articles from Memory Dump Analysis Anthology volumes 1 – 10 related to theoretical aspects of pattern-oriented software diagnostics. Some articles from the forthcoming volume 11 are also included. In addition to 13 new articles, the second edition also includes one relevant article from Debugged! MZ/PE magazine issue and the former Debugging Experts Magazine Online that was referenced in the first edition of this book.

For any errors, please send a personal message using this contact e-mail:

dmitry.vostokov@dumpanalysis.org

Alternatively, via Twitter @DumpAnalysis

Facebook pages and group:

http://www.facebook.com/DumpAnalysis
http://www.facebook.com/TraceAnalysis
http://www.facebook.com/groups/dumpanalysis

The Software Diagnostics Group on LinkedIn:

https://www.linkedin.com/groups/8473045

About the Author

Dmitry Vostokov is an internationally recognized expert, speaker, educator, scientist, inventor, and author. He founded the pattern-oriented software diagnostics, forensics, and prognostics discipline (Systematic Software Diagnostics) and Software Diagnostics Institute (DA+TA: DumpAnalysis.org + TraceAnalysis.org). Vostokov has also authored over 50 books on software diagnostics, anomaly detection and analysis, software and memory forensics, root cause analysis and problem solving, memory dump analysis, debugging, software trace and log analysis, reverse engineering, and malware analysis. He has over 25 years of experience in software architecture, design, development, and maintenance in various industries, including leadership, technical, and people management roles. Dmitry also founded Syndromatix, Anolog.io, BriteTrace, DiaThings, Logtellect, OpenTask Iterative and Incremental Publishing (OpenTask.com), Software Diagnostics Technology and Services (former Memory Dump Analysis Services) PatternDiagnostics.com, and Software Prognostics. In his spare time, he presents various topics on Debugging.TV and explores Software Narratology, its further development as Narratology of Things and Diagnostics of Things (DoT), Software Pathology, and Quantum Software Diagnostics. His current interest areas are theoretical software diagnostics and its mathematical and computer science foundations, application of formal logic, artificial intelligence, machine learning and data mining to diagnostics and anomaly detection, software diagnostics engineering and diagnostics-driven development, diagnostics workflow and interaction. Recent interest areas also include cloud native computing, security, automation, functional programming, applications of category theory to software development and big data, and artificial intelligence diagnostics.

Threads of Thinking

Here we chronologically review articles that started various threads of thinking. We use periodization based on time spanned by each Memory Dump Analysis Anthology volume. Because we rearrange articles within each volume according to related topics, they may not be reprinted chronologically.

Volume 1: August 2006 – December 2007

The article Multiple Exceptions, published on the 30th of October, 2006 opened the thread of crash dump analysis patterns. There are more than 350 such patterns at the time of this writing, with examples from Windows, Mac OS X, and Linux (September 2020).

After crash dump analysis pattern innovation, the author started thinking about terminology, methodological principles, and questions related to software technical support, troubleshooting, causes of software problems, general principles of artifact analysis:

- Four Pillars
- Five Golden Rules
- Critical Thinking
- Troubleshooting as Debugging
- What is a Software Defect?
- Four Causes of Crash Dumps
- What is Memory Dump Analysis?
- Crashes and Hangs Differentiated

During that time, the author started applying mathematical ideas to software execution artifact analysis:

- Memory Dump - A Mathematical Definition
- Threads as Braided Strings in Abstract Space

Volume 2: January 2008 – September 2008

On the 19th of July 2008, the author published the first pattern from Debugware Patterns thread as an effort to bring pattern-oriented design approaches to chaotic software troubleshooting and debugging tool development prevalent in software companies. UML notation was used for describing many such patterns.

The author continued thinking about software technical support, troubleshooting, debugging, root cause analysis, and the role of memory dump analysis:

- Three Main Ideas of Debugging
- The Hidden Tomb in Pyramid of Software Change
- Ceteris Paribus in Comparative Troubleshooting
- Object-Oriented Debugging and Troubleshooting
- Component-Based Debugging and Troubleshooting
- Domain-Driven Debugging and Troubleshooting
- Causal Models

PARTS: Problem Solving Power of Thought was the first attempt to create problem analysis and resolution methodology.

Recognizing the need to name the emerging discipline, the author proposed Memoretics, Memiotics, and Memory Analysis classification that included memory forensics and intelligence.

Volume 3: October 2008 – June 2009

Introduction to Software Trace Analysis Patterns opened the thread of trace and log analysis patterns. There are more than 200 such patterns at the time of this writing (October 2020). Such pattern-oriented trace and log analysis thinking led to Software Narratology: A Definition.

The author also attempted to unify software traces and memory dump, and continued to apply mathematical ideas:

- Software Trace: A Mathematical Definition
- Geometrical Debugging
- Riemann Programming Language
- The Measure of Debugging and Memory Dump Analysis Complexity

A few articles continued the thinking thread of problem analysis, troubleshooting, debugging, analysis reporting, efficient and effective strategies, scientific thinking, and the foundational role of memory dump analysis:

- I'm RARE
- T&D Labyrinth
- Efficient vs. Effective: DATA View
- A Copernican Revolution in Debugging
- Is Memory Dump Analysis a Science?
- Universal Memory Dump: A Definition

The author also continued to apply ideas from other disciplines:

- Quantum Memory Dumps
- On Subjectivity of Software Defects
- My Dangerous Idea: Parameterized Science
- Unique Events and Historical Narratives
- Chemistry of Virtual Memory
- Graphical Notation for Memory Dumps

Volume 4: July 2009 – January 2010

Succession of Patterns introduced a pattern-oriented approach to root cause analysis.

The new Workaround Patterns catalog was added to pattern-oriented problem solving.

The author also continued applying mathematical concepts to software artifact analysis:

- Metaphorical Bijectionism: A Method of Inquiry
- Memory Dumps as Posets
- MemD Category
- Operating Closure of Memory
- Fiber Bundle of Memory Space
- Extending Multithreading to Multibraiding (Adjoint Threading)
- Manifold Memory Space
- Cubic Memory Representation

Volume 5: February 2010 – October 2010

The author introduced Software Behavior Patterns and Structural Memory Patterns together with pattern unification, the new pattern language, and experimental notation:

- General Memory Analysis
- Notation for Memory and Trace Analysis
- Memory Systems Language

Models of Software Behavior were also introduced as a useful tool for building pattern catalogs.

The author continued to apply ideas from other disciplines:

- Category Theory and Troubleshooting
- Collective Pointer
- On Unconscious
- Psychoanalysis of Software Troubleshooting and Debugging
- Archaeological Foundations for Memory Analysis
- Software Chorography and Chorology: A Definition

Software narratology was also further explored:

- Basic Software PLOTs
- The Extended Software Trace
- Presenting a Software Story
- Two Readings of a Software Trace

Volume 6: November 2010 – October 2011

This period continued the gestation of pattern-oriented software diagnostics with the recognition of its systemic aspect before the explosion of ideas during its maturation period that started in 2012.

The most important articles from this period are about pattern-oriented root cause analysis, unified debugging pattern language, and software defect periodicity:

- A.C.P. Root Cause Analysis Methodology
- Analysis, Architectural, Design, Implementation and Usage Debugging Patterns
- A Periodic Table of Software Defects

Intelligence Analysis Patterns catalog was also incepted during that period.

Volumes 7 – 10: November 2011 – May 2017

The formative years when Software Diagnostics Discipline was defined, including its scope, and most theoretical work was done and the majority of trace and log analysis Pattern Repertoire. During 2016, the accumulated mathematical ideas gave rise to Topological Software Trace and Log Analysis and its unification with the previous software narratological work by introducing Software Diagnostic Space as a General Graph of Software Narratives.

Many more pattern catalogs were added:

- Software Problem Description Patterns
- Patterns of Software Diagnostics
- Network Trace Analysis Patterns
- Software Disruption Patterns
- Static Code Analysis Patterns
- Elementary Software Diagnostics Patterns
- ADDR Pattern Catalog
- Memory Acquisition Pattern Catalog
- Trace Acquisition Pattern Catalog
- Patterns of Software Diagnostics Architecture
- Vulnerability Analysis Patterns (VAP)
- Malware Analysis Patterns
- A Pattern Language for Performance Analysis

We consider introducing mechanisms as the most important addition to Patterns-Based Root Cause Analysis Methodology, a part of the pattern-oriented problem-solving methodology where diagnostics plays a major role compared to many black box problem analysis and resolution methods.

Volumes 11 – 13: June 2017 – July 2020

The years 2017 and 2020 expanded the application of category theory:

- Categorical Foundations of Software Diagnostics
- Software Codiagnostics
- Diagnostic Operads
- Debugging and Category Theory
- Introducing Diags: Diagnostic Analysis Gestures and Logues

The new interdisciplinary approaches for software diagnostic analysis have also been introduced since the year 2018:

- Artificial Chemistry Approach to Software Trace and Log Analysis
- Introducing Software Pathology
- Log's Loxels and Trace Message's Mexels Graphical Representation of Software Traces and Logs
- Application of Trace and Log Analysis Patterns to Image Analysis: Introducing Space-like Narratology

Volumes 14 – 16 and Beyond: August 2020 – Present

The main ideas during this period are the metaphor of bias and variance: traces and logs as models of computation and environment as input data, traces and logs as 2-categories, cloud analysis patterns, analysis pattern networks, language of visualization, diagrams of memory analysis patterns, and defect mechanism patterns:

- Traces and Logs as 2-categories
- Introducing Methodology and System of Cloud Analysis Patterns (CAPS)
- General Architecture of Analysis Pattern Networks
- Introducing Lov Language
- Dia|gram Language and Memory Dump Analysis Patterns
- Defect Mechanism Patterns (DMP)

Multiple Exceptions

After doing crash dump analysis for some time, we decided to organize our knowledge into a set of patterns (to speak in a memory dump analysis pattern language and facilitate its common vocabulary).

What is a pattern? It is a general solution we can apply in a specific context to a common recurrent problem.

The first pattern we are going to introduce is **Multiple Exceptions**. This pattern captures the known fact that there could be as many exceptions ("crashes") as many threads in a process. The following UML diagram depicts the relationship between Process, Thread, and Exception entities:

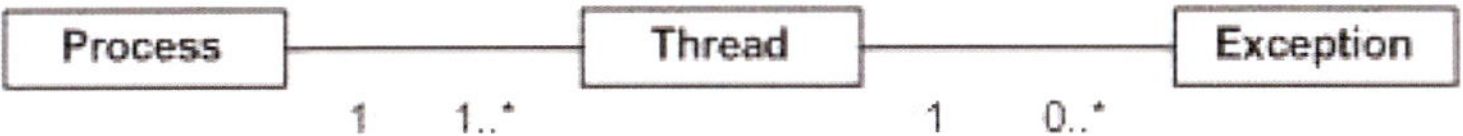

Every process in Windows has at least one execution thread, so there could be at least one exception per thread (like invalid memory reference) if things go wrong. There could be the second exception in that thread if exception handling code experiences another exception or the first exception was handled, and we have another one and so on.

So what is the **general solution** to that common problem when an application or service crashes, and we have a crash dump file **(common recurrent problem)** from a customer **(specific context)**? The general solution is to look at all threads and their stacks and not rely on what tools say.

Here is a concrete example from one of the dumps. Internet Explorer crashed, and we opened it in WinDbg and ran **!analyze -v** command. This is what we got in our WinDbg output:

```
ExceptionAddress: 7c822583 (ntdll!DbgBreakPoint)
   ExceptionCode: 80000003 (Break instruction exception)
  ExceptionFlags: 00000000
NumberParameters: 3
   Parameter[0]: 00000000
   Parameter[1]: 8fb834b8
   Parameter[2]: 00000003
```

Break instruction, we might think, shows that the dump was taken manually from the running application, and there was no crash - the customer sent the wrong dump or misunderstood troubleshooting instructions. However, we looked at all threads and noticed the following two stacks (threads 15 and 16):

```
0:016>~*kL
...
15  Id: 1734.8f4 Suspend: 1 Teb: 7ffab000 Unfrozen
ntdll!KiFastSystemCallRet
ntdll!NtRaiseHardError+0xc
kernel32!UnhandledExceptionFilter+0x54b
kernel32!BaseThreadStart+0x4a
kernel32!_except_handler3+0x61
ntdll!ExecuteHandler2+0x26
ntdll!ExecuteHandler+0x24
ntdll!KiUserExceptionDispatcher+0xe
componentA!xxx
componentB!xxx
mshtml!xxx
kernel32!BaseThreadStart+0x34

# 16  Id: 1734.11a4 Suspend: 1 Teb: 7ffaa000 Unfrozen
ntdll!DbgBreakPoint
ntdll!DbgUiRemoteBreakin+0x36
```

We see here that the real crash happened in *componentA.dll,* and *componentB.dll* or *mshtml.dll* might have influenced that. Why did this happen? The customer might have dumped Internet Explorer manually while it was displaying an exception message box. *NtRaiseHardError* displays a message box containing an error message.

Perhaps something else happened. Many cases where we see multiple thread exceptions in one process dump happened because crashed threads displayed message boxes like Visual C++ debug message box and preventing that process from termination. In our dump under discussion, WinDbg automatic analysis command recognized only the last breakpoint exception (shown as # 16). In conclusion, we should not rely on "automatic analysis" often.

Four Pillars

They are (sorted alphabetically):

1. Crash Dump Analysis (also called Memory Dump Analysis or Core Dump Analysis)
2. Problem Reproduction
3. Trace and Log Analysis
4. Virtual Assistance (also called Remote Assistance)

Five Golden Rules

It is difficult to analyze a problem when we have crash dumps and traces from various tracing tools and supporting information we have is incomplete or missing. We came up with this easy to remember **4WS** questions to ask when sending or requesting traces and memory dumps:

- ***What*** - What had happened or had been observed? Crash or hang, for example?
- ***When*** - When did the problem happen if traces were recorded for hours?
- ***Where*** - What server or workstation had been used for tracing, or where memory dumps came from? For example, one trace is from a primary server, and two others are from backup servers, or one trace is from a client workstation, and the other is from a server.
- ***Why*** - Why did a customer or a support engineer request a dump file or a trace? This could shed light on various assumptions, including presuppositions hidden in the problem description.
- ***Supporting information*** - needed to find a needle in a haystack: for example, process id and thread id. Also, the answer to the following question is important: how were memory dumps and traces created?

Every trace or memory dump shall be accompanied by **4WS** answers.

4WS rule can be applied to any troubleshooting because even the problem description itself is a trace.

Critical Thinking

Faulty thinking happens all the time in technical support environments, partly due to hectic and demanding business realities.

There is an interesting website that taxonomically organizes fallacies[1].

Take, for example, **False Cause** fallacy. Technical examples might include false causes inferred from trace analysis, customer problem description that includes steps to reproduce the problem. This also applies to debugging, and the importance of critical thinking skills has already been emphasized[2].

False cause fallacies less influence surface-level of basic crash dump analysis because it does not have explicitly recorded a sequence of events, although some caution should be exercised during the detailed analysis of thread waiting times and other historical information.

Troubleshooting as Debugging

This post is motivated by TRAFFIC steps introduced by Andreas Zeller in his book[3]. This book is wonderful, and it gives practical debugging skills a coherent and solid systematical foundation.

However, these steps are for fixing defects in code, the traditional view of the software debugging process. Based on an analogy with systems theories where we have different levels of abstraction like psychology, biology, chemistry, and physics, We would say that debugging starts when we have a failure at the system level.

If we compare systems to applications, troubleshooting to source code debugging, the question we ask at the higher level is "Who caused the product to fail?" which also has a business and political flavor. Therefore, we propose a different acronym: **VERSION**. If we always try to fix system problems at the code level, we get a huge "traffic" in all sense, but if we troubleshoot them first, we get a different system/subsystem/ component version and get your problem solved faster. This is why we have technical support departments in organizations.

There are some parallels between TRAFFIC and VERSION steps:

Track	**V**iew the problem
Reproduce	**E**nvironment/repro steps
Automate (and simplify)	**R**elevant description
Find origins	**S**ubsystem/component identification
Focus	**I**dentify the origin (subsystem/component)
Isolate (defect in code)	**O**btain the solution (replace/eliminate subsystem/component)
Correct (defect in code)	**N**ew case study (document, postmortem analysis)

Troubleshooting does not eliminate the need to look at the source code. In many cases, a support engineer must be proficient in code reading skills to map from traces to source code. This helps in component identification, especially if the product has an extensive tracing facility.

What is a Software Defect?

Software can be considered as models of real or imagined systems which may be models themselves. Any modeling act involves a mapping between a system and a model that preserves causal, ordering, and inclusion relationships, and a mapping from the model to the system that translates emerging relationships and causal structures back to that system. The latter we call modeling expectations, and any observed deviations in structure and behavior between the model and the system we call software defects, which can be functional failures, error messages, crashes or hangs (bold line on diagrams below):

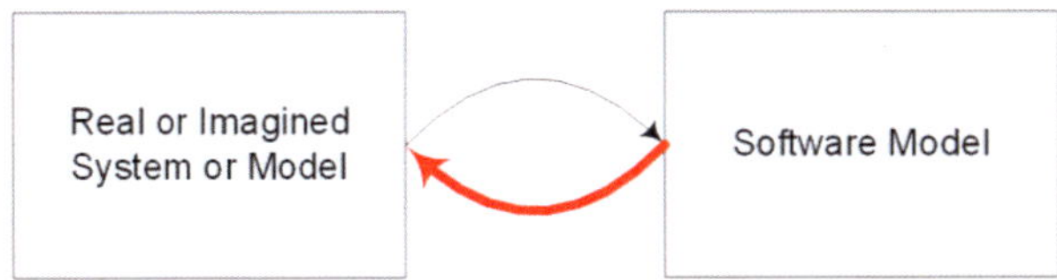

Consider ATM software as a venerable example. It models an imagined world of ATM transactions that we call ATM software requirements. The latter specifies ACID (atomic, consistent, isolated, and durable) transaction rules. If the written software breaks them, we have the defect:

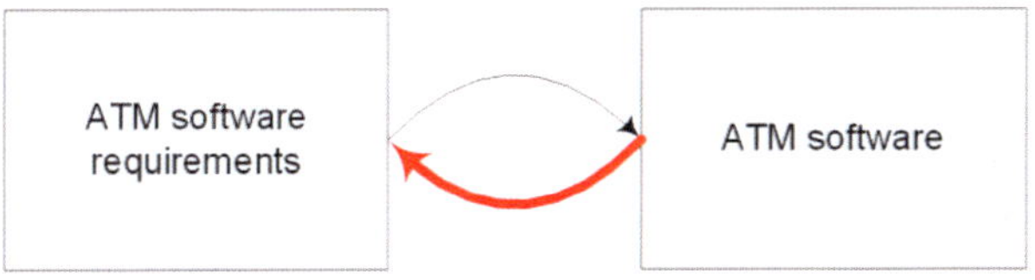

What are the software requirements? They are models of real or imagined systems or can be models of past causal and relationship experiences. If requirements are wrong, they do not translate back, and we still consider software as having a defect:

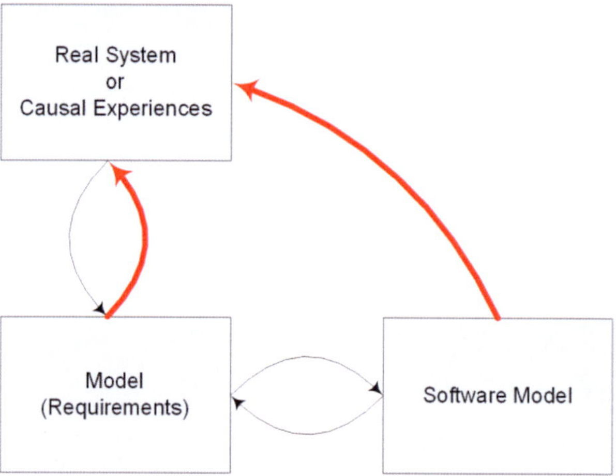

Translating this to the ATM example, we have:

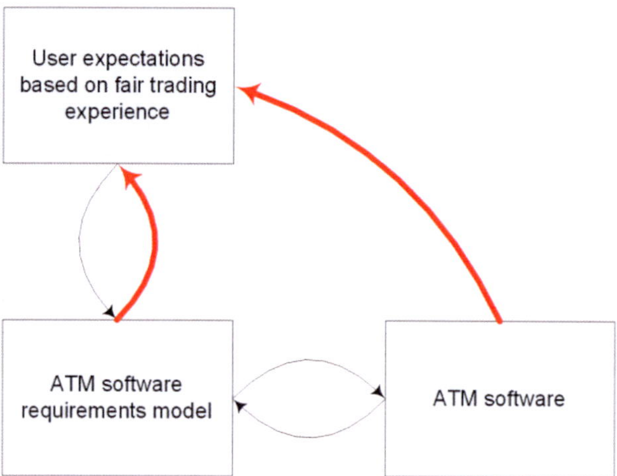

Another example where the perceived absence of failures can be considered a defect is the program designed to model memory leaks that might not be leaking due to a defect in its source code.

Four Causes of Crash Dumps

The appearance of crash dumps on a computer was caused by something. Was it a bug, a fault, a defect, or something else?

Aristotle suggested four types of causation two millennia ago, and they are:

- ***Material cause*** - the presence of some substance, usually material one (hardware), can be machine code (software). The distinction between hardware and software is often blurred today because of virtualization.
- ***Formal cause*** - some form or arrangement (an algorithm)
- ***Efficient cause*** - an agent (data flow or event caused an algorithm to be executed)
- ***Final cause*** - the desire of someone (or something, operating system, for example).

We skip material causes because hardware and software are always involved. Final causality should be among the crash dump causes because they were either anticipated or made deliberately. Let's look at three examples and their possible causes:

Buffer Overflow

- *Formal cause* - a defect in the code which might have arisen from an incomplete or wrong model
- *Efficient cause* - data is too big to fit in a buffer
- *Final cause* - operating system and runtime library support decided to save a crash dump

Bugcheck (NMI)

- *Formal cause* - NMI handler
- *Efficient cause* - a button on a hardware panel or *KeBugCheckEx*

- *Final cause* - "I need a memory dump" desire. Also, crash dump saving functions were written before by kernel developers in anticipation of future crash dumps.

Bugcheck (A)

- *Formal cause* - a defect in the code again or a particular disposition of threads
- *Efficient cause* - Driver Verifier triggered paging out data
- *Final cause* - deliberate OS bugcheck (here we can also say that it was anticipated by OS designers)

Concrete causes depend on the organizational level we use, for example, software/hardware systems/components or modeling acts by humans.

What is Memory Dump Analysis?

From a computer system, we get a memory dump composed of fixed size observable values called bit or byte values. Then we impose some structure on it in order to extract various derived objects like threads and processes, build some organization, and understand what had happened. This activity is called modeling and memory, crash, or core dump analysis is all about modeling a dynamical computer system based on its memory slice. Then we can make predictions and test them via controlled experiments called troubleshooting advice. Tools like WinDbg or GDB can be considered as abstract computers whose job is to model another computer when we feed memory dumps to them.

Crashes and Hangs Differentiated

In the articles **Crashes Explained**[4] and **Hangs Explained**[5], we highlighted the difference between crashes and hangs. In this part, we elaborate on this terminology a bit further. First of all, we have to unify them as manifestations of functional failure. Considering a computer as a system of components having certain functions, we shall subdivide failures into system and component failures. Of course, systems themselves may be components in some larger hierarchy, like in the case of virtualization. Application and service process failures fall under component failures category. Blue screen and server freezes fall under the system failures category. Now it is obvious why most computer users confuse crashes and hangs. They are just failures, and often the distinction between them is blurred from the user perspective.

Software developers tend to make a sharp distinction between crashes and hangs because they consider a situation when a computer accesses a wrong memory address or gets and executes an invalid instruction as a crash. However, after such a situation, a computer system may or may not terminate that application or service.

Therefore, we propose to consider crashes as situations when a system or a component is not observed anymore. For example, a running application or service disappears from Task Manager; a computer system shows a bluescreen or reboots. In hang situations, we can observe the existence of a failed component in Task Manager, or a computer system does not reboot automatically and shows some screen image different from BSOD or a panic message. The so-called sluggish behavior or long response time can also be considered as hang situations.

Memory Dump - A Mathematical Definition

This post was inspired by reading the book written by Robert Rosen, where computers are depicted as direct sums of states[6]. As shown in that book, in the case of machines, their synthetic models (direct sums) are equivalent to analytic models (a direct product of observables). Taking every single bit as an observable having its values in Z_2 set {0, 1}, we can make a definition of *an ideal memory dump* as a direct product or a direct sum of bits saved instantaneously at the given time:

$$\prod_i s_i = \sum_i s_i$$

Of course, we can also consider 8-bit bytes as observables having their values from the Z_{256} set.

In our case, we can simply rewrite the direct sum or product as the list of bits, bytes, words, or double words:

$(\ldots, s_{i-1}, s_i, s_{i+1}, \ldots, s_{j-1}, s_j, s_{j+1}, \ldots)$

According to Rosen, we include hardware states (registers, for example) and partition the memory into the input, output states for a particular computation and other states.

Saving a memory dump takes a certain amount of time. Suppose that it takes three discrete-time events (ticks). During the first tick, we save memory up to $(\ldots, s_{i-1}, s_i)$, and that memory has some relationship to s_j state. During the second tick, s_j state changes its value, and during the 3rd tick, we copy the rest of the memory $(s_{i+1}, \ldots, s_{j-1}, \mathbf{s_j}, s_{j+1}, \ldots)$. Now we see that the final memory dump is inconsistent:

$(\ldots, s_{i-1}, s_i, s_{i+1}, \ldots, s_{j-1}, \mathbf{s_j}, s_{j+1}, \ldots)$

It is explained earlier in plain words in **Inconsistent Dump** memory analysis pattern[7]. Therefore, we may consider *a real memory dump* as a direct sum of disjoint memory areas M_t that were taken during some time interval (t_0, ..., t_n)

$$M = \sum_t M_t \text{ where } M_t = \sum_k S_{tk} \text{ or simply } M = \sum_t \sum_k S_{tk}$$

Threads as Braided Strings in Abstract Space

In the past, we were trying to find a way to depict running and blocked threads graphically perhaps as strings in some abstract n-dimensional space (manifold), preferably a 3-dimensional manifold. If you have never encountered manifolds, here is their informal definition:

> *A 3-dimensional manifold is a 3-dimensional space that looks like a 3-dimensional Euclidean space locally (in small regions), so we can explore the manifold space as we do in our 3-dimensional spatial world.*

Example: the surface of a sphere where small regions look like 2-dimensional rectangles (compare Earth surface and a football field on it)

Our earlier attempts were not satisfactory, and only recently we found that it might be good to represent threads as n-string braids.

Braids are strings that raise monotonically without reversing their direction. It sounds like an arrow of time during the computation. Braid theory is related to knot theory and might be a good metaphor to explore. To picture thread strings, we need to find abstract coordinates for our space. One of the axes is the time axis, and the other is the program counter axis (for example, the value of EIP register).

Here is a thread running through code sequentially without jumps or loops, acquiring and releasing a spinlock on its way:

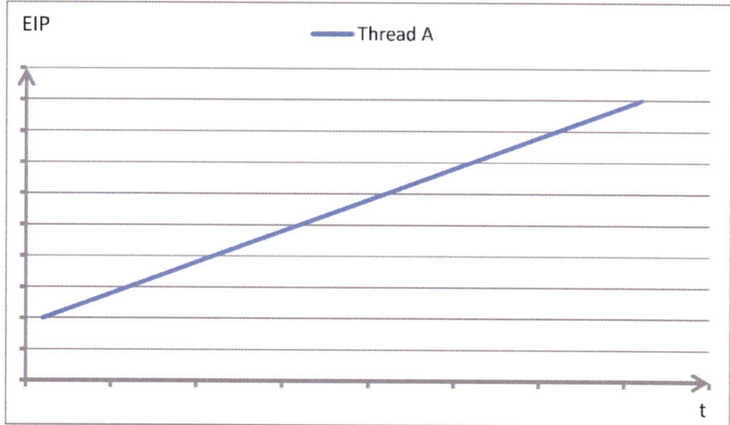

Here is another thread looping while trying to acquire a spinlock and finally taking ownership of it and then running the same code sequentially:

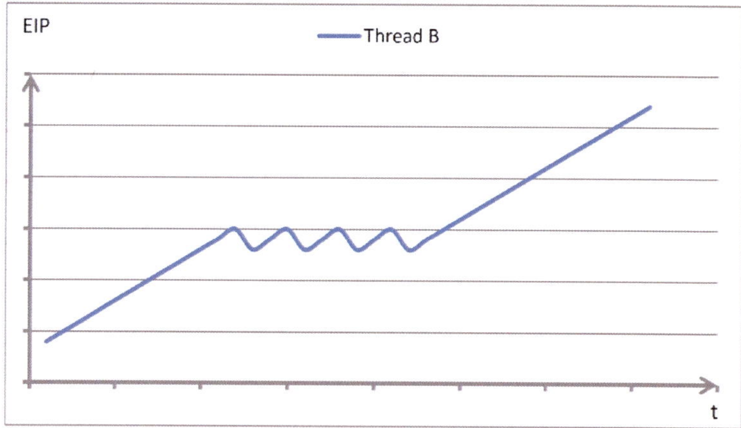

Suppose that both threads contend for the same spinlock, and there is a third thread doing the same. Let's overlay them on one single diagram:

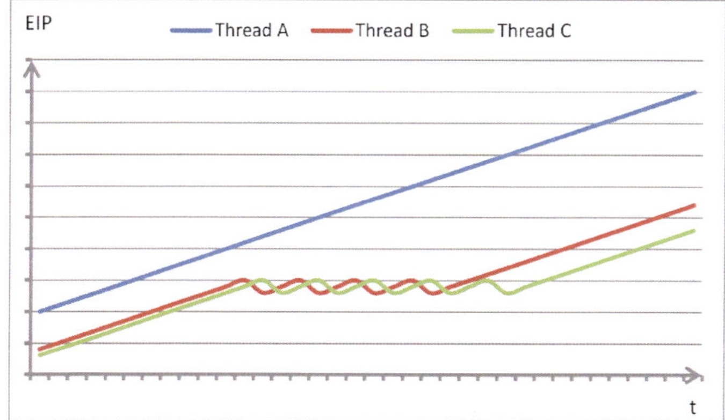

To have a perspective, we can add the third dimension: thread number or ID (TID):

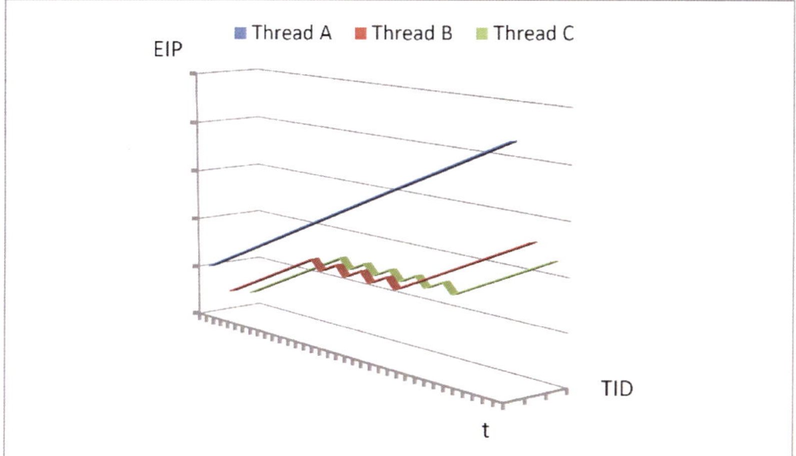

Instead of the TID axis, we can use the data address axis (the data address accessed by the current instruction) or have it as the fourth dimension. If we want to differentiate between *read* and *write* addresses, we can add the fifth axis. We try to do it in the next part.

[This page is intentionally left blank]

Volume 2

Debugware Patterns

Debugware patterns are solutions for common recurrent problems occurring during design of troubleshooting and debugging tools.

Note: These patterns can be found in Memory Dump Analysis Anthology volumes 2 and 6. Recently we came to the necessity of separating diagware patterns from debugware patterns.

Three Main Ideas of Debugging

There is a common tripartite view of intellectual history[8]. The history of debugging can also be divided into main three ideas:

- Forward debugging

Conventional debugging where an engineer starts with initial conditions and during debugging tries to reproduce the problem or see the anomalies on the way to it. Delta debugging[9] also falls into this category.

- Memory dump analysis

It is best described as taking memory slices for remote or postmortem analysis. It helps in problem identification, effective and efficient troubleshooting, and also in debugging hard to reproduce or non-reproducible bugs.

- Backward debugging

It is also called time travel debugging[10]. Although in its early stages of development, this debugging method is the future. Most simply, but technologically infeasible at the moment, it can be implemented as recording memory dumps in succession with every tick. Currently, to avoid saving redundant information and conserve storage, the code is altered to save context-dependent information for every processor instruction or high-level programming language statement. Another approach that comes with virtualization is coarse-grained backward debugging where memory and execution state is saved at certain important points or after specified time intervals.

The Hidden Tomb in Pyramid of Software Change

How does software change in a production environment? Our experience suggests three major ways:

1. The executive decision to replace the whole software product with another competing product.
2. Software troubleshooting at a component level like upgrading or eliminating suspicious components and unrelated products that influence behavior.
3. Correction of individual components after debugging to address implementation and functional defects, non-functional, design or architecture deficiencies.

This can be shown in the following rough diagram (excluding possible overlapping of levels) highlighting the often hidden role of memory dump analysis in software change:

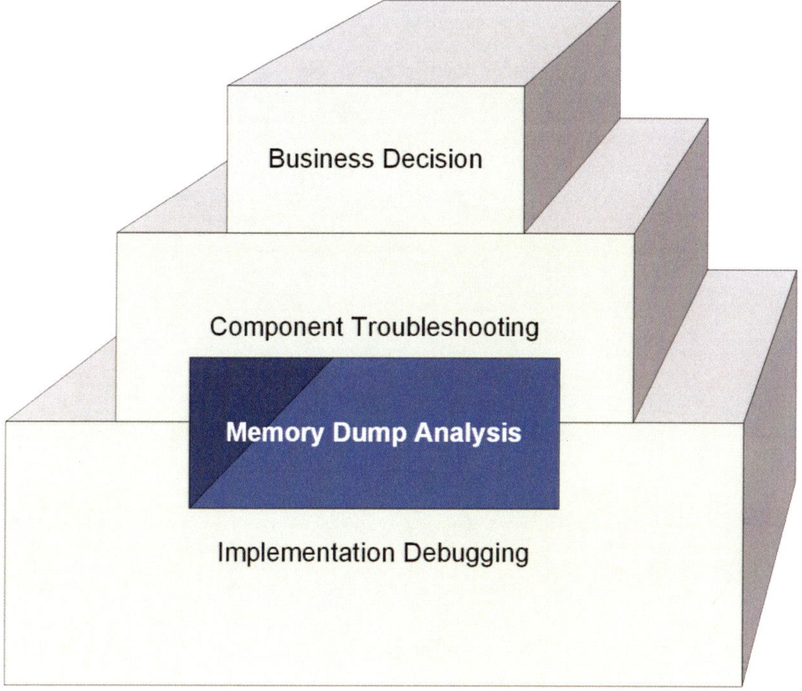

Ceteris Paribus in Comparative Troubleshooting

Ceteris Paribus means *"with other things being the same"* (Latin), and when applied to software troubleshooting and debugging, it means equal environment and configuration. Our favorite example is troubleshooting an issue using two Citrix CDF traces (ETW based): one is for the problem and another for the expected behavior. Say we have a terminal services connectivity problem where a published application does not start on the one particular server in Citrix farm. Here **Ceteris Paribus** means that the application, connection method, configuration, username are all the same for both traces.

It looks like Latin is used here to obfuscate something obvious, but surely many engineers forget it when facing complex issues. This equally applies to debugging as well.

Object-Oriented Debugging and Troubleshooting

OODT (pronounced "oddity") is not a paradigm shift for support and software maintenance environments but a recognized way to solve problems using object-oriented techniques. In contrast to **Structured Debugging and Troubleshooting** methods (**SDT**), where engineers have a sequence of questions and structure troubleshooting plans around them, **OODT** is based on targeting specific objects, subsystems, and systems (sending "messages" to them) and evaluating response and changes in their behavior.

Note: **OODT** does not mean troubleshooting OO systems - it means applying OO techniques to troubleshooting.

Component-Based Debugging and Troubleshooting

Component identification is one of the main goals of post-mortem memory dump analysis and troubleshooting process, in general. Using the definition of components as units of deployment and 3rd-party composition, taken from Clemens Szyperski's seminal book discussing component software in general, and COM, CORBA, Java, and .NET in particular[11], we can say that **CBDT** is focused on component isolation and replacement.

Domain-Driven Debugging and Troubleshooting

SDT (Structured Debugging and Troubleshooting) is procedural (action-based). Once we get the description of the problem, we jump to actions:

1. Ask this
2. Ask that
3. Do this
4. Do that
5. ...

Whereas **OODT** (page 49) is focused on objects (systems and customers are also objects):

1. Get objects from the problem description and problem environment
2. Interrogate them sending messages (could be an email at high levels of organizational structure) like changing a registry key is a message to configuration management subsystem
3. ...

OODT depends on a troubleshooting domain, and therefore, we finally come to **DDDT**.

Causal Models

Looking at traces, system and application event logs, and logs from other tools, technical support engineers see correlations between various events and build causal models used to trace symptoms back to their causes. They use prior knowledge, assumptions, informed guessing, and event order to discern causal structure. Event order in logs influences that, so it is important to understand how we think in causal terms to learn about our biases.

Another essential question from a software engineering perspective is how to design tracing components to help technical support and software maintenance engineers build correct causal models of software issues.

PARTS: Problem Solving Power of Thought

Problem **A**nalysis and **R**esolution **T**roubleshooting **S**ystem (**PARTS**) is the new troubleshooting methodology for critical problem analysis and resolution. It consists of **P**roblem **A**nalysis and **R**esolution **T**asks (**PART**s). The motivation to create this system came to us after looking at various software support processes in various companies around the globe, how they relate to software engineering methodologies and the scientific method, and finally, after looking at "The Master Key System" devised by Charles Haanel almost 100 years ago. Borrowing the idea of "Creative Power of Thought," we subtitle PARTS as *Problem Solving Power of Thought*.

Memoretics

Memory dump analysis needs relevant scientific grounds, and this branch of science needs its name. After considering different alternative names, we finally chose the word **Memoretics**. Here is the brief definition:

> ***Computer Memoretics*** *studies computer memory snapshots (page 37) and their evolution in time.*

This domain of research has many links with application and system debugging. However, its scope is wider than debugging because it does not necessarily study memory snapshots from systems and applications experiencing faulty behavior.

Memiotics

Analysis of computer memory snapshots (memory dumps, page 37) and their evolution is the domain of memoretics (page 54). Computer memory semiotics (**mem**iotics or **memo**semiotics) is the branch of memoretics that studies the interpretation of computer memory, its meaning, signs, and symbols.

Memory Analysis

Here is an attempt to come up with memory analysis classification:

Memory Analysis Forensics:

Answering questions related to committed computer crime. The suspect may be a human or a software/hardware component. Incident response, troubleshooting, and debugging belong to this category. Postmortem memory analysis is usually an analysis of dump files saved and detached from the original system or operating conditions.

Memory Analysis Intelligence:

Monitoring memory state for behavioral and structural patterns to prevent certain events from occurring. It is usually done in situ. However, digital dumpster divers and spies may also collect and analyze memory data detached from the original computer system.

Each category can be further subdivided into:

Functional Memory Analysis: Tracing of events.

Memoretics (page 54)**:** Analysis of memory states and their evolution.

The latter can be subdivided into:

Static Memory Analysis: Traditional memory dump analysis.

Dynamic Memory Analysis: Live debugging.

Volume 3

Introduction to Software Trace Analysis Patterns

We expand the domain of software defect research into **Trace Analysis Patterns**. In addition to Citrix CDF / Microsoft ETW traces, we cover other variants based on extensive software engineering background in the past where we used tracing in software products ranging from soft multi-platform real-time systems to static code analysis tools. Connection with memory dump analysis is covered too because, sometimes, the combination of static and dynamic data leads to interesting observations and helps to troubleshoot and resolve customer problems, especially when not all data can be collected dynamically.

Stack Traces[12] and their **Stack Trace Collections**[13] are specializations of more general traces. Another example is **Historical Information**[14] in memory dump files, especially when it is somehow time stamped.

Note: These patterns can be found in all Memory Dump Analysis Anthology volumes starting from volume 3.

Software Narratology: A Definition

Let's define a software or computer narratology as an application of the theory and methods of literary narratology[15] to the domain of software execution where software traces and logs are considered as narratives, stories of computation[16]. As an example, we have the following correspondence between 4-tiers of literary and software narrative models:

```
Events              Instructions, statements, functions
History             Concrete execution path
Narrative           Software trace
Presentation        View (from a trace viewer)
```

Software Trace: A Mathematical Definition

What is a software trace from a mathematical standpoint? Before any software writes its trace data, it assembles it in memory. Therefore, a software trace is a linear ordered sequence of specifically prepared memory fragments (trace statements):

$(ts_1, ts_2, ..., ts_n)$

where every ts_i is a sequence of bits, bytes, or other discrete units (see the definition of a memory dump, page 39):

$(s_{11}, s_{12}, ..., s_{1k}, s_{21}, s_{22}, ..., s_{2l}, ..., ..., ..., s_{n1}, s_{n2}, ..., s_{nm})$

These trace statements can also be minidumps, selected regions of memory space. In the limit, if every ts_i is a full memory snapshot saved at an instant of time (t_i), we have a sequence of memory dumps:

$(m_{t1}, m_{t2}, ..., m_{tn})$

Like with memory dump analysis, we need symbol files to interpret saved memory fragments unless they were already interpreted during their construction. For example, traces written according to ETW specification (Event Tracing for Windows) need TMF files (Trace Message Format) for their interpretation and viewing. Usually, these files are generated from PDB files, and therefore we have this correspondence:

- memory dump file -> software trace file
- PDB file -> TMF file

Geometrical Debugging

Most of (if not all) debugging is arithmetical. Here we would like to introduce a new kind of debugging and troubleshooting approach that interprets observables as objects in their spaces, for example, the possible space of various GUI forms. These spaces are not necessarily rational-valued spaces of simulation output or discreet arithmetic spaces of memory locations and values.

This geometrical approach applies modeling and systems theory to debugging and troubleshooting by treating them as mappings (or functions in the case of one-to-one or many-to-one mappings) from the space of all possible software environment states (SE) to the space(s) of observables. Here we have a family of mappings to different spaces:

f_i: SE → SO_i

Some observables can be found fixed like the list of components, and the number of mappings can be reduced (i < j):

f_j: $SE_{a,b,c,d,\ldots}$ → SO_j

In every system and its environment, we have something fixed as parameters (a, b, c, d, …) and this could be the list of components as high level "genotype," or it could be just specific code (low-level "genotype"), specific data or hardware specification. The whole family of mappings becomes parameterized. If we want, we can reduce mappings even more, to treat them as many-valued (one-to-many or many-to-many) if several observables belong to the same kind of space.

Let's illustrate this by analogy with the modeling of a natural system. The system to be modeled is a falling ball together with its environment (Earth). The system has some internal structure (the abstract space of states, E), but we do not know it. Fortunately, we can observe some measurable values like the ball position at any time (Q). So we have these mappings for balls with different masses:

f_m: E → Q

We also find that for any individual ball, its mass does not change, so we abstract it as a parameter:

f: E_m → Q

The same modeling approach can be applied to a software system, be it an application or a service running on an operating system or a software system itself running on hardware. The case of a pure software system abstracted from hardware is simple. In such a case, SE space theoretically could be the space of abstract memory dumps (page 39). Practically, we deal with the space of observables (universal memory dumps, page 70) that approximate SE and spaces of software "phenotypes," observable behavior, like distorted GUI, for example, or measured values of memory and CPU consumption or disk I/O throughput.

Riemann Programming Language

Named after Bernhard Riemann[17], this programming language gives software defects first-class status as alternative branches of computation, comparable with multivalued functions[18] and Riemann surfaces[19]. Bugs become first-class constructs. It is reflected in the language syntax, semantics, and pragmatics.

The Measure of Debugging and Memory Dump Analysis Complexity

Recently we were asked how to measure the complexity of technical support cases, especially ones that require memory dump analysis. Our first response was that it is a subjective qualitative measure based mostly on experience and feeling. However, after careful consideration, we understood that nothing has changed for many years: the nature and causes of system or application hangs and crashes still the same regardless of OS types and versions. Therefore, the complexity measure shifts from a case description and its artifacts to an analyst, a memory dump reader. Here the number of queries, questions asked, or commands executed to gather information for analysis can be a good approximation to the measure of complexity. For example, many years ago, we started with a few commands like **!analyze -v**, **kv,** and **dd** and progressed to an elaborate checklist[20]. Here the natural logarithm can be used to approximate the measure:

$C = \ln(N_{dc})$, where N_{dc} is the number of debugging commands used.

Initially, the complexity was $\ln(3) \approx 1.1$, and now, if someone uses ten commands on average or asks ten questions, the complexity is $\ln(10) \approx 2.3$. The analysis is more than two times complex than it was.

I'm RARE

It is a reciprocal counterpart to **five golden rules of troubleshooting** (page 29). Whereas the former rules are for artifact submitters, internal and external customers of memory dump analysts, and complex trace readers, **I'm RARE** are rules for writing analysis reports with easy to remember mnemonic:

I'm RARE - **I**ridium **R**ules of **A**nalysis **R**eport **E**xcellence

Note about **Iridium** metal from Wikipedia: "It is one of the rarest elements in the Earth's crust, with annual production and consumption of only three tonnes."[21]

Here are 5 of them (subject to change):

1. Use a template.
2. Structure a report according to the audience's technical level and organizational processes.
3. Use checklists not only for commands and tools but also for things to avoid in reports and things to encourage.
4. Put all relevant data for later search and other engineers to reproduce the analysis.
5. Provide appropriate explanations and narrative in the cases where analysis is inconclusive.

T&D Labyrinth

Here is a picture of a troubleshooting and debugging labyrinth resting on a notion of universal memory dumps that are observational snapshots, and it includes both memory and various traces we collect to resolve problems.

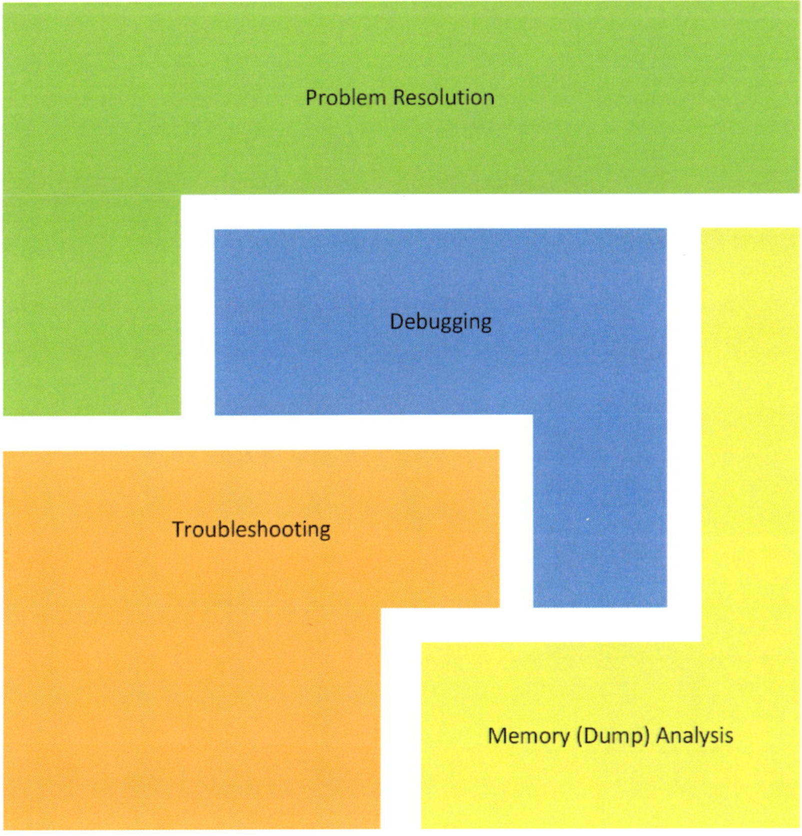

This picture shows possible paths on how we arrive at problem resolution. For example:

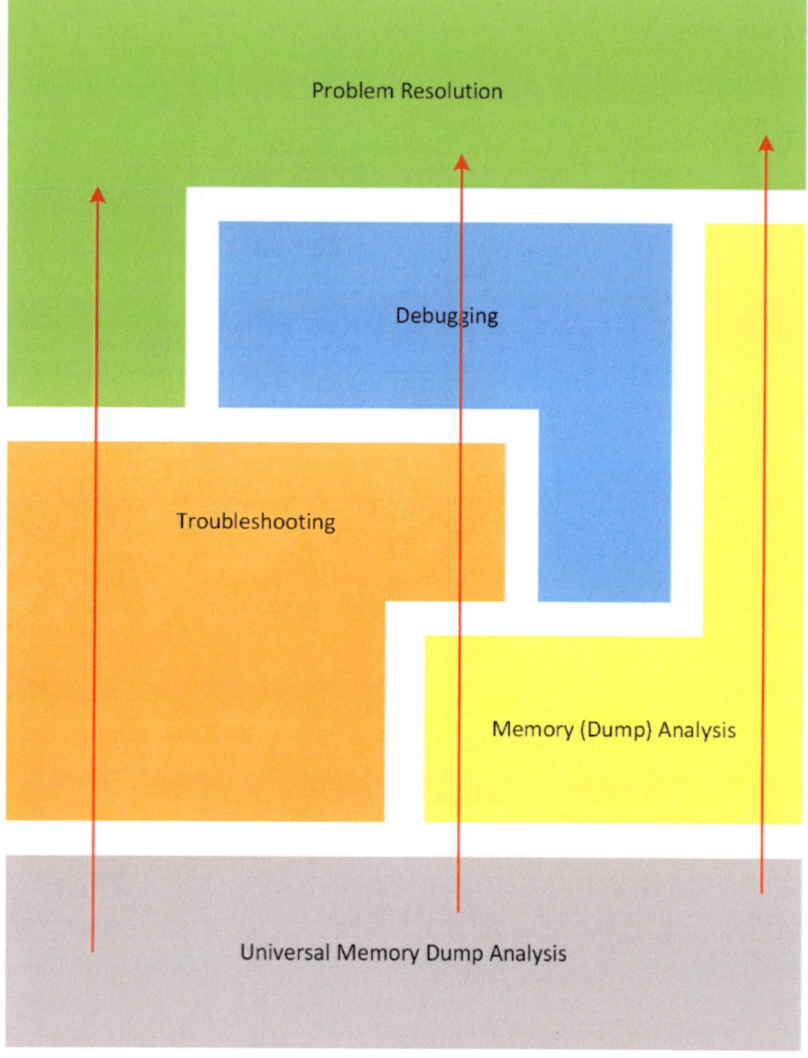

Efficient vs. Effective: DATA View

DATA (**D**ump **A**rtifact + **T**race **A**rtifact) - > DATA (**D**ump **A**nalysis + **T**race **A**nalysis) examples:

1. *Efficient*

- Our 64 GB server bluescreens. We set a complete memory dump option in Control Panel.
- A user cannot connect. We started tracing yesterday and stopped today.
- We analyze all these artifacts every day.

2. *Effective*

- Our 64 GB server bluescreens. We set a kernel memory dump option in Control Panel.
- A user cannot connect. We started tracing, tried to connect, stopped tracing.

We analyze all these artifacts every day and write articles to reduce DATA load.

A Copernican Revolution in Debugging

A number of Copernican revolutions occurred or announced in various branches of various sciences. Now it is our turn to say that action-based ″earth-centric″ debugging is replaced by memory (dump) analysis as a “heliocentric” foundation of debugging. Even in live debugging, we have memory snapshots and differential memory analysis. A trace in trace-based debugging is another example of a universal memory dump. Therefore, memory (dump) analysis comes first.

Is Memory Dump Analysis a Science?

Based on John Moore's eight science criteria, we can consider Memory Dump Analysis (**MDA**) as a science:

1. **MDA** is based on data (memory dumps) collected in the field or repro/test environment.
2. Data (memory dumps) is collected to answer troubleshooting, debugging or forensics and intelligence questions. Observations in memory dumps are made to support or refute these questions.
3. Analysis of data (via memory dump analyzers, debuggers, and log analyzers) is done objectively.
4. Troubleshooting, debugging, or forensics hypotheses are developed, and they are consistent with observations and compatible with the general conceptual computer memory framework.
5. Troubleshooting, debugging, or forensics hypotheses are tested, and several comparable competing ones may be developed at any one time.
6. Generalizations are made that are valid universally within the domain of **MDA**.
7. The facts are confirmed independently.
8. Previously puzzling facts are explained.

It is also interesting to generalize the domain of **MDA** to empirical data collection via the so-called universal memory dumps (page 70).

Universal Memory Dump: A Definition

Applying a mathematical definition of a memory dump (page 37) to natural systems, we can introduce a Universal Memory Dump as a snapshot of observables describing the system. Similar to software memory dump analysis, we need a suitable reader and a set of Universal Symbol Files as semantical mappings or NDB (Nature DataBase) files.

Therefore we have these two categories of universal memory dumps:

- Natural Memory Dumps
- Software Memory Dumps

Quantum Memory Dumps

Quantum computation[22] and quantum information[23] are hot topics at the time of this writing (including quantum memory). Unfortunately, quantum mechanics forbids perfect (ideal) memory dumps due to the so-called no-cloning theorem[24]. Still, it is possible to get inconsistent (imperfect) memory dumps, and perfect ones can be made from quantum computer simulators. The analysis of quantum memory snapshots is the domain of Quantum Memoretics (page 54).

On Subjectivity of Software Defects

If we assume the model-based definition of software defects (page 33), we can easily see that any changes to an underlying model can surface the new, unanticipated defects and hide the known ones. New and evolving disciplines like software security engineering can change our views about solid code and create defects by introducing non-functional constraints on models. Another aspect of this is the interaction of a human debugger with code; the very act of reading code can create defects.

My Dangerous Idea: Parameterized Science

In the future, all sciences, engineering, and technology are ultimately fused and concerned with universal memory dumps (page 70) of empirical data where appropriate symbol files are used for every science as we know today, these files are called *science files.* The set of science files can be considered as a parameter, hence the name of this idea. In other words, there is one Science of memory dump analysis and many sciences. All sciences are finally unified.

Now the question is: would it also be possible to discover new sciences by finding a suitable set of science files corresponding to a collected dump of empirical data?

Unique Events and Historical Narratives

Sometimes a problem such as a crash or hang never happens again, the so-called unique computational event, like the extinction of dinosaurs if we apply biological metaphors. Biology science copes with such events via constructing historical narratives and multiple probabilistic explanations with cross data examinations. The same is true for memory dump analysis, where we construct possible explanations based on evidence and collected supporting data. Like Ernst Mayr[25] pointed, we try to answer both questions: "How?" and "Why?" Usually, the answer to the first question is very simple and straightforward, like NULL pointer access (proximate, functional causation), and the answer to the second question is provided by testing various possible historical narratives (ultimate or evolutionary causation) possibly involving an animate agent (a human user of a system).

Chemistry of Virtual Memory

We can use a nice basic chemical formula representation for processes in memory. In this nomenclature, the class of modules developed by a particular vendor constitutes an element. For example, **M** is for Microsoft modules, **C** is for Citrix modules. Individual modules of particular elements are similar to "atoms" and denoted as numbers in subscript. For example, net.exe command running in a typical Citrix terminal services environment has the following loaded modules where we highlighted Citrix modules in bold and Microsoft modules in italics:

```
0:000> lm1m
net
wdmaudhook
tzhook
twnhook
scardhook
mmhook
mfaphook
cxinjime
CtxSbxHook
MPR
NETAPI32
Secur32
USER32
msvcrt
GDI32
RPCRT4
kernel32
ADVAPI32
MSVCR71
ntdll
```

Therefore, the formula is this: $\mathbf{M_{12}C_8}$.

We put the element of the main process module first in such formulae.

The formula is for the IE process from the case study[26]: $\mathbf{M_{126}A_5U}$, where **A** is for Adobe modules, and **U** is for an unknown module that needs identification; see **Unknown Component** pattern[27].

These formulas can be useful to highlight various **Hooksware** components[28] and distinguish memory dumps generated after eliminating modules for troubleshooting and debugging purposes. It also forms the basis for one of many classificatory schemes for micro- and macro-taxonomy of software discussed in the forthcoming book[29].

We also plan to discuss the structural formulas as well, similar to the ones used in organic chemistry.

Graphical Notation for Memory Dumps

Inspired by Penrose tensor notation[30] and Feynman diagrams,[31] we introduce **V**isual **D**ump **O**bjects (**VDO**) graphical notation to depict and communicate memory dump analysis patterns, their combinations, and analysis results. Let's look at some basic visual objects.

1. Thread:

2. Function:

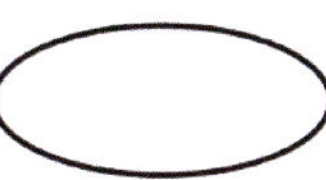

3. Module:

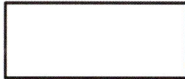

4. Thread, running through functions, modules, or both (stack trace). Optional arrowhead can indicate stack trace direction:

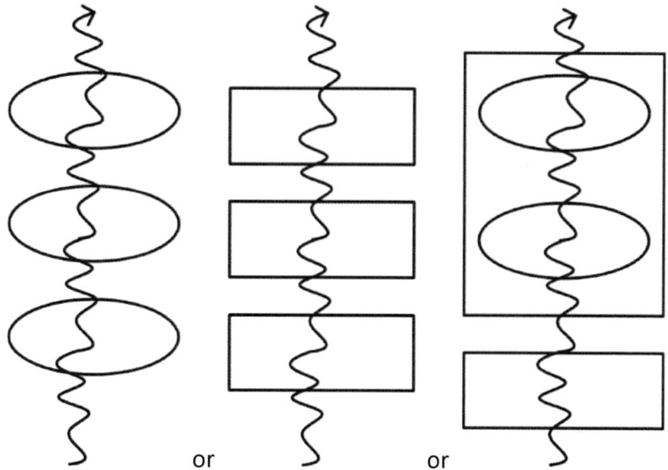

Threads running through modules depict collapsed stack traces[32].

5. Blocked thread:

An example of three threads blocked by another thread (an arrowhead can disambiguate the direction of the waiting chain):

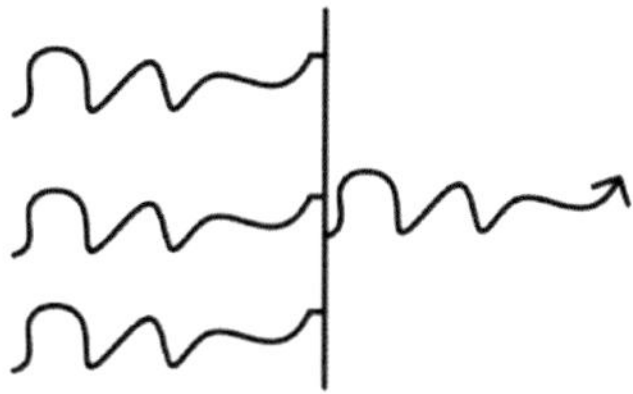

6. Spiking thread (colors are encouraged in VDO notation):

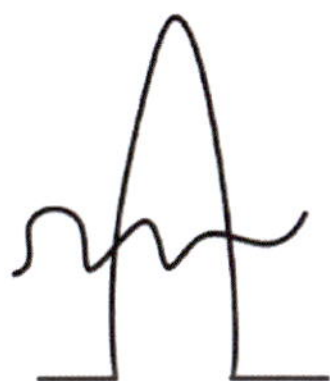

7. Space boundary between user space and kernel space:

Here is an example of a thread spiking in kernel space:

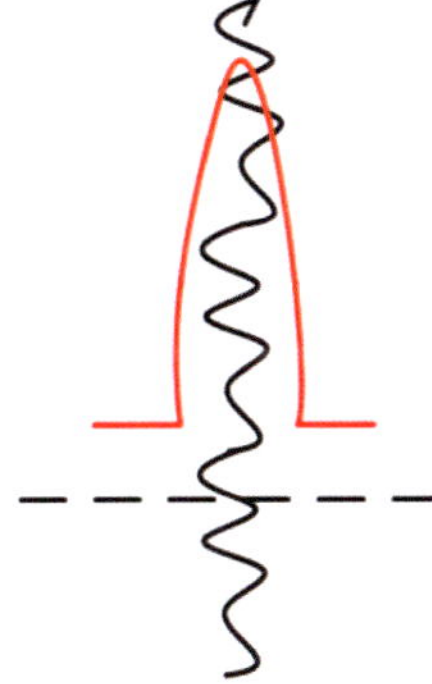

The same thread but depicted with modules from its stack trace:

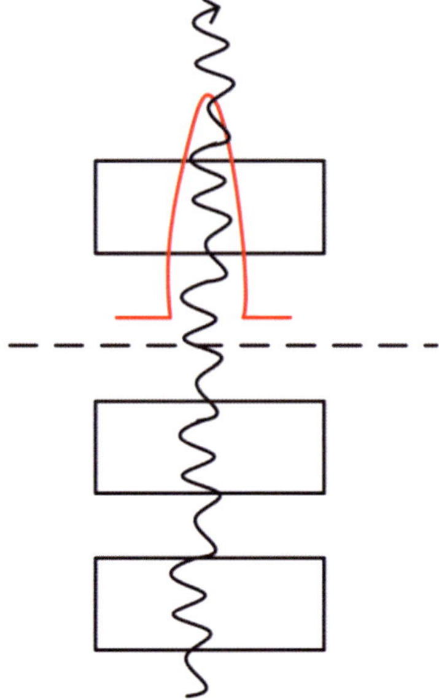

Succession of Patterns

When looking at pattern cooperation studies,[33] it is easy to see that some patterns precede others; for example, **Heap Corruption**[34] might follow by a hard error[35] or **Message Box**[36] and therefore block other threads, creating conditions for another pattern to appear, **Wait Chains**[37]. **Blocked Threads**[38] may block other **Coupled Processes**[39] creating inter-process **Wait Chains**[40]. Successive patterns reach the climax in the end, and the system is no longer able to generate any other patterns.

Such pattern sequences can help in troubleshooting and finding root causes.

Workaround Patterns

After fighting HTML comments in Safari and Chrome, we came to an idea to name and catalog workaround[41] patterns in troubleshooting and debugging.

Note: These patterns can be found in Memory Dump Analysis Anthology volumes 4, 6, 9a, and further patterns are planned for publishing.

Metaphorical Bijectionism: A Method of Inquiry

Where all the author's ideas come from? Consider this example mapping (taken metaphorically from the mathematical notion of injection[42]) of one domain of knowledge to another:

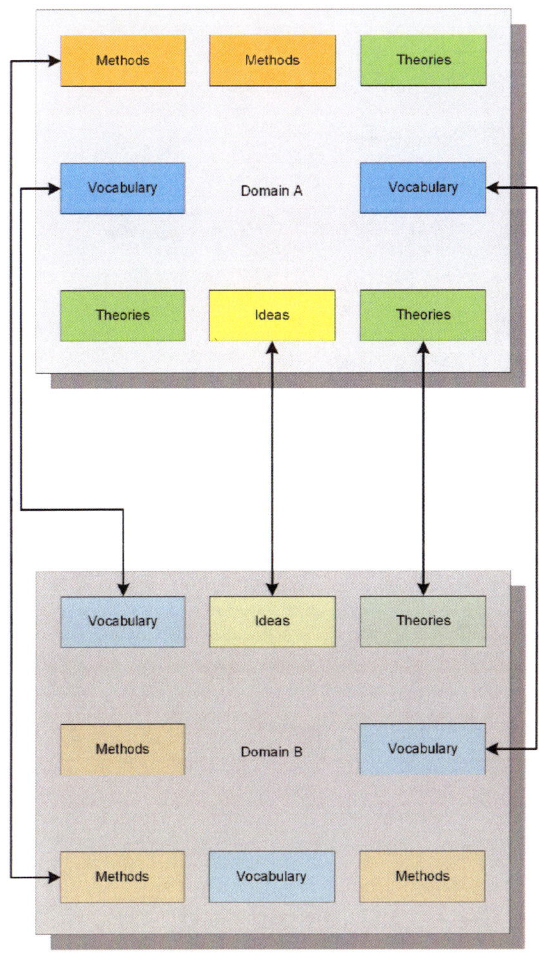

This mapping between concepts and ideas was once called "bijectivism" but was trivially described either as one to one mapping between two domains (like physical vs. mathematical) or fusing different concepts together to get another emerging concept. We have also proposed a similar mapping and called it a metaphorical bijection[43].

Now consider another mapping metaphorically equivalent to a mathematical notion of a surjection[44] where all constituents of the second domain are covered metaphorically by the first domain:

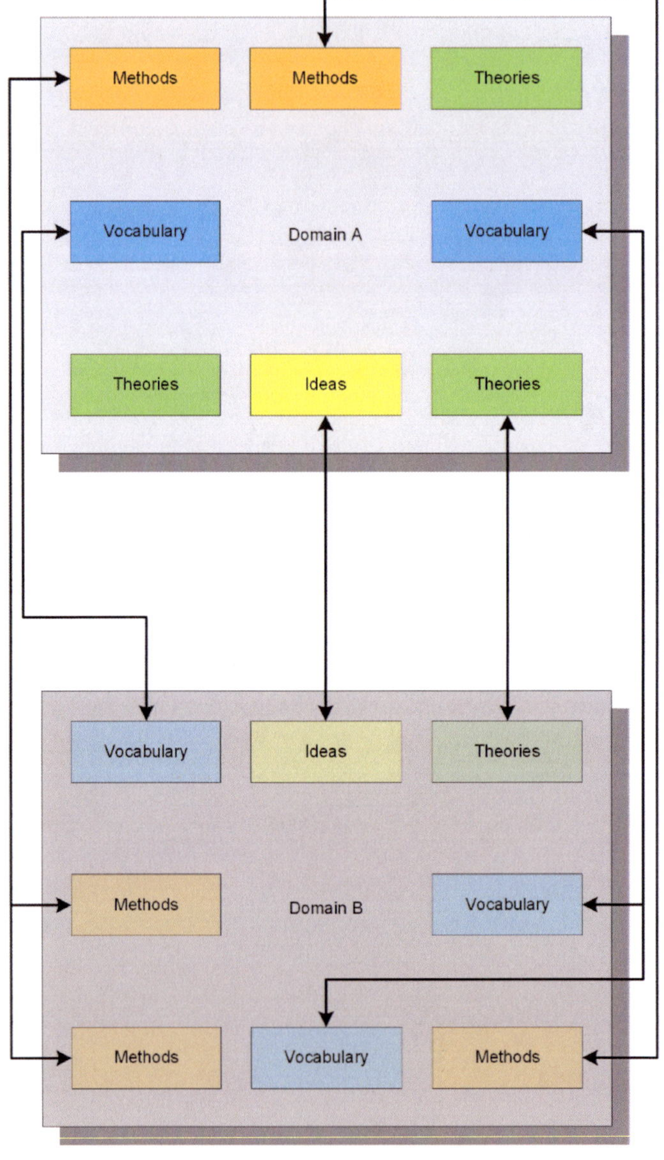

What we strive for is to establish the complete bijective mapping[45] and reorganize our knowledge of both domains to achieve that:

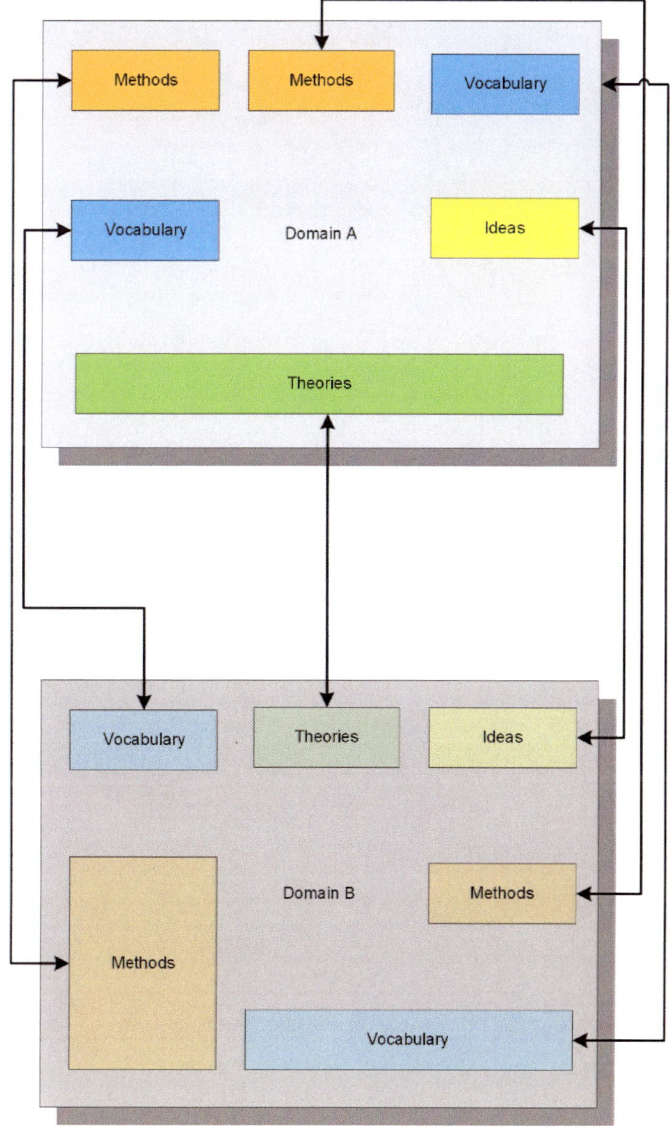

In the diagrams above, small boxes can represent sets of ideas, methods, or individual ideas and methods. The established metaphorical bijection can divide sets or combine them if needed. There can be several such bijections, of course, and we can use other methods of inquiry (for example, the so-called scientific method[46]) to choose between competing metaphorical bijections.

Memory Dumps as Posets

We can compare the existing collection of memory dump analysis patterns[47] to the collection of trace analysis patterns[48] and search for an isomorphism (or more correctly, general morphism). It is not a coincidence that such pattern pairs can be formed. For example, it is possible to discern deadlocks from both crash dumps and software traces (if the appropriate information is available there). Fundamentally, it is implied by the definition of a software trace (page 59) as some sort of a memory dump. Moreover, we can see traces in memory dumps too, for example, **Execution Residue** pattern[49]. Because raw stack data resides in stack pages, and, in contemporary operating systems, they are created from zero pages (metaphorically, out of the void) we can say that stack regions of threads are sorted by their creation time, for example, in this process user memory dump:

```
0:017> !runaway 4
 Elapsed Time
  Thread       Time
   0:49c       0 days 5:16:31.076
   4:4d8       0 days 5:16:30.967
   3:4d0       0 days 5:16:30.967
   2:4cc       0 days 5:16:30.967
   1:4c8       0 days 5:16:30.967
   5:4e8       0 days 5:16:30.936
   6:b6c       0 days 5:16:15.695
   7:b70       0 days 5:16:15.679
   9:b88       0 days 5:16:15.586
   8:b84       0 days 5:16:15.586
  11:348       0 days 5:16:12.934
  10:bfc       0 days 5:16:12.934
  12:1200      0 days 5:15:16.528
  15:1298      0 days 5:15:15.220
  14:1290      0 days 5:15:15.220
  13:128c      0 days 5:15:15.220
  17:12e4      0 days 5:15:13.257
  16:12dc      0 days 5:15:13.257
  18:12ec      0 days 5:15:13.117
  20:12f4      0 days 5:15:13.085
  19:12f0      0 days 5:15:13.085
  21:17a0      0 days 5:13:16.321
  22:1628      0 days 5:13:15.729
  24:1778      0 days 1:35:50.773
```

```
23:17ec      0 days 1:35:50.773
25:1570      0 days 1:27:54.190
26:1724      0 days 1:27:10.151
27:1490      0 days 0:05:46.732
28:1950      0 days 0:02:28.153
29:19b4      0 days 0:00:58.108
30:177c      0 days 0:00:38.358
31:1798      0 days 0:00:23.351
32:1a7c      0 days 0:00:08.343
```

If we have complete memory dumps, we can also account for other processes and their elapsed time. Within stack pages, we have partial stack traces but do not have exact timing information between them except for stack frames from the frozen current thread stack trace or, if we are lucky, from a partial stack trace from the past execution. However, the timing between frames from different stacks is undefined, and we can only guess it from higher-level considerations like the semantics of procedure calls and other information.

These considerations and the notion of a poset[50] (partially ordered set) suggest that memory dumps are posets. We can even create an interpretation of **POSET** abbreviation for this occasion: **P**artially **O**rdered **S**oftware **E**xecution **T**race.

MemD Category

We started applying category theory[51] (as an alternative to the traditional set-theoretic approach of memory bits) to memory dump analysis, debugging, and software trace analysis. In addition to modeled complex systems[52], we apply an evolutive systems approach to computer memory. Here is a picture illustrating the **Mem*D*** category of memory dumps (snapshots) as category objects and category arrows as different ways of arriving at the same memory picture:

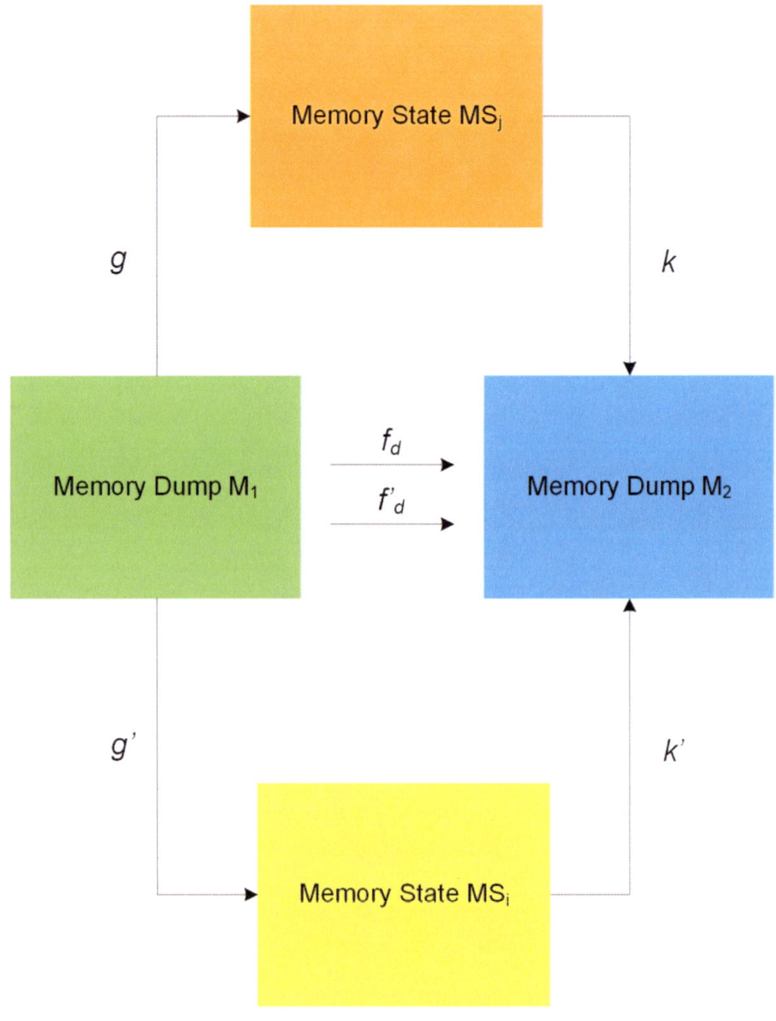

This category applies to software traces as well if we consider every individual trace message or statement as a minidump (page 59). We currently consider software trace category **Mem*T*** as a subcategory of **Mem*D***.

The configuration category of a computer memory dump represents its memory internals at an instant *t* (ideal memory dumps) or at a time interval T: components and links, pointers, wait chains, causal relations, data flows.

Pointers and their links are also objects and arrows to form a category, called **Mem*P***(tr). The following picture illustrates it with the last pointer shown as a dereference fixpoint[53]:

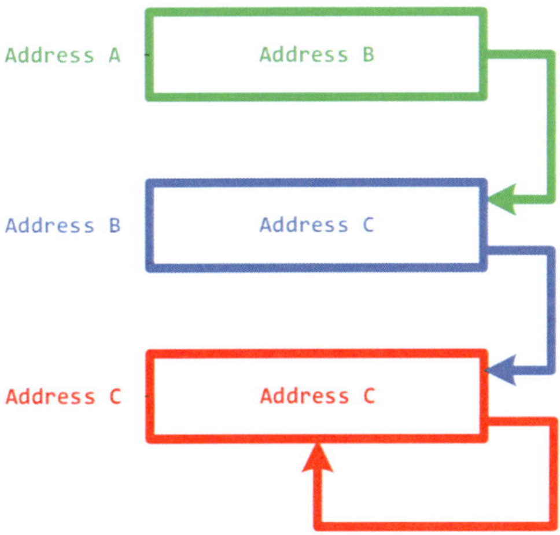

The perception field of a pointer is a category of all links to its memory location:

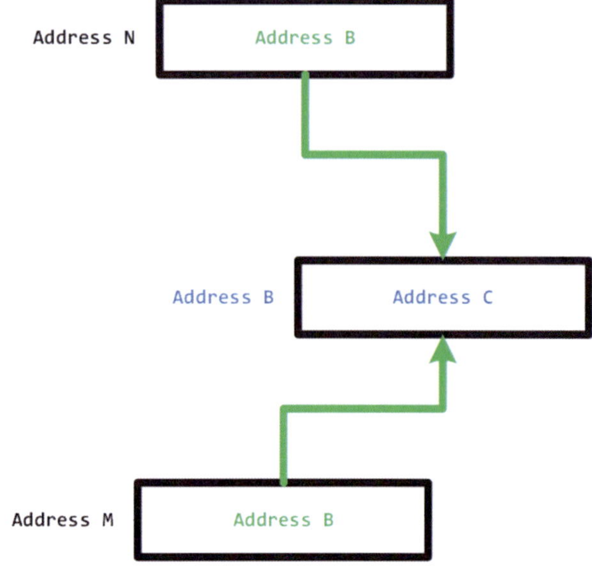

However, the operating field of a pointer is its link to a memory location it is pointing to.

Operating Closure of Memory

Previously we defined the **MemP** category and the operating field of a pointer as its link to a memory location it is pointing to. This operating field value can be in a different pseudo-memory plane if its value is outside memory bounds, for example, 8FFFFFF0 for memory with the highest possible address 7FFFFFFF:

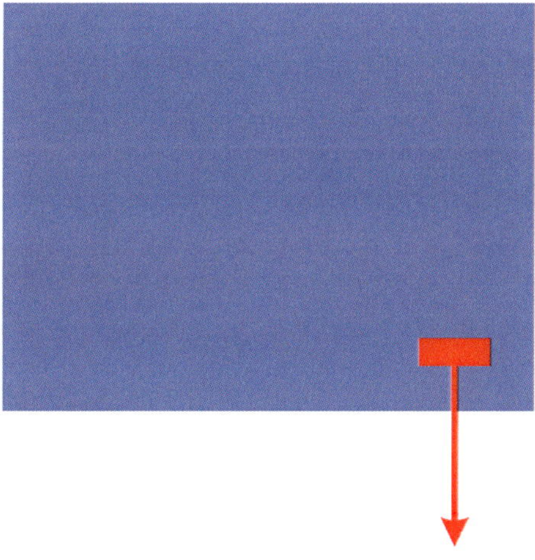

We define the closure of memory as the smallest MemP category that includes memory for operating fields of every pointer for the current memory snapshot. For the example above, by adding another memory location that has a pointer value pointing back to the original memory region, we have the following operating closure:

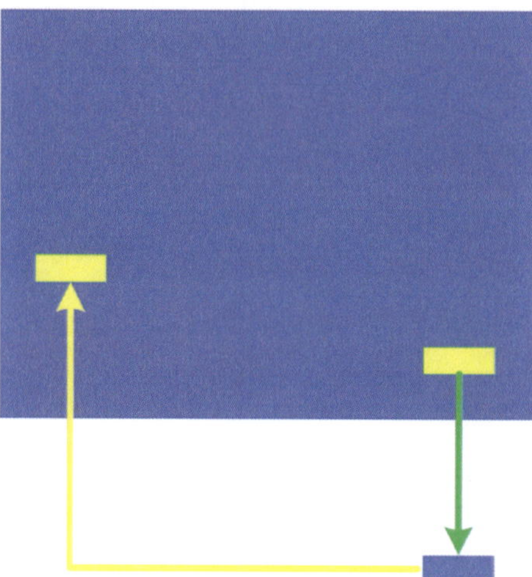

We can also add more memory, as well:

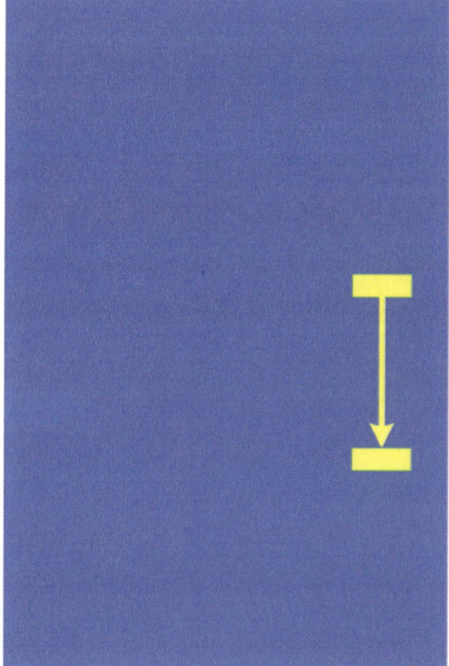

Fiber Bundle of Memory Space

When complete memory dumps are huge (in the case of x64 systems), we can dump specific processes and then force a kernel memory dump. Here we have a product of spaces similar to a fiber bundle[54] illustrated by the following intuitive picture:

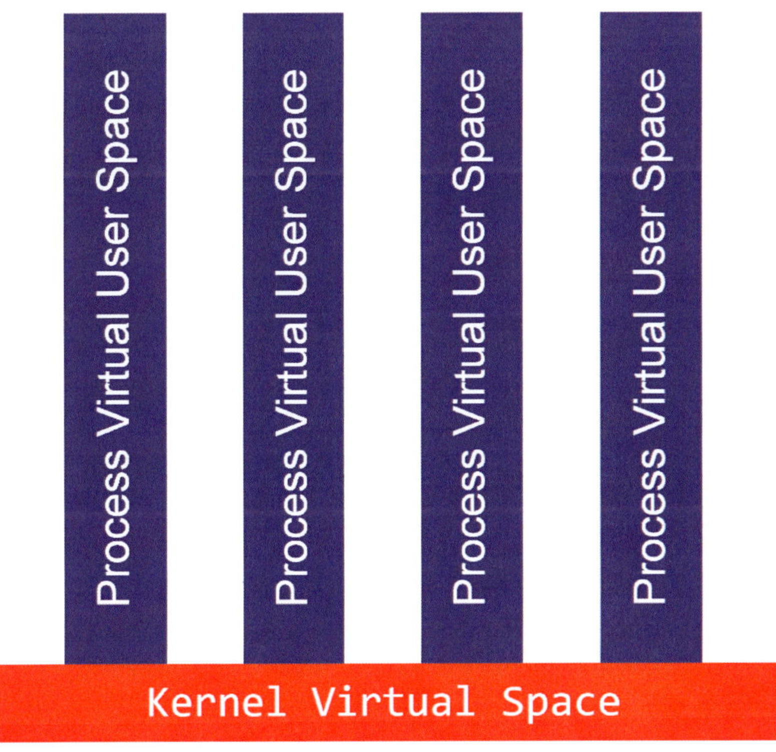

Cubic Memory Representation

A nibble is a (0,1)-matrix, a byte is a cubic 0,1-lattice, and the next cubic byte-boundary 0,1-lattice represents a 64-bit qword:

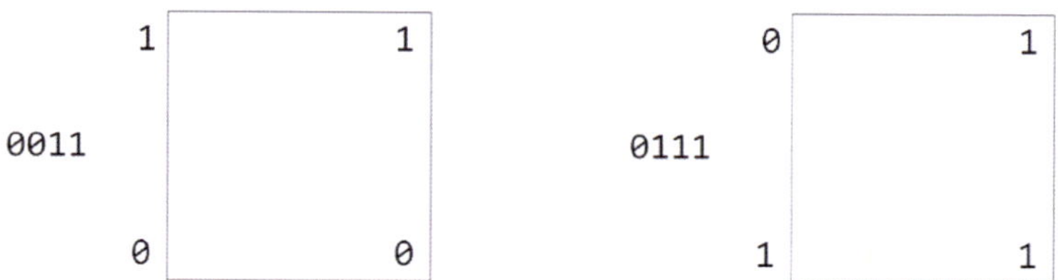

0
1
1
1
01110011
1
0
0

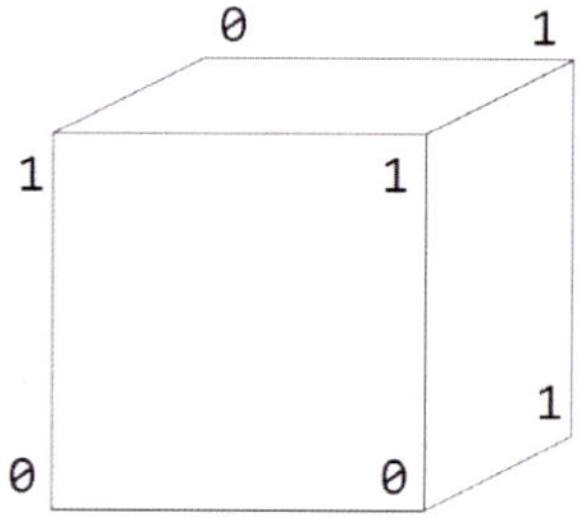

We call this a **natural memory representation** of memory building blocks or **qubic memory** (do not mistake it with qubit memory). It elevates bytes and 64-bit quadruple words as natural addresses and shows that 32-bit addresses are unnatural.

Qubic memory also allows visualizing specific overlapped memory patterns in dump files (same vertice, edge, or side).

Manifold Memory Space

We propose such a name for a multiple virtual memory space view taking into account code and data sharing:

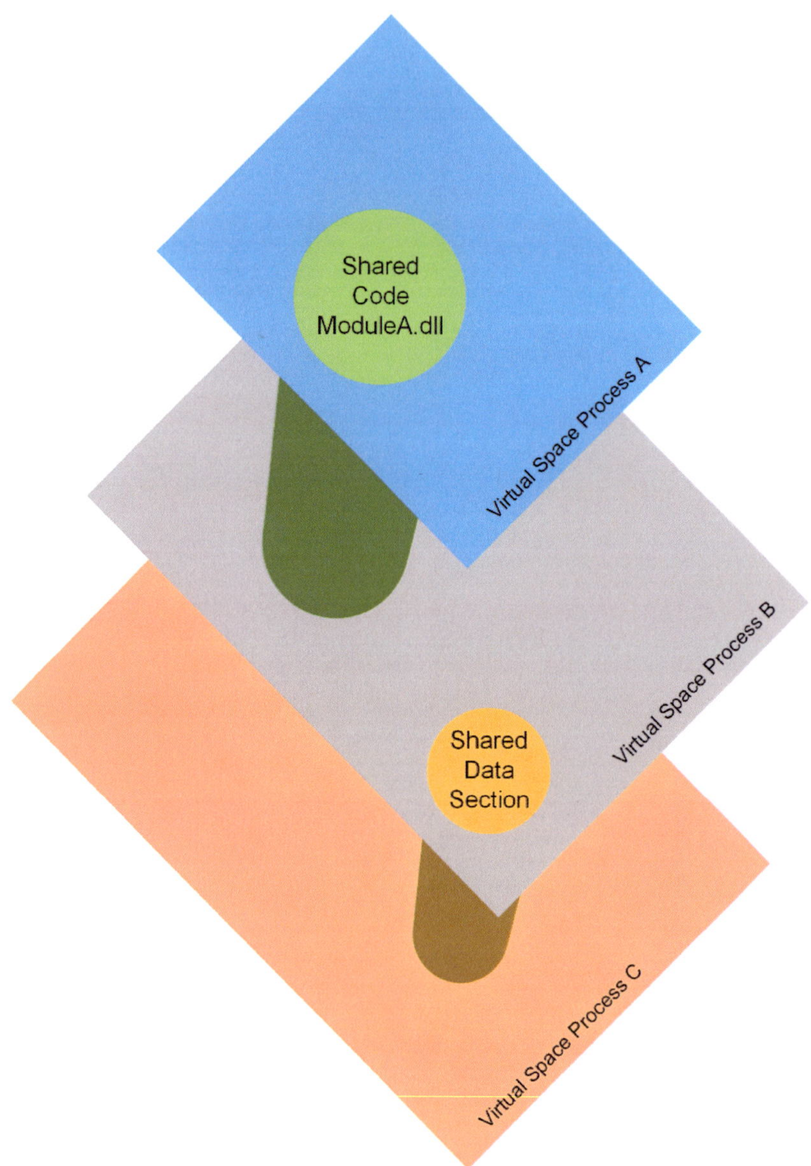

The same physical memory region can be mapped to different virtual memory regions. Here is another example of a sample manifold memory space where a physical memory region is mapped to the same virtual memory address range [N, M] of 3 OS processes:

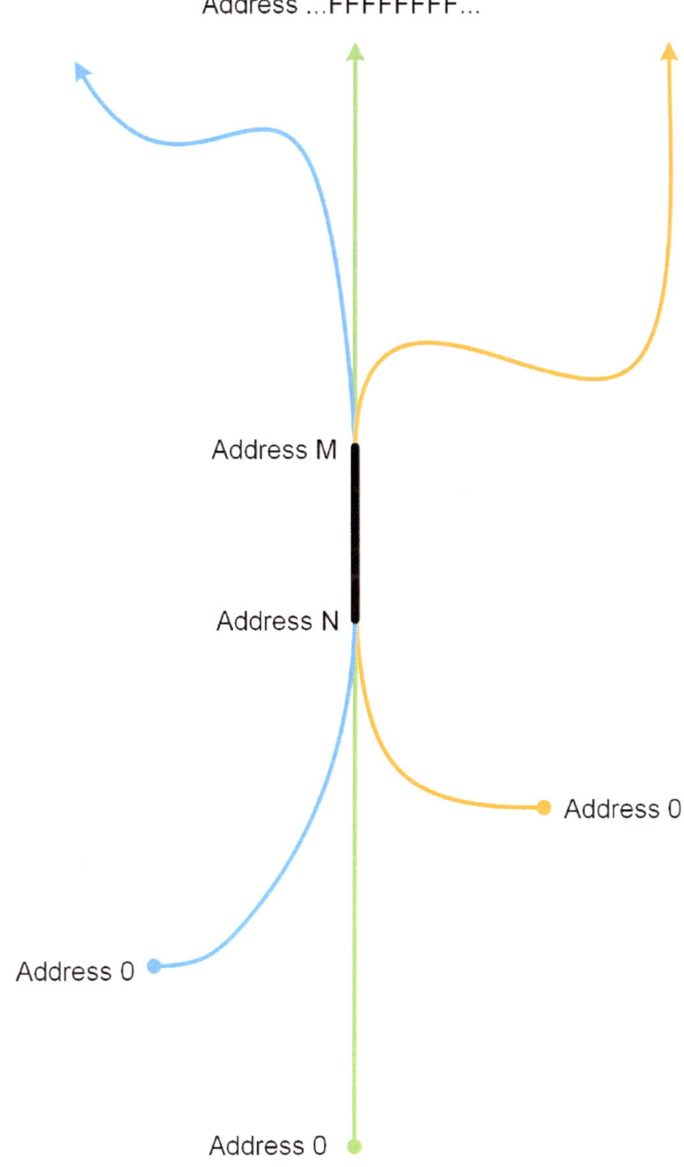

Extending Multithreading to Multibraiding (Adjoint Threading)

Having considered computational threads as braided strings (page 41) and after discerning software trace analysis patterns,[55] we can see formatted and tabulated software trace output in a new light and employ the "fabric of traces" and braid metaphors for an **Adjoint Thread** concept. This new concept was motivated by reading about *Extended Phenotype*[56] and extensive analysis of Citrix ETW-based CDF traces. The term *Adjoint* was borrowed from mathematics[57] because the concept we discuss below resembles this metaphorical formula: (Thread A, B) = [A, Thread B]. Let us first illustrate adjoint threading using simplified trace tables. Consider this generalized software trace example (date and time column are omitted for visual clarity):

#	Source Dir	PID	TID	File Name	Function	Message
1	\src\subsystemA	2792	5676	file1.cpp	fooA	Message text…
2	\src\subsystemA	2792	5676	file1.cpp	fooA	Message text…
3	\src\subsystemA	2792	5676	file1.cpp	fooA	Message text…
4	\src\lib	2792	5680	file2.cpp	barA	Message text…
5	\src\subsystemA	2792	5680	file1.cpp	fooA	Message text…
6	\src\subsystemA	2792	5676	file1.cpp	fooA	Message text…
7	\src\lib	2792	5680	file2.cpp	fooA	Message text…
8	\src\lib	2792	5680	file2.cpp	fooA	Message text…
9	\src\subsystemB	2792	3912	file3.cpp	barB	Message text…
10	\src\subsystemB	2792	3912	file3.cpp	barB	Message text…
11	\src\subsystemB	2792	3912	file3.cpp	barB	Message text…
12	\src\subsystemB	2792	3912	file3.cpp	barB	Message text…
13	\src\subsystemB	2792	3912	file3.cpp	barB	Message text…
14	\src\subsystemB	2792	3912	file3.cpp	barB	Message text…
15	\src\subsystemB	2792	2992	file4.cpp	fooB	Message text…
16	\src\subsystemB	2792	3008	file4.cpp	fooB	Message text…
…	…	…	…	…	…	…

We see several threads in a process PID 2792. In CDFAnalyzer, we can filter trace messages that belong to any column, and if we filter by TID, we get a view of any **Thread of Activity**[58]. However, each thread can "run" through any source directory, file name or function. If a function belongs to a library, multiple threads access it. This source location (can be considered as a subsystem), file, or function view of activity is called an **Adjoint Thread.** For example, if we filter only subsystemA column in the trace above, we get this table:

#	*Source Dir*	PID	TID	File Name	Function	Message
1	***\src\subsystemA***	2792	5676	file1.cpp	fooA	Message ...
2	***\src\subsystemA***	2792	5676	file1.cpp	fooA	Message ...
3	***\src\subsystemA***	2792	5676	file1.cpp	fooA	Message ...
5	***\src\subsystemA***	2792	5680	file1.cpp	fooA	Message ...
6	***\src\subsystemA***	2792	5676	file1.cpp	fooA	Message ...
7005	***\src\subsystemA***	2792	**5664**	file1.cpp	fooA	Message ...
10198	***\src\subsystemA***	2792	**5664**	file1.cpp	fooA	Message ...
10364	***\src\subsystemA***	2792	**5664**	file1.cpp	fooA	Message ...
10417	***\src\subsystemA***	2792	**5664**	file1.cpp	fooA	Message ...
10420	***\src\subsystemA***	2792	5676	file1.cpp	fooA	Message ...
10422	***\src\subsystemA***	2792	5680	file1.cpp	fooA	Message ...
10587	***\src\subsystemA***	2792	**5664**	file1.cpp	fooA	Message ...
10767	***\src\subsystemA***	2792	5680	file1.cpp	fooA	Message ...
11126	***\src\subsystemA***	2792	**5668**	file1.cpp	fooA	Message ...
11131	***\src\subsystemA***	2792	5680	file1.cpp	fooA	Message ...
11398	***\src\subsystemA***	2792	5676	file1.cpp	fooA	Message ...
11501	***\src\subsystemA***	2792	**5668**	file1.cpp	fooA	Message ...
11507	***\src\subsystemA***	2792	**5668**	file1.cpp	fooA	Message ...
11509	***\src\subsystemA***	2792	**5664**	file1.cpp	fooA	Message ...
11513	***\src\subsystemA***	2792	5680	file1.cpp	fooA	Message ...
11524	***\src\subsystemA***	2792	**5668**	file1.cpp	fooA	Message ...
...	...	...	...	...	...	...

We can graphically view subsystemA as a braid string that "permeates the fabric of threads":

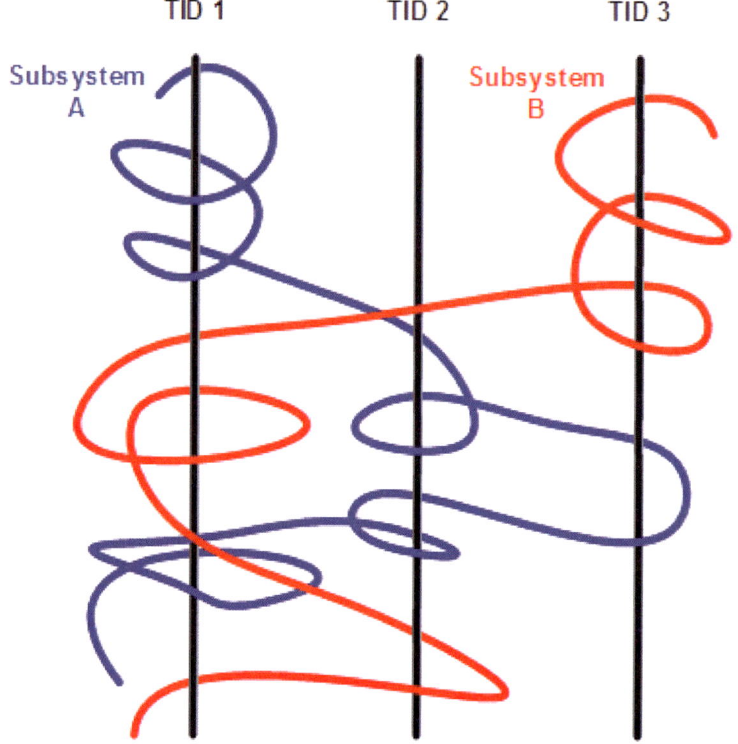

We can get many different braids by changing filters, hence *multi*braiding. Here is another example of a driver source file view initially permeating two process contexts and four threads:

#	Source Dir	PID	TID	*File Name*	Function	Message
41	\src\sys\driver	3636	3848	*entry.c*	DriverEntry	IOCTL ...
80	\src\sys\driver	3636	3896	*entry.c*	DriverEntry	IOCTL ...
99	\src\sys\driver	3636	3896	*entry.c*	DriverEntry	IOCTL ...
102	\src\sys\driver	3636	3896	*entry.c*	DriverEntry	IOCTL ...
179	\src\sys\driver	3636	3896	*entry.c*	DriverEntry	IOCTL ...
180	\src\sys\driver	3636	3896	*entry.c*	DriverEntry	IOCTL ...

311	\src\sys\driver	3636	3896	***entry.c***	DriverEntry	IOCTL	...
447	\src\sys\driver	3636	3896	***entry.c***	DriverEntry	IOCTL	...
448	\src\sys\driver	3636	3896	***entry.c***	DriverEntry	IOCTL	...
457	\src\sys\driver	2792	5108	***entry.c***	DriverEntry	IOCTL	...
608	\src\sys\driver	3636	3896	***entry.c***	DriverEntry	IOCTL	...
614	\src\sys\driver	3636	3896	***entry.c***	DriverEntry	IOCTL	...
655	\src\sys\driver	3636	3896	***entry.c***	DriverEntry	IOCTL	...
675	\src\sys\driver	3636	3896	***entry.c***	DriverEntry	IOCTL	...
678	\src\sys\driver	3636	3896	***entry.c***	DriverEntry	IOCTL	...
680	\src\sys\driver	3636	3896	***entry.c***	DriverEntry	IOCTL	...
681	\src\sys\driver	3636	3896	***entry.c***	DriverEntry	IOCTL	...
1145	\src\sys\driver	3636	4960	***entry.c***	DriverEntry	IOCTL	...
1153	\src\sys\driver	3636	4960	***entry.c***	DriverEntry	IOCTL	...
1154	\src\sys\driver	3636	4960	***entry.c***	DriverEntry	IOCTL	...
...	...	...	...	...	...	...	

[This page is intentionally left blank]

Volume 5

Software Behavior Patterns

Forthcoming CARE[59] and STARE[60] online systems additionally aim to provide software behavior pattern identification via debugger log and trace analysis and suggest possible software troubleshooting patterns. This work started in October 2006 with the identification of computer memory patterns[61] and later continued with software trace patterns[62]. Bringing all of them under a unified linked framework seems quite natural to the author.

Structural Memory Patterns

In this part, we divide memory analysis patterns discerned so far as mostly abnormal software behavior memory dump[63] and software trace[64] patterns into behavioral and structural catalogs. The goal is to account for normal system-independent structural entities and relationships visible in memory like modules, threads, processes.

Note: These patterns can be found in Memory Dump Analysis Anthology volumes 5, 9b, and further patterns are planned for publishing.

General Memory Analysis

General Memory Analysis is another name for Memoretics (page 54), a discipline that studies memory snapshots, including their similarities and differences on different system platforms such as Windows, Linus, Mac OS X, embedded and mobile systems, historical architectures. The analysis of memory helps solve problems in various domains such as software troubleshooting and debugging, computer forensic analysis, cyber warfare.

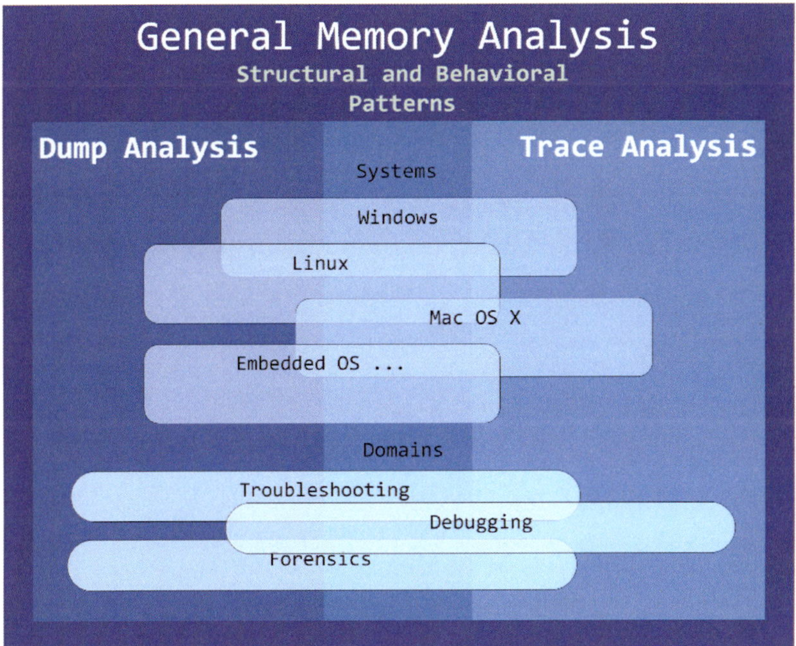

The current focus of interdisciplinary research is to build a unified memory pattern language (page 106) that covers both behavioral and structural patterns, and also to study the possibility of building memory systems from below, not from requirements -> architecture -> design -> implementation -> compilation -> linking -> loading -> execution but from directly modeling and assembling memory systems using memory patterns.

Memory Systems Language

Computer memory analysis is based on interconnected structures of symbols. We state that there exists a memory language that extends a hierarchy of modeling and implementation languages (both domain-specific and general-purpose):

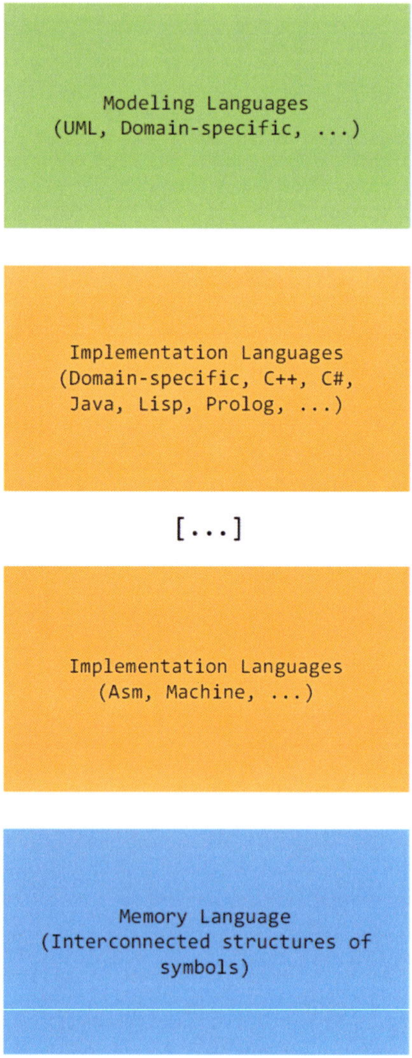

Modeling Languages
(UML, Domain-specific, ...)

Implementation Languages
(Domain-specific, C++, C#, Java, Lisp, Prolog, ...)

[...]

Implementation Languages
(Asm, Machine, ...)

Memory Language
(Interconnected structures of symbols)

Notation for Memory and Trace Analysis

Here we introduce a syntactical notation for memory (dump) and software trace and log analysis pattern languages (in addition to graphical notation proposed earlier, page 77). It is simple and concise: allow easy grammar with plain syntax and obvious reading semantics. We propose to use capitalized letters for major pattern categories, for example, **W** for **Wait Chains**[65] and **D** for **Deadlocks**[66]. Then use subscripts (or small letters) for pattern subcategories, for example, **Wcs** and **Dlpc**. Several categories and subcategories can be combined by using a slash (/), for example, **Wcs/Dcs/lpc**. Slash notation is better viewed using subscripts:

$$\mathbf{W}_{cs}/\mathbf{D}_{cs/lpc}$$

In the next volumes, we introduce more categories and propose notational adornments for pattern succession (page 81), space differentiation, and the inclusion of details in notational sentences.

Models of Software Behavior

Due to many requests for memory dumps corresponding to crash dump analysis patterns, we started modeling software behavior and defects. Every pattern has an example application(s), service(s) or driver(s) or a combination of them. Their execution results in a memory layout that corresponds to memory or trace analysis patterns. Some initial examples can be found in Volume 6[67].

Category Theory and Troubleshooting

Troubleshooting can be represented as a category[68] of memory states (or collections of proximate states) as objects and troubleshooting tools as arrows:

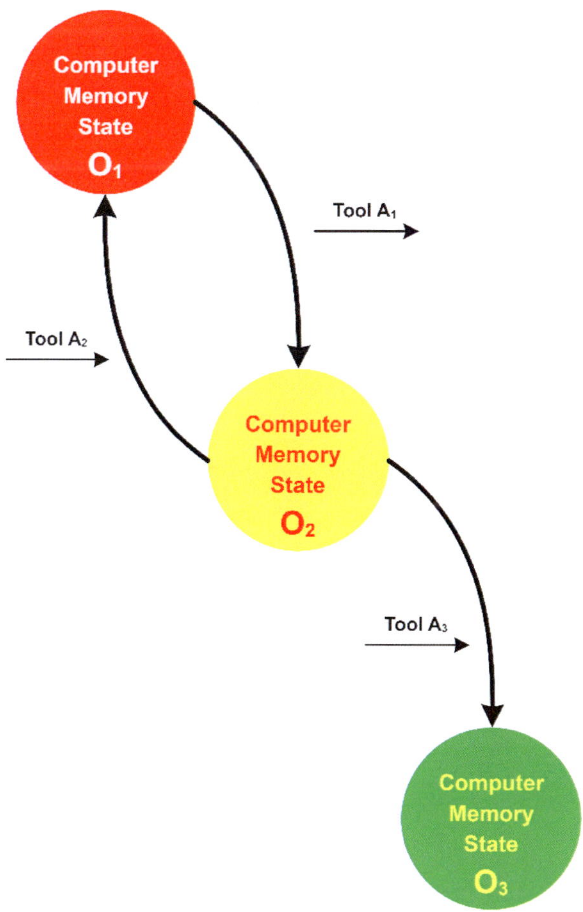

We can also consider tools as categories with arrows as troubleshooting actions. In the latter case, we can model a collection of tools and transformations (morphisms) between them as a functor.

Collective Pointer

We now introduce collective pointers or pointer cones. Suppose we have a set of pointers pointing to the fields of some memory structure. This set of pointers could be another structure as well or just a collection of pointers that can be logically brought together:

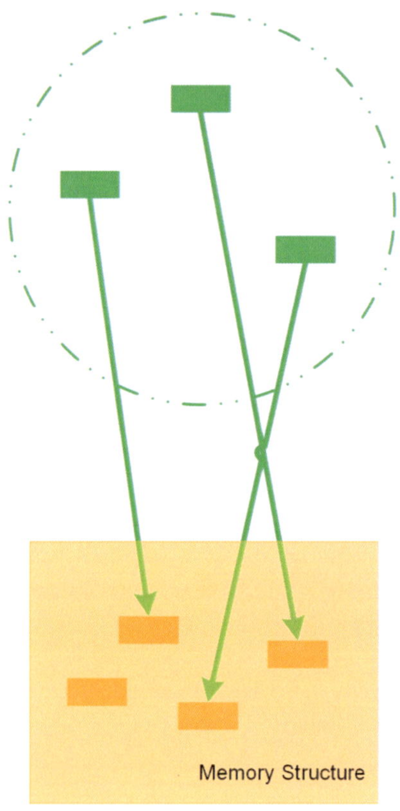

If we make the boundary opaque, we can name such set of pointers as **Collective Pointer** (or **Pointer Cone**):

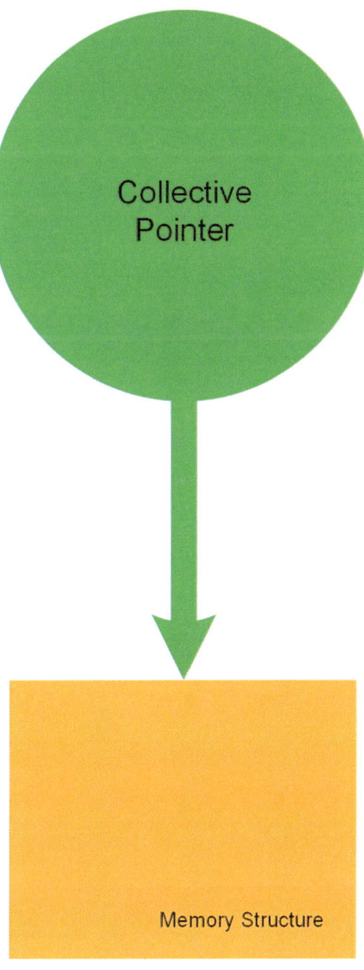

Another example is when we split the perception field (page 88) of a pointer into disjoint collective pointers (the perception field as a whole is already a trivial collective pointer):

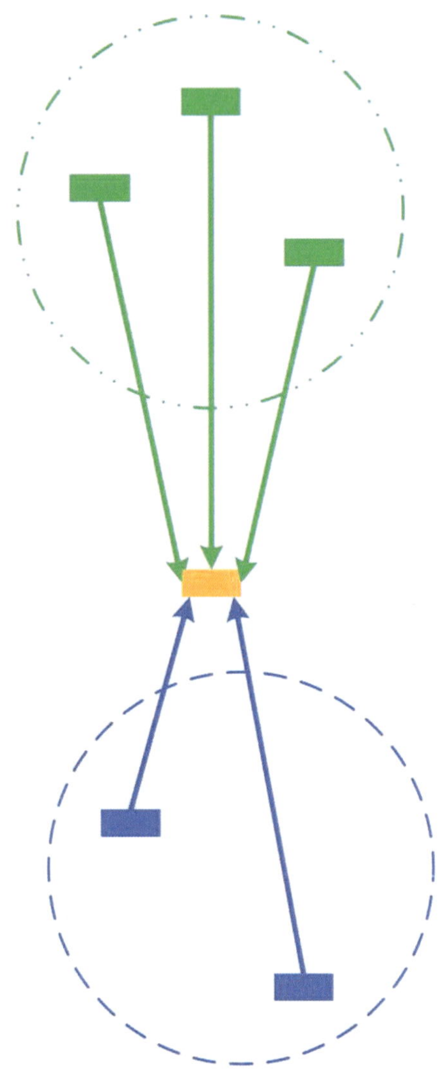

On Unconscious

Computer software is said to be simple and predictable as any mechanism[69]. We can debug it. We can completely trace what it is doing. It seems rational to us. Let's then label it as Conscious. On the outside, there is an irrational human being who programmed that software. Let's then label that person's mind as Unconscious. What about hardware and body? They form parts of HCI (Human-Computer Interaction or Interface).

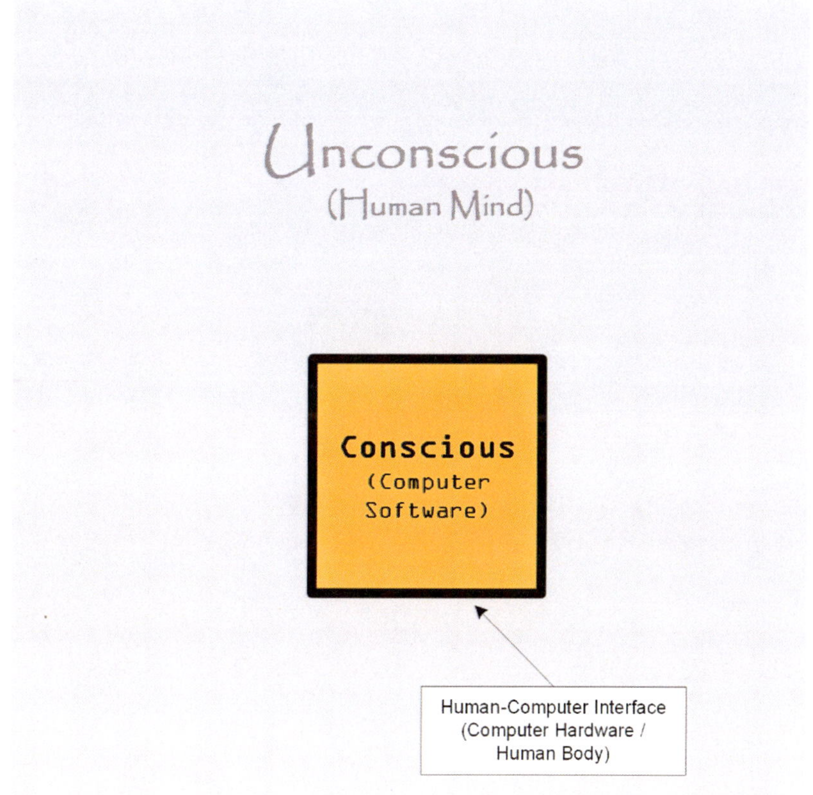

Psychoanalysis of Software Troubleshooting and Debugging

We would like to introduce the notion of **Forgotten Facts** in opposition to **Basic Facts**[70] or **Supporting Information** (page 29). These are facts that engineers often feel uncomfortable to mention because they are troubleshooting information they could not obtain (if they tried) due to some time or customer pressures, failures, incorrectly understood troubleshooting procedures, or some other obstacles. Therefore, it is important to have a set of counter questions or checklists mapped from common software behavior patterns to software troubleshooting patterns. Problem descriptions should also be subjected to close reading to reveal unconsciously concealed information.

Archaeological Foundations for Memory Analysis

We can adapt archaeological classificatory framework (using the method of inquiry called metaphorical bijectionism, page 83) to lay out foundations for yet another attempt to classify DA+TA patterns (Dump Analysis + Trace Analysis):

```
Attribute  ⇔ Pattern
Artifact   ⇔ Component Artifact71
Assemblage ⇔ Component Assemblage
Culture    ⇔ Memory System Culture72
```

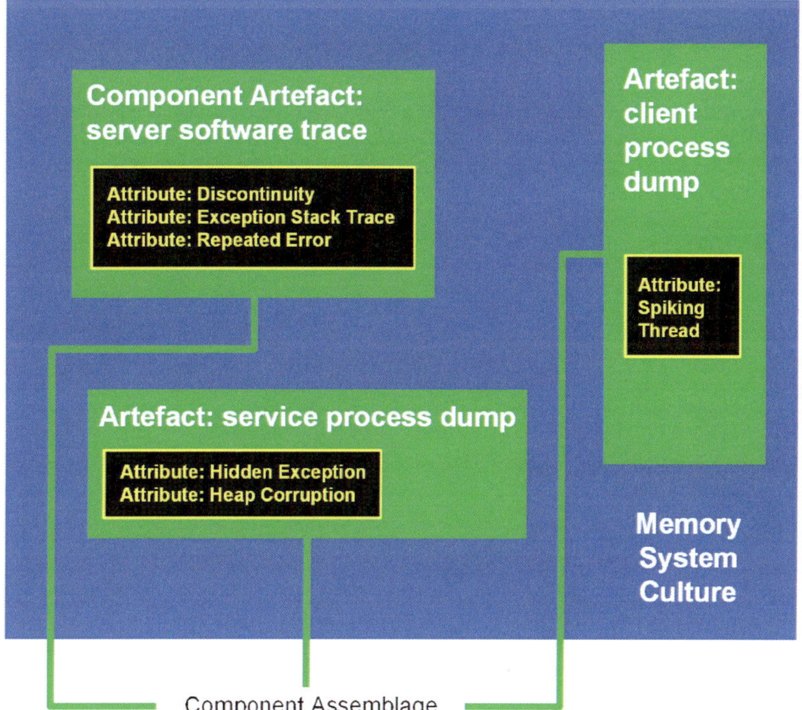

We propose a word *Memoarchaeological* for such a framework and Memoarchaeology for a branch of Memoretics (page 54) that studies saved computer memory artifacts from past computations (as opposed to live memory).

Software Chorography and Chorology: A Definition

In addition to software narratology (page 58), we would like to introduce another two branches of memoretics (borrowed from "geographical" chorography[73] and chorology[74]), the science of memory snapshots (page 54):

Software Chorography

The study and visualization of small memory regions compared to the full memory dumps.

Software Chorology

The spatial equivalent of software narratology where the latter is considered in chronological terms. Studies spatial distribution and causal relations between software behavioral and structural phenomena inside particular memory regions.

To give a perspective where usual software traces and memory dumps reside in terms of narrativity and non-narrativity (spatiality), we created this diagram:

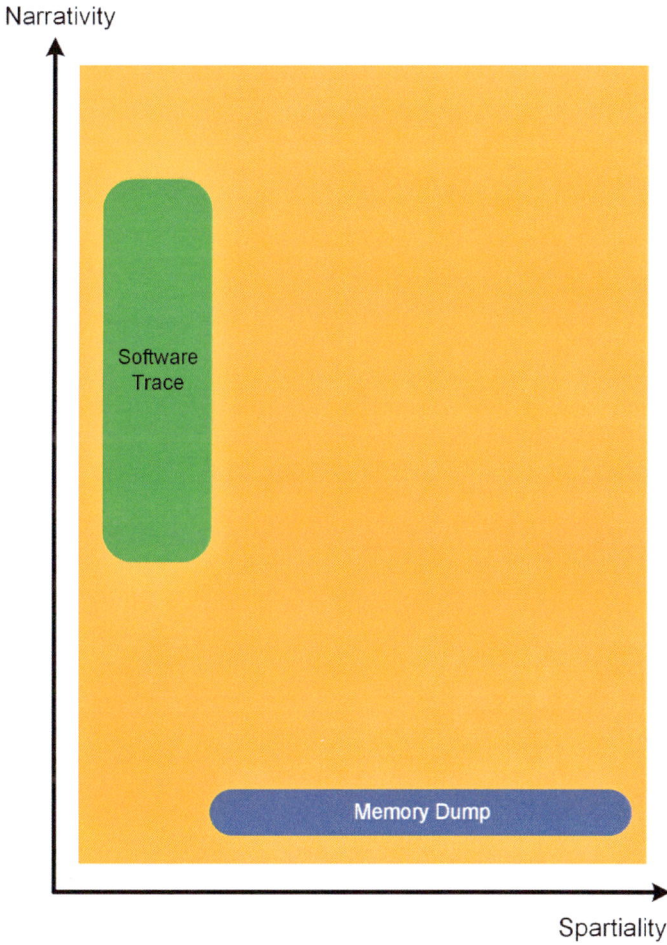

Memory dumps have some extension in the dimension of narrativity because it is possible to get **Stack Trace Collection**[75] and other **Execution Residues**[76] from them that provide partial fragments of a software narrative.

Basic Software PLOTs

Behind every trace and its messages is source code:

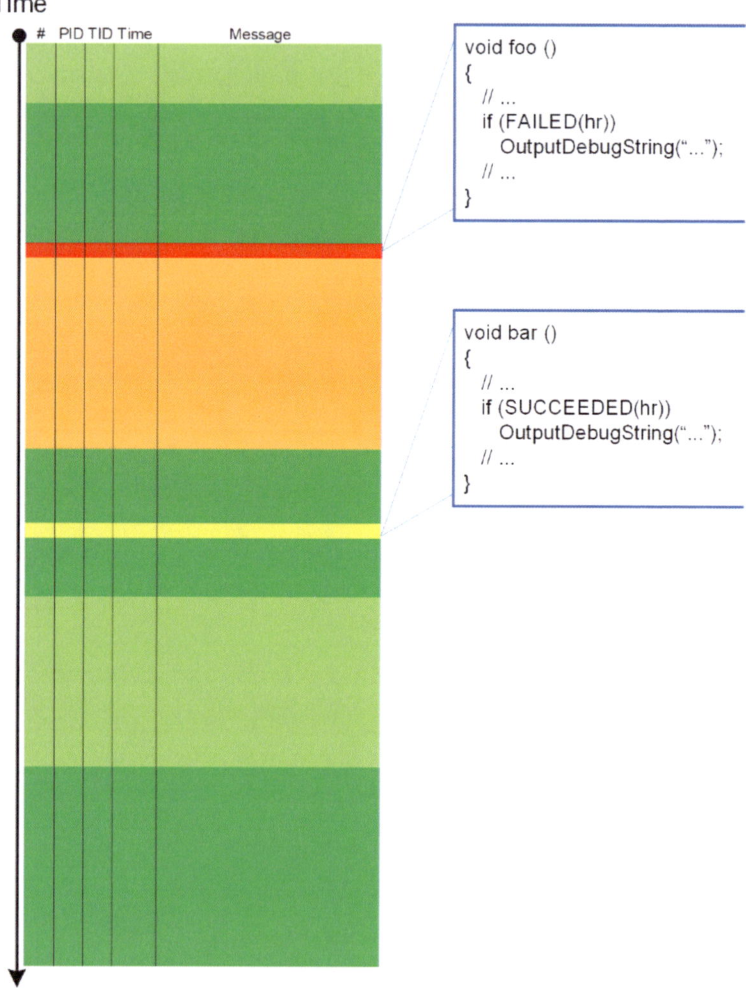

Borrowing the acronym PLOT (Program Lines of Trace[77]), we now try to discern basic source code patterns that give rise to simple message patterns in software traces. There are only a few distinct PLOTs, and the ability to mentally map trace statements to source code is crucial to software trace reading and comprehension. More complex message patterns (for example, specific message blocks or correlated messages) arise from supportable and maintainable realizations of architectural, design, and implementation patterns.

We were thinking about the acronym SLOT (Source Lines of Trace) but decided to use PLOT because it metaphorically bijects (page 83) into literary theory[78] and narrative plots[79].

The Extended Software Trace

By analogy with paratext,[80] let us introduce a software narratological concept of the extended software trace that consists of a software trace plus additional supporting information that makes troubleshooting and debugging easier. Such "paratextual" information can consist of pictures, videos, accounts of scenarios and past problem histories, customer interviews, and even software trace delivery medium and format (if preformatted).

Presenting a Software Story

It is time to introduce a conceptual software narratological framework for viewing software traces (using rich ETW / CDF tracing as our main focus). Here we consider a software story (fabula[81]) as a full trace when every component was selected for tracing and emits debug messages during code execution paths. However, during viewing, we can filter on and off certain modules, threads, processes, messages (adjoint threading, page 98), and see a different sub-story or plot (sujet[82]). Every software plot (please do not confuse with PLOT acronym, page 118) can be presented differently (by using appropriate discourse[83]). Some presentational examples include temporal rearrangement, the collapse of repetitive regions, source code hypertext (lexia), and allegorical devices such as message tool-tip comments. Here is a diagram that depicts story (fable, fabula) - plot (sujet) - presentation (discourse):

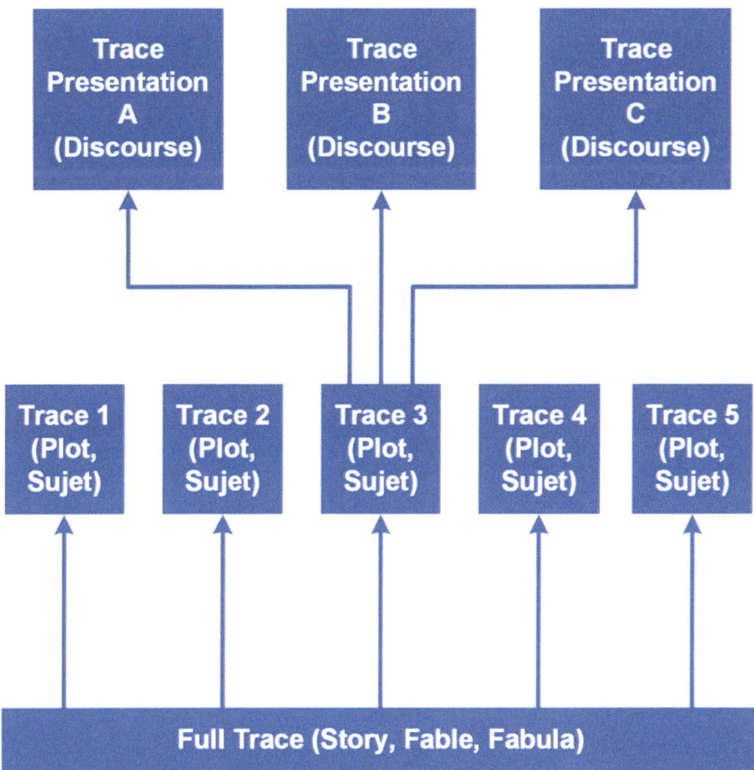

Two Readings of a Software Trace

When we have a software trace, we read it in two directions. The first one is to deconstruct it into linear ordered source code based on PLOT fragments (page 118). The second direction is to construct an interpretation that serves as an explanation for reported software behavior. During the interpretive reading, we remove irrelevant information, compress relevant activity regions, and construct the new fictional software trace based on discovered patterns and our problem description.

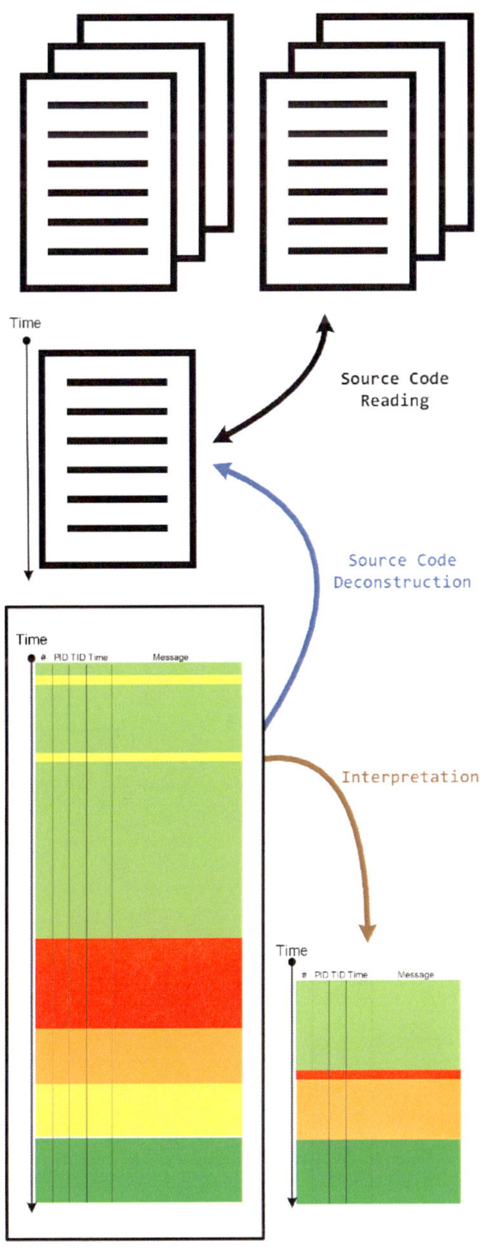
Time
Source Code
Reading
Source Code
Deconstruction
Time
PID TID Time
Message
Interpretation
Time
PID TID Time
Message

[This page is intentionally left blank]

Volume 6

Intelligence Analysis Patterns

Being deep into studying intelligence analysis[84] while preparing for a cyber warfare memory dump analysis presentation, we came to an idea of intelligence analysis patterns based on software trace analysis patterns[85] and Software Narratology (page 58). We consider intelligence data as pseudo-software trace messages with an additional probability field (column). Most of the patterns can be transferred and used immediately in intelligence analysis, and we are working on such a map. Because real software trace messages are quite certain (deterministic), but their sequences sometimes are not (for example, **Impossible Trace** pattern[86]), there are some unique patterns applicable only in the intelligence analysis domain.

A.C.P. Root Cause Analysis Methodology

It is a very simple methodology summarized in just three words applicable to any problem-solving domain. Its activities include software troubleshooting and debugging:

Artifacts. Checklists. Patterns.

As an example of checklists and patterns, please see these three presentations related to memory dump and software trace artifacts:

- Introduction to Pattern-Driven Software Problem Solving[87]
- Fundamentals of Complete Crash and Hang Memory Dump Analysis[88]
- Software Trace and Memory Dump Analysis: Patterns, Tools, Processes and Best Practices[89]

Function Activity Theory

Borrowing routine activity theory[90] (RAT) from criminology, we would like to introduce the similar approach to abnormal software behavior with patterning activities that adds additional unmotivated offenders to combine malware (software rats) with unintentional ordinary common bugware:

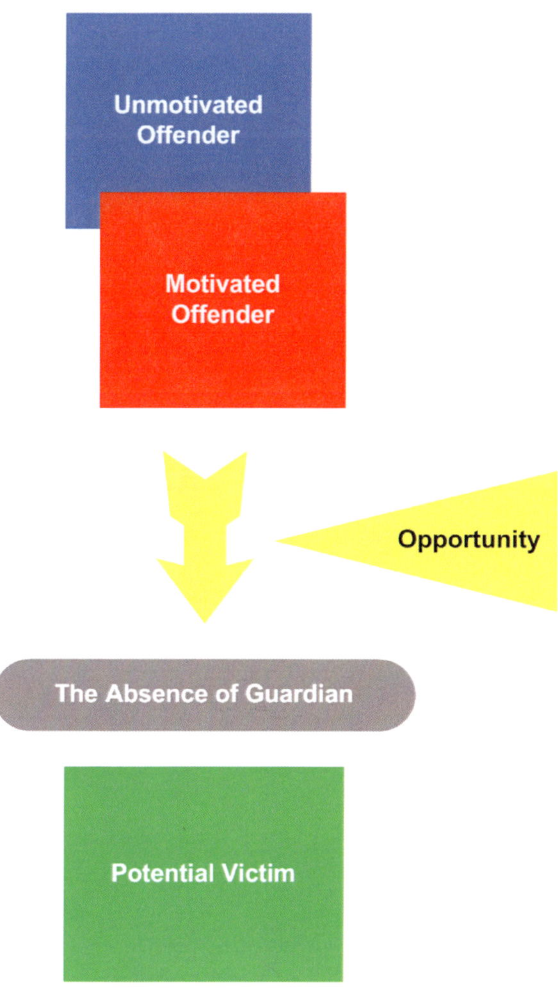

The application of RAT to software can be metaphorically named as Function Activity Theory (FAT).

Close and Deconstructive Readings of a Software Trace

There are two trace reading practices with techniques borrowed from structuralist and post-structuralist narratology:

1. Close reading

- emphasizes structural patterns;
- looks at a software trace as a unity of messages;
- searches for similarities, repetitions, and contrasts;
- reveals code reflections in message texts.

2. Deconstructive reading

- reveals subconscious (page 114) exposed in message texts;
- searches for conflicting and absent messages;
- looks at a software trace as disunity of messages from conflicting components.

Analysis, Architectural, Design, Implementation and Usage Debugging Patterns

We now start unifying software behavior analysis patterns with debugging architecture, design, implementation, and usage. This is analogous to software construction, where a problem analysis leads to various software engineering phases. The important difference here is the addition of debugging usage patterns. Let's look at an example:

- Analysis Patterns

  Shared Buffer Overwrite[91]

- Architectural Patterns

  Debug Event Subscription/Notification

- Design Patterns

  Punctuated Execution

- Implementation Patterns

  Breakpoint (software and hardware)

- Usage Patterns

  Kernel vs. user space breakpoints

To differentiate this systematic approach from the published ad hoc debugging patterns, we call it **Unified Debugging Pattern Language**. **ADI** parts can also correspond to various **DebugWare** patterns, page 45.

Generative Debugging

Followed by our search for a periodic table of software defects (page 138), we came up with a novel approach called **Generative Debugging,** partially borrowed from principles and parameters [92] generative linguistics framework. For debugging and post-construction software problem-solving [93] purposes, we have *Behavioral Principles* and *Structural Parameters*. The parameters allow us to describe existing and even generate new software defects (We are also considering *Structural Principles* and *Behavioral Parameters,* but whether this is fruitful needs to be explored and seen). We may also consider the name "generative debugging" as a "naming" counterpart to software construction problem solving called generative programming[94]. So the former could also be used to generate problem solutions faster in an automated fashion. Both, in the future, maybe combined into a unified generative software problem solving.

As a first example, consider functional hang of an application with a thread blocked by a pending I/O request packet (IRP). It is composed of the general behavioral principle of blocked (or unresponsive) activity and structural parameters, including Thread and IRP.

Metadefect Template Library

To model software behavior at application and system levels, test generative debugging (page 130) scenarios, and construct software defects using metaprogramming[95], we started working on **MdTL** (**M**eta**d**efect **T**emplate **L**ibrary). It consists of C++ templates for structural and behavioral patterns. The simplest examples include *Threads<Spike>* and *Spike<Thread>*. The template classes can be more complex, of course, utilizing the full power of C++, STL, and existing libraries like Boost. The unique and novel feature of this library is the inclusion of dual classes of behavior such as *Leak<>*, *Deadlock<>*, *Overflow<>*, *Residue<>*, *Exception<>*, *Contention<>* parameterized by various structural memory classes like *Process<>*, *Thread<>*, *Heap<>*, *Stack<>*, *Region<>*, and *Buffer<>*. MdTL also includes classes to model software tracing, and this can be used for simultaneous software trace and memory dump analysis. We also plan to extend this metaprogramming approach in the future to model malware analysis patterns by introducing Metamalware Template Library (MmTL).

Orbifold Memory Space

This is a multiple virtual/physical memory space view taking into account multiple computers:

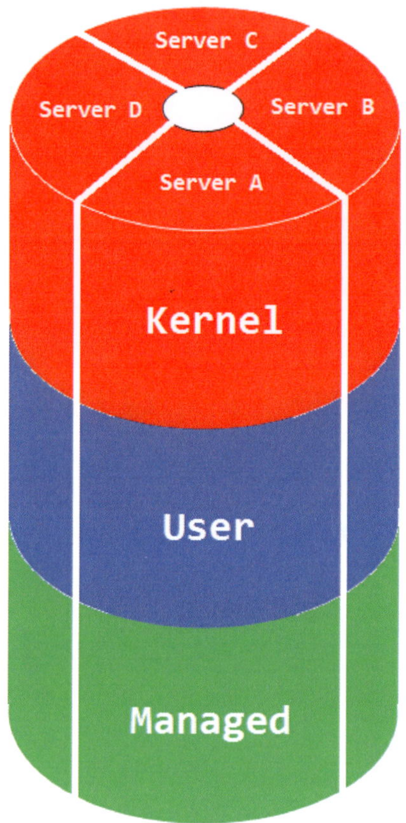

The picture can be much more complex if we glue different manifold memory spaces (page 96). The space name comes from a mathematical orbifold[96], the generalization of a manifold[97]. It is also a good metaphor for a cloud memory space[98].

Uses of Memoretics

Memoretics (page 54) promotes pattern-driven memory dump and software trace analysis, which has many uses but not limited to:

- Software and Site Reliability
- Software Diagnostics
- Software Debugging
- QA and Software Testing
- Computer Security
- Software Troubleshooting
- Malware Research and Analysis
- Tools as a Service (TaaS)
- Supportability

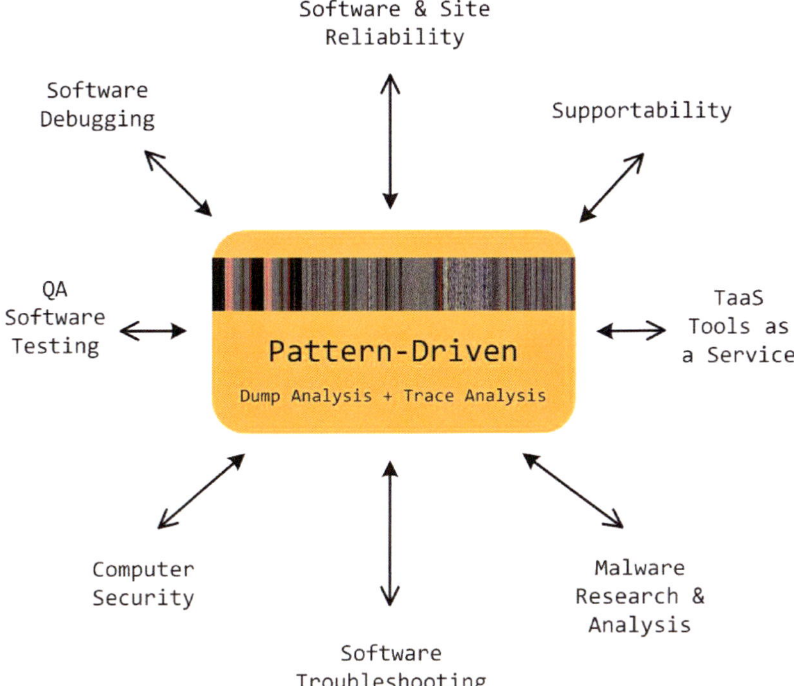

Crossdisciplinary Memoretics as Interdisciplinary Science

Memoretics (page 54) as a science of memory snapshots borrows many ideas from the following disciplines (the list is not exhaustive):

- Troubleshooting and Debugging
- Intelligence Analysis
- Critical Thinking
- Forensics
- Linguistics
- Archaeology
- Psychoanalysis
- History
- Mathematics: Sets and Categories
- Literary Criticism and Narratology

It also contributes many ideas back. The following diagram depicts such an interaction:

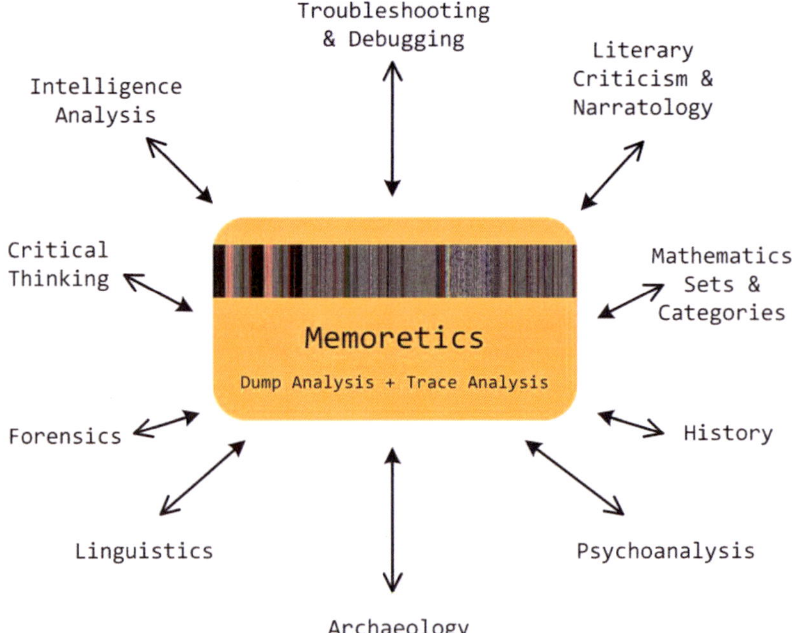

Coarse vs. Fine Grained DNA of Software Behavior

Whereas DNA of a ruptured computation[99] is coarse-grained, the software behavioral genome, in general, is fine-grained, consisting of multiple behavioral patterns such as seen in memory dumps[100] and software traces[101]. Here is a nice "memory DNA" metaphorical picture from the 3D memory visualization article[102]:

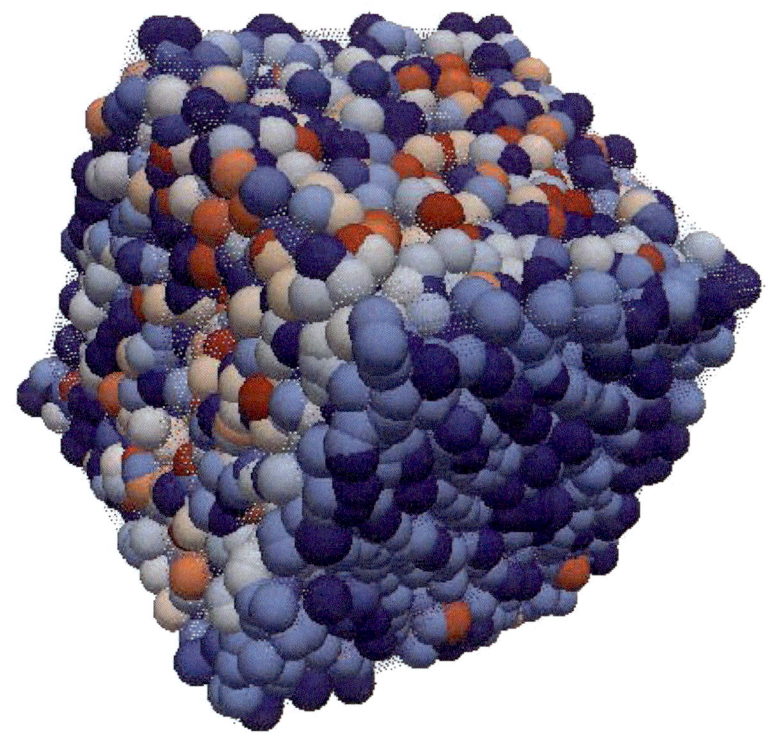

The Way of Philip Marlowe: Abductive Reasoning for Troubleshooting and Debugging

After working for more than seven years in a technical support environment, we found that many support incidents were resolved more easily by abductive reasoning[103] than by induction and deduction practiced by Sherlock Holmes and observed by Dr. Watson. Abduction as a way to build an incident theory to advance in problem resolution was practiced by a USA colleague of Holmes: Philip Marlowe[104]. Because technical support is less detached from customers ("the world") when compared to software engineering departments, we see the way of Marlowe as more natural. Of course, from time to time, the way of Holmes is also appropriate. It all depends on a support case. We found that abductive reasoning is also appropriate for memory dump and software trace analysis where "leaps of faith" are necessary because of insufficient information. Such leaps of abduction happen all the time when analysts give troubleshooting advice based on patterns.

We are grateful for Clive Gamble for pointing this way out in his book[105].

The New School of Debugging

It is a new initiative to integrate traditional multidisciplinary debugging[106] approaches and methodologies with multiplatform pattern-driven software problem-solving[107], unified debugging patterns (page 129), best practices in memory dump analysis[108] and software tracing[109], computer security, economics, and the new emerging trends[110].

The New School of Debugging places pattern-driven memory and software trace analysis as a solid foundation for any debugging methodology, processes, tools, and techniques. *Unified Debugging Patterns* and *Generative Debugging Framework* (page 130) are additional features of the new school.

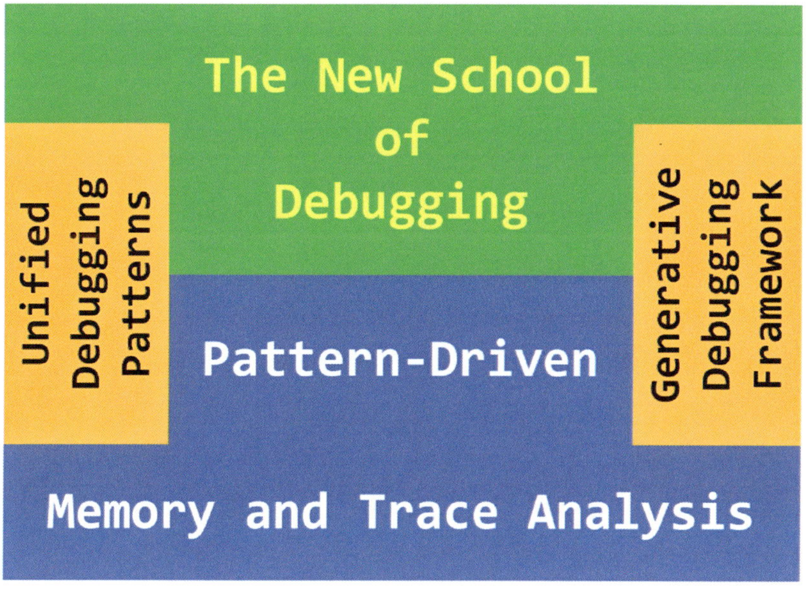

A Periodic Table of Software Defects

The author discovered rules that make it possible to devise a memory dump and software trace analysis equivalent of the Periodic Table of Elements in Chemistry. It allows predicting abnormal software behavior and structural defects and what patterns to look for after deploying software and collecting its artifacts.

User Interface Problem Analysis Patterns

As a part of the unified debugging (page 129) patterns and generative debugging (page 130) approach, we extend software behavior analysis patterns such as memory dump[111] and software trace[112] analysis with UI abnormal behavior patterns. Here, by abnormality, we mean behavior that users should not encounter while using software. A typical example is some error message or GUI distortion during the execution of a functional use case. Such patterns extend a pattern language for software behavior analysis we use to describe post-construction software problems.

Note: These patterns can be found in Memory Dump Analysis Anthology volumes 6, 7, and further patterns are planned for publishing.

[This page is intentionally left blank]

Volume 7

Software Anti-Narrative

In narratology, anti-narrative denotes a narrative which has sequences of events impossible in reality. In software traces, such sequences usually depict abnormal software behavior. Here are some parallels with corresponding trace analysis patterns:

Fiction	Software Trace
Repeated unrepeatable	Periodic Error[113] (?)
Denarration (erasure)	No Activity[114] / Incomplete History[115]
Chronological contradiction	Impossible Trace[116]

The question mark means that possibly another pattern is needed there.

Narremes in Software Narratology

Reading about narremes[117] suggested us to elaborate on a basic software trace (log) unit. One candidate is a trace message invariant, a skeleton trace message similar to a format string. There is also a corresponding software trace analysis pattern called **Message Invariant**[118]. Although this might be too an elementary unit akin to a sentence level and another possible candidate is a macromessage, a combination of several messages serving some semantic function. There are a corresponding general pattern **Macrofunction**[119] and an example of a concrete analysis pattern called **Exception Stack Trace**[120]. The actual software narreme might be situated between these two extremes: invariants and macrofunctions.

For additional information about software narratology, please look at these articles placed in chronological order (except a pattern catalog):

- Software Narratology: A Definition (page 58)
- Basic Software PLOTs (page 118)
- Two Readings of a Software Trace (page 122)
- The Extended Software Trace (page 120)
- Presenting a Software Story (page 121)
- Close and Deconstructive Readings of a Software Trace (page 128)
- Software Trace Analysis Pattern Catalog[121]

Narralog - A Software Trace Modeling Language

Teaching Accelerated Software Trace Analysis training[122] requires extensive real life like software logs with multiple software behavior patterns. The similar accelerated memory dump analysis courses (unmanaged/native Windows[123] and .NET[124]) also require good memory dumps, but this problem was solved by modeling patterns of abnormal software behavior in an appropriate implementation language such as C, C++, and C#. Modeling software traces with hundreds of software components, processes, and threads would require enormous programming efforts. Therefore, the natural approach is to describe the desired software trace in some declarative language (or minimally imperative) and get a million line software log that models a specific combination of trace analysis patterns. So, welcome to such a language called **Narralog**: Software **Narra**tive **Log** or **Narra**tive **Log**ic. This language is different from Riemann programming language (page 62), which is a language to describe software problems and generate software problem-solving tools.

What is a Software Narrative?

The previous definition (page 58) of software narratology was restricted to software traces and logs (the top left quadrant on a software narrative square (page 147). Now with the broadening of the domain of software narratology to the whole world of software narrative stories, including actor interactions with software in construction requirements use cases and post-construction incidents, we give another definition:

> **Software narrative** is a representation of software events and changes of state. **Software Narratology** is a discipline that studies such software narratives (software narrative science).

Software Narrative Planes

Using an idea of expression and content planes from glossematics[125] and a basic unit of glosseme we can organize software traces with corresponding patterns and software trace narremes (basic units of software narrative such as traces and event logs, page 142) into two planes: software trace narrative plane (*expression plane*) with narremes and the corresponding program lines of traces (PLOTs, page 118) source code and design plane (*content plane*) with their own set of construction narremes such as related to collaboration of software constructs. All this corresponds to the following diagram:

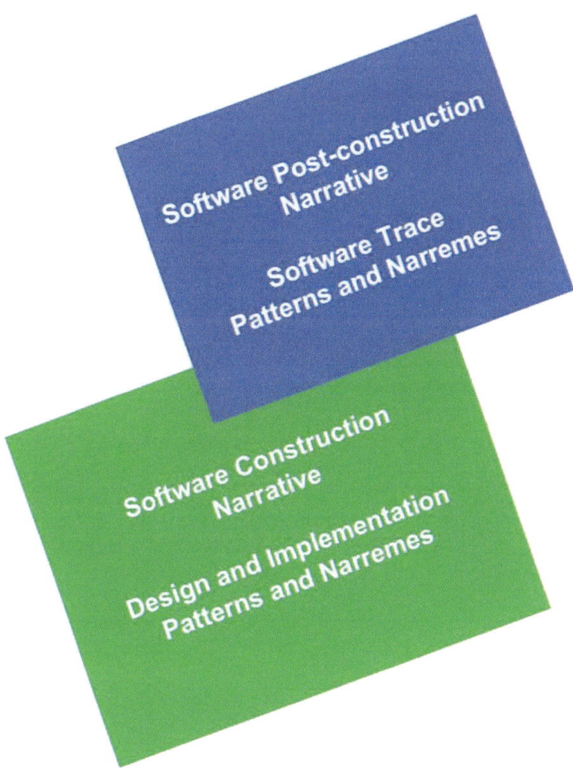

The same can be said about actor interaction level of software construction (*what ought to be*) and post-construction (*what is*) phases having their construction and post-construction narratives, patterns, and narremes such as in requirements (use cases) and problem and software incident descriptions:

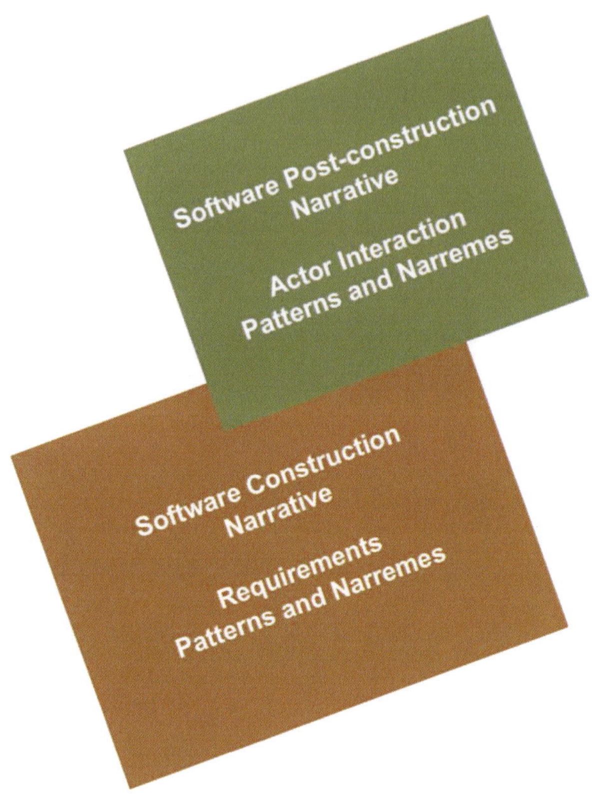

Software Narratology Square

After introducing software narrative planes (page 145), it is logical to expand the field of software narratology (page 58) to cover the whole domain of software construction and post-construction. We, therefore, combine both pairs of planes to create a narratological square:

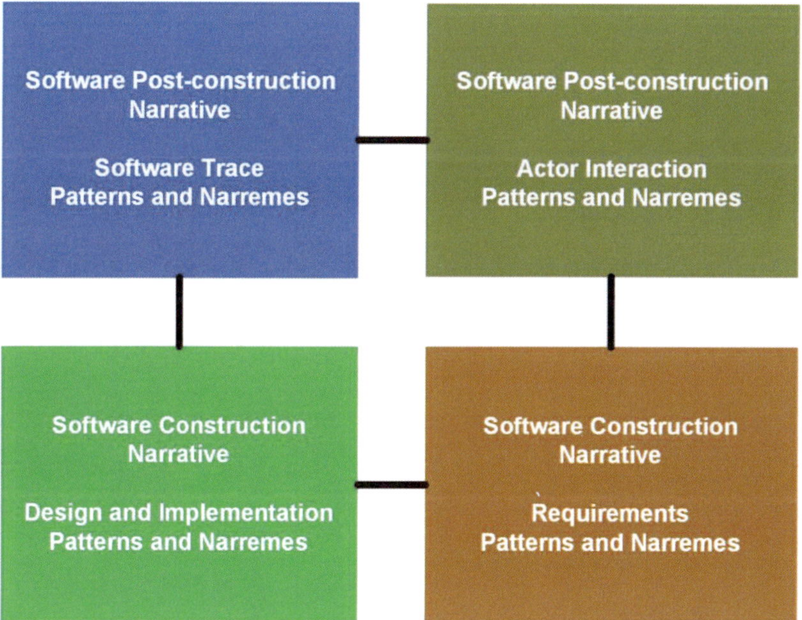

Software Trace Analysis Patterns Domain Hierarchy

We get many questions on whether software log analysis patterns from Software Diagnostics Institute[126] are OS or platform or product-specific. We answer that they are independent of all of them because they are based on viewing software logs as stories of computation and were discovered by applying narratological analysis (software narratology[127]). In addition to these patterns, there exist domain-specific problem patterns such as wrong hotfix level or specific product error code during software installation or execution.

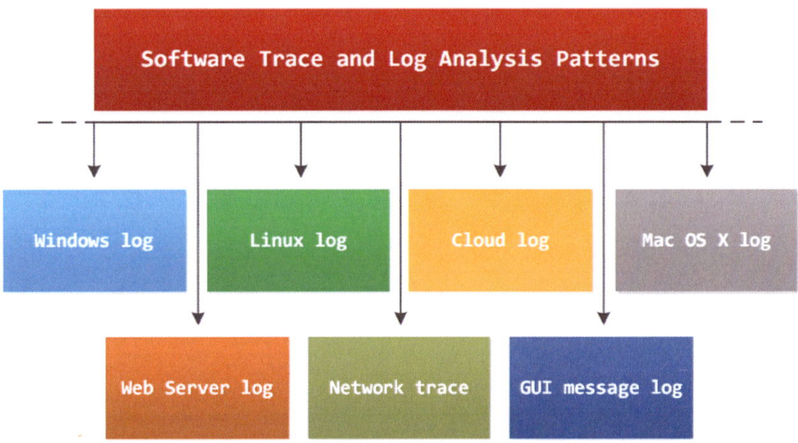

Generalized Software Narrative and Trace

In the past, we viewed software traces and logs as temporarily ordered event sequences. Since events are just memory data, we have a map:

T -> M

This can be seen in the definition of a software trace (page 59). Here we generalize the domain to any arbitrary set; for example, it can be a list of indexes or pointers or even memory itself. The latter map can give us narrative chains such as:

M -> M -> M -> M

Moreover, it can even give us a grand unification of memory and log analysis and the possibility to apply software narratology to memory dump analysis as well.

Unified Computer Diagnostics: Incorporating Hardware Narratology

Interpretation of hardware signals as messages and messages as signals allows us to apply Software Narratology and software trace analysis patterns to the domain of hardware diagnostics:

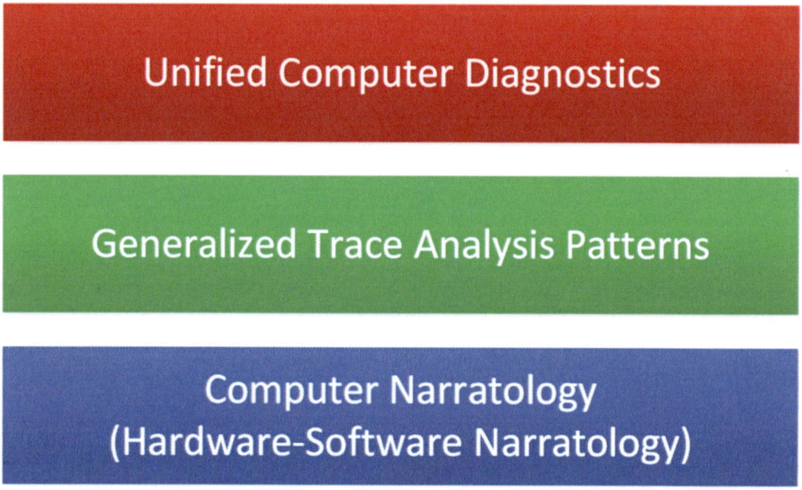

Unified Computer Diagnostics

Generalized Trace Analysis Patterns

Computer Narratology
(Hardware-Software Narratology)

Generalized trace analysis patterns and narrative extends the view of hardware-software traces and logs as temporarily ordered event sequences. The time domain is generalized to any arbitrary set, such as a list of indexes or pointers or even memory itself. This gives a unification of memory and log analysis, and application of Computer Narratology to memory dump analysis.

We call the application of methods of literary narratology to computer trace and log analysis and computer-related stories in general as Hardware-Software Narratology or simply Computer Narratology as it was originally done when we first introduced Software Narratology (page 58).

Introducing Software Narratology of Things (Software NT)

This is the further development of Software Narratology (T -> M) and Generalized Software Narratives (M -> M -> M -> ..., page 149). Now it incorporates devices (things) and IoT. Whereas the general narrative space is 2M1T:

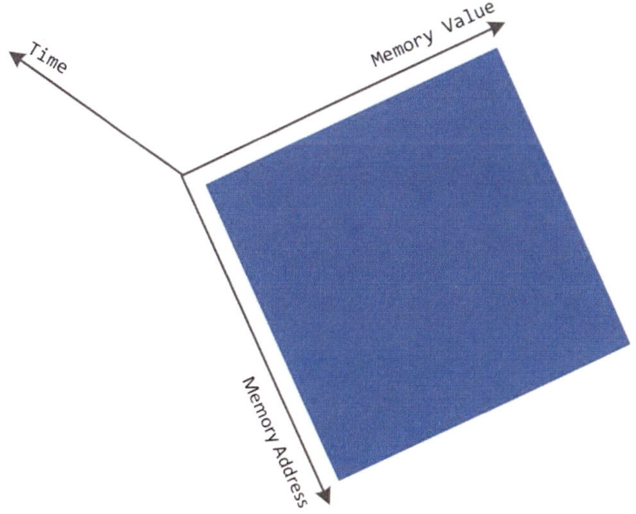

The narrative space of NT is "complex" 2M2T:

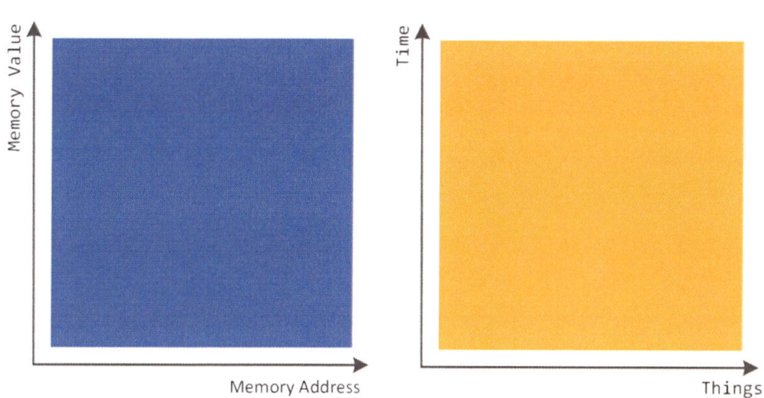

Narratology of Things also incorporates Hardware Narratology (page 150).

What are Software Trace and Memory Dump Analysis? A One Sentence Definition

Many years passed since we provided a longer structuralist definition (page 37). Recently we came to recognize pattern-driven iterative and incremental nature of memory and software trace analysis[128] and post-construction software problem solving[129] in general, and, therefore, a one-sentence definition became necessary: **recognition and interpretation of patterns of software behavior.**

Software Problem Description Language

The purpose of **SPDL** (Software Problem Description Language) is an automatic generation of a software troubleshooting tool based on the description of a problem. Here software problem means a post-construction problem as outlined in Introduction to Pattern-Driven Software Problem Solving[130]. The tool construction utilizes an expanded set of DebugWare (page 45) and Workaround (page 82) patterns together with the refined version of RADII[131] software development process. This also provides necessary effectiveness, efficiency and enhanced problem-solving capabilities to existing TaaS (Tools as a Service) implementations that are limited in the number of tools they offer.

Software Problem Description Patterns

The development of SPDL (page 153) requires extending the pattern-driven analysis approach to software problems such as software defect and software incident descriptions. Such a pattern language should help with accurate problem identification and problem resolution through software behavior analysis and with choosing, for example, appropriate workaround patterns (page 82) or, for a debugging strategy, unified debugging patterns (page 129). This also applies to software security incident descriptions as well.

Note: These patterns can be found in Memory Dump Analysis Anthology volume 7, and further patterns are planned for publishing.

Software Behavior Pattern Prediction

Sometimes we hear voices saying that Linux, FreeBSD, and Mac OS X core dumps are uninteresting. This is not true. If we have not seen anything interesting there, it just simply means that we only encountered a limited amount of abnormal software behavior. The widespread usage of Windows OS means that most patterns have been diagnosed and described first for it, and other operating systems are waiting for their turn.

Our goal is to have a pattern catalog with examples from different OS. For example, currently, all Mac OS X patterns we provide are just examples of existing Windows pattern names. All operating systems share the same structure and behavior, for example, structural memory analysis patterns (page 104) and the same computational model. Although structural patterns are different from behavioral patterns, we also plan to extend the structural list significantly, especially in relation to memory forensics training. Regarding behavioral patterns, it is possible to model and predict specific pattern examples for another OS by using the already existing catalog.

Patterns of Software Diagnostics

While preparing a seminar on Software Diagnostics,[132] we made many notes and realized that a system of patterns, corresponding vocabulary, and pattern language are all needed for this discipline. Here patterns are supposed to be broad in nature and different from patterns for specific artifacts such as memory dumps[133] and software traces[134]. So the first pattern addresses a *diagnostic encounter* with **First Fault** in comparison to subsequent faults where the problem becomes noticeable and diagnostic resources are allocated. Such faults should not be dismissed. Dan Skwire is a passionate advocate of first fault software problem solving and wrote a book[135].

The following paper proposes distributed control flow reconstruction for first fault diagnosis: *TraceBack: First Fault Diagnosis by Reconstruction of Distributed Control Flow*[136].

Software Diagnostics Services (former Memory Dump Analysis Services) uses patterns of abnormal software behavior for its first fault diagnostics that does not require any special instrumentation: *Join Debugging Diagnostics Revolution!*[137]

Highly Effective Diagnostics

Motivated by an article *7 Habits of Highly Effective Debuggers,*[138] we would like to reflect on a distinction between diagnostics and problem solving as separate processes (although highly related). First, we reverse the precept from that article because stories such as software logs and traces are of primary importance to software diagnostics (and not only). Moreover, without diagnostics, there is no effective debugging (treatment, problem solving).

The principle precept of diagnostics: stories, *not* statistics, secure certainty.

Network Trace Analysis Patterns

We can apply the software trace analysis pattern approach to network trace analysis, which lacks a unified pattern language. Here we consider a network trace as essentially a software trace where packet headers represent software trace messages coupled with associated transmitted data:

Since we have a trace message stream formatted by a network trace visualization tool, we can apply most, if not all, trace and log analysis patterns for diagnostics [139], including software narratology [140] for interpretation, discourse, and different representations. We provide a few trivial examples here, and more are covered in the separate seminar[141]. The first example is **Discontinuity** pattern[142]:

Other similar patterns are **No Activity**[143], **Truncated Trace**[144]**,** and **Time Delta**[145]. The second example is **Anchor Messages**[146]:

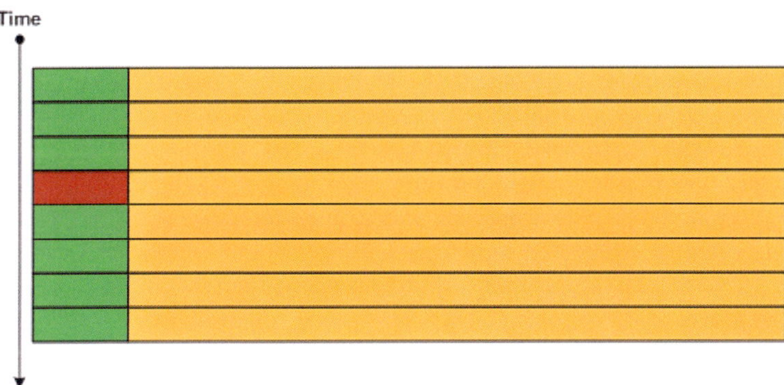

Additional examples there include **Significant Event** [147] and **Bifurcation Point** [148] patterns. Layered protocols are represented by **Embedded Message** pattern (to be described and added to the pattern list). Such traces can be filtered for their embedded protocol headers and therefore naturally represent **Adjoint Thread** pattern [149] (for a more detailed description of adjoint threads as an extension of multithreading, please see the article *What is an Adjoint Thread,* page 371):

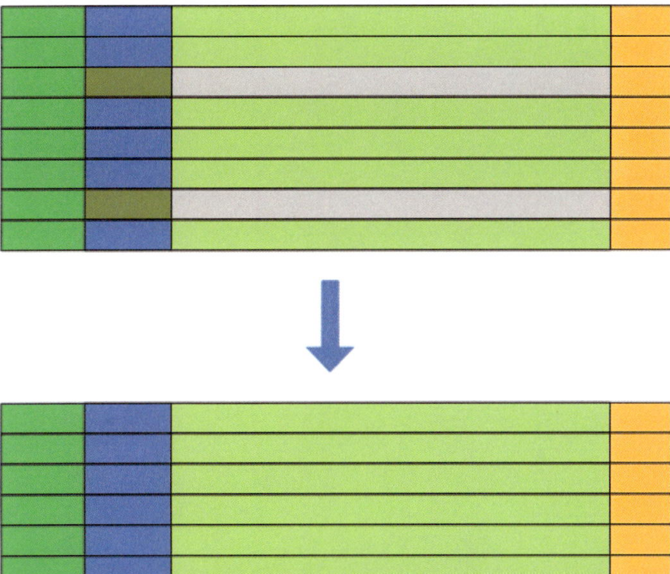

Pattern-Based Software Diagnostics

Pattern-driven[150] software post-construction problem solving involves using preexisting pattern languages and pattern catalogs for software diagnostics, troubleshooting, and debugging. ***Pattern-based*** software post-construction problem-solving addresses PLS (Pattern Life Cycle) - from the discovery of a new pattern through its integration into an existing catalog and language, testing, packaging, and delivering to pattern consumers with subsequent usage, refactoring, and writing case studies:

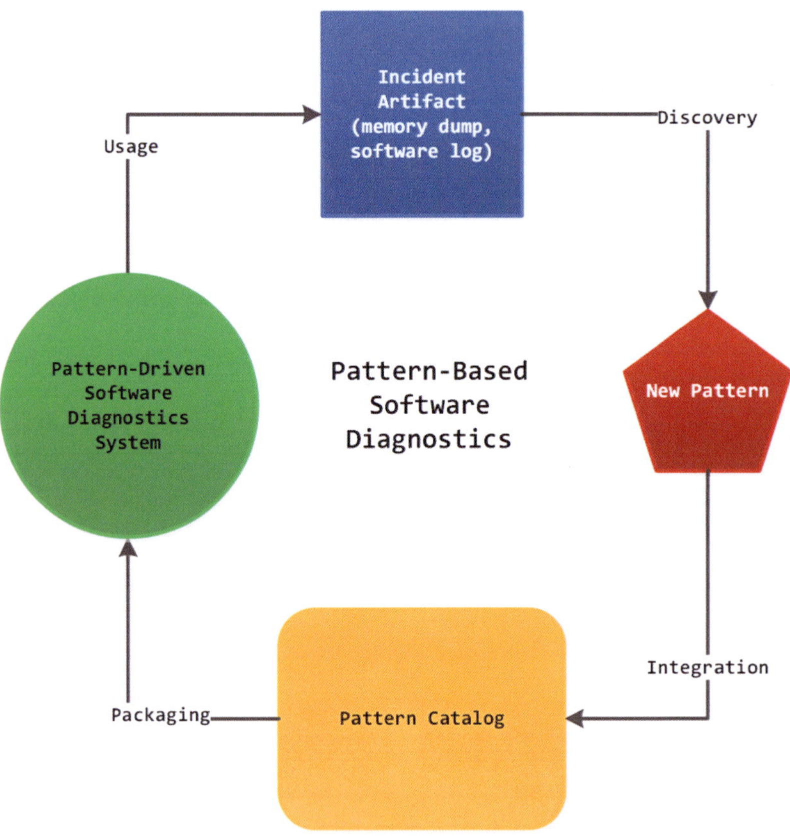

Software Diagnostics Discipline

Let us define software diagnostics as a discipline studying abnormal software structure and behavior in software execution artifacts (such as memory dumps, software and network traces and logs) using pattern-driven[151], systemic[152], and pattern-based[153] analysis methodologies.

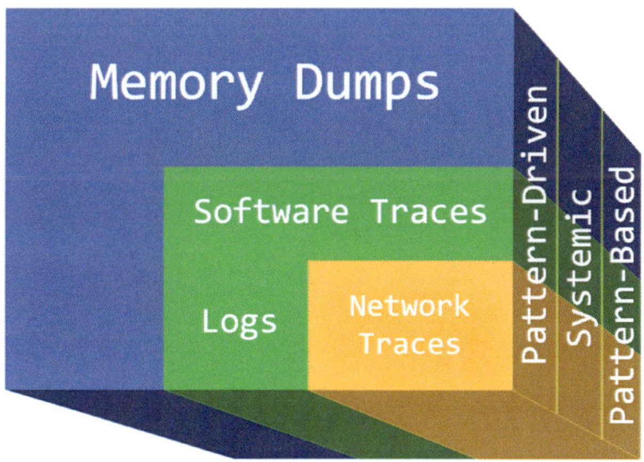

Architecture of memCPU

In addition to MemOS (Memory OS), we propose a memCPU architecture where software diagnostics is built from the very start. Every CPU instruction from memISA (Memory Instruction Set Architecture) has its previous memory state saved in a memory dump. Plus, there are special instructions to facilitate software tracing. Here is a conceptual diagram depicting data and code input streams and continuous output memory dump stream:

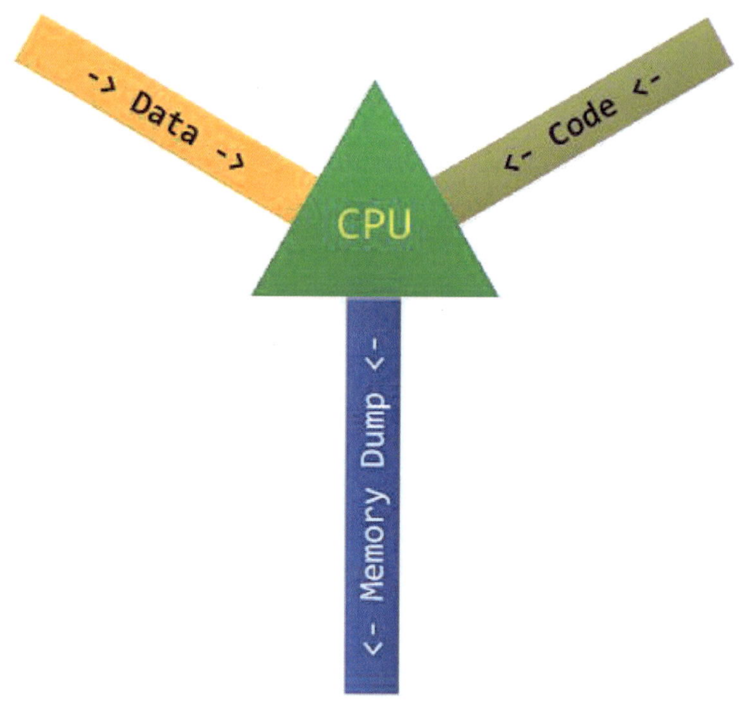

Phenomenology of Software Diagnostics: A First Sketch

Influenced by stages of Husserlian[154] phenomenological investigation, we propose the following stages of the investigation of phenomena as it appears in software execution artifacts such as memory dumps, traces, and logs:

1. Bracketing the outside source code as a reduction to patterns of phenomena independent from causal software engineering explanations.
2. Constructing the computational world for the given incident (the so-called horizon of computation).
3. Comparing with "computed-in" experience of past computational worlds from which all universal patterns of computational structural and behavioral phenomena emerged.

According to the above, software diagnostics is a phenomenological science of patterns.

Software Diagnostics Report Schemes

Report schemes are important meta-patterns of monitoring and software problem analysis reports. It is often the case that we have software artifacts and some problem description, and we need to provide recommendations for further troubleshooting. Most of the time, such an analysis and associated response fit into abstract schemes where we can just substitute variables for concrete states, actions, artifacts, and behavioral descriptions. Sometimes we also have difficulty in writing such analysis reports, so we hope report schemes are of help here to provide organizing templates for the thought process.

Here's the first such scheme:

1. If **A**ction then **B**ehavior
2. We have a trace of **B**ehavior
3. We need a trace of **A**ction and **B**ehavior

The difference with **Truncated Trace**[155] pattern here is that in a truncated trace, it was intended to trace certain behavior, but the tracing session was stopped prematurely or started too late. In a missing cause trace, only a part of the necessary activity was traced, and the missing part was not thought of or considered for tracing.

Software Diagnostics Training: Two Approaches

Doing memory dump analysis training for several years, we found that students are divided into two types: those who prefer to see source code first and those who want to see a memory dump first. We prefer to show a memory dump first and then explore it to find certain patterns of abnormal structure and behavior. Software Diagnostics Services[156] used this approach to design its Accelerated Windows Memory Dump Analysis[157] and Accelerated .NET Memory Dump Analysis[158] courses. Students explore memory dumps and debugger logs to find memory dump analysis patterns that are introduced when necessary. After that, they can check the source code of modeling applications if they have development experience. Accelerated Windows Software Trace Analysis[159] course uses a different approach. It introduces all software trace analysis patterns at once because they are patterns from software narratology[160] independent from programming languages and software platforms. After that, they explore and analyze software traces and logs. We can summarize these two approaches on this diagram:

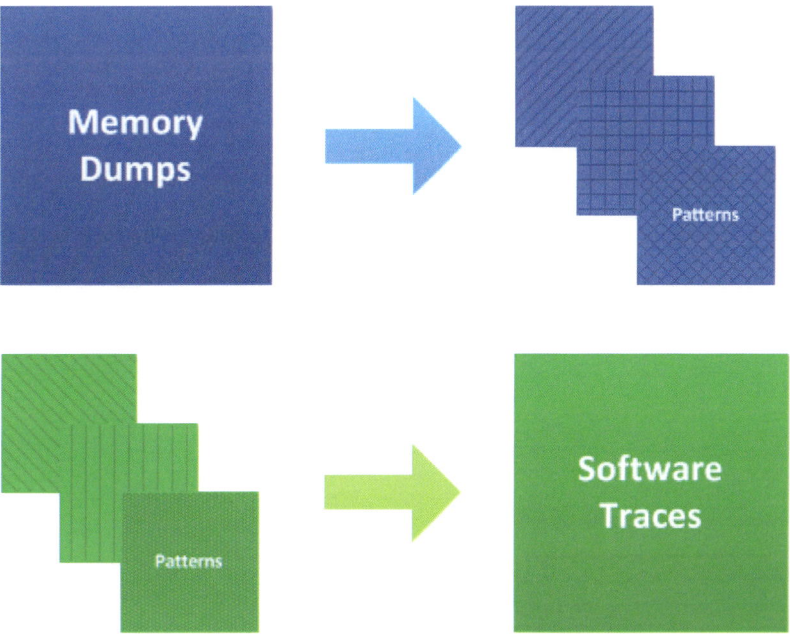

The Structure of Software Problem Solving Organization

Based on the separation of problem-solving powers, we propose the following software problem-solving triangle with a separate software diagnostics department:

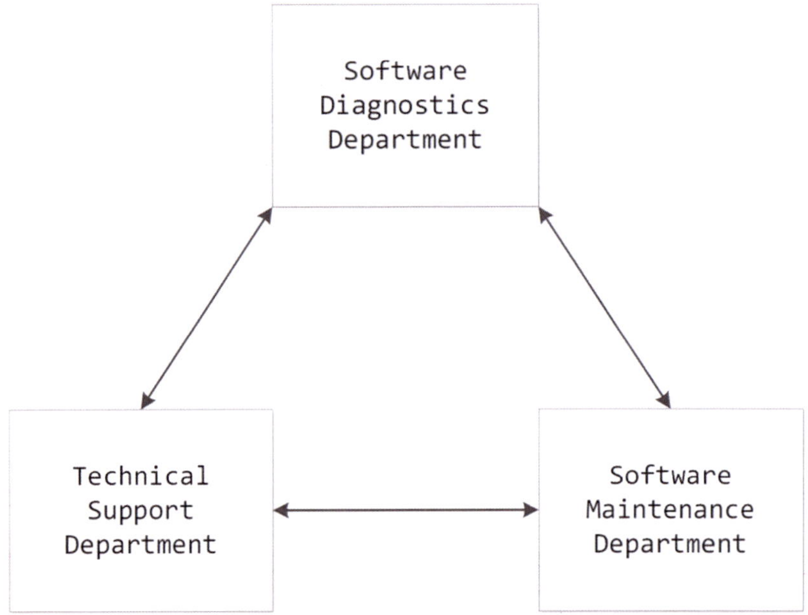

Software Disruption Patterns

These are not patterns of software testing but patterns of user or program behavior resulting in abnormalities such as colored screens (blue and gray), crash dumps, and other support artifacts, including performance alerts and UI problem patterns (page 139).

Note: The first pattern can be found in Memory Dump Analysis Anthology volume 7, and further patterns are planned for publishing.

Static Code Analysis Patterns

Static program analysis[161] is used to eliminate certain coding errors that may lead to abnormal software behavior. Therefore, it is naturally a part of software diagnostics but at source code level. Our goal here is to identify certain patterns directly linkable to patterns we see in memory dumps and software logs and collect them into a catalog.

Note: The first pattern can be found in Memory Dump Analysis Anthology volume 7, and further patterns are planned for publishing.

Bridging the Great Divide

In Pattern-Based Software Diagnostics[162] presentation, we proposed to use pattern catalogs to bridge the separation of software construction and memory dump software diagnostics. With an introduction of **Motifs**[163] to trace and log analysis pattern catalog, it is now possible (at least conceptually) to bridge construction and trace analysis too:

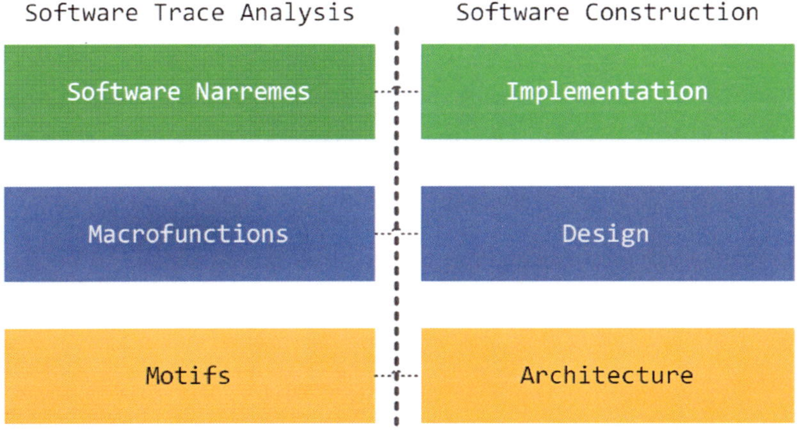

Elementary Software Diagnostics Patterns

These are patterns of abnormal software behavior that affect software users and trigger the application of pattern-oriented software diagnostics and debugging if necessary. The initial list of relevant elementary patterns includes:

- Functional

    ✓ **Use-case Deviation**

- Non-functional

    ✓ **Crash**
    ✓ **Hang** (includes delays)
    ✓ **Counter Value** (includes resource leaks, CPU spikes)
    ✓ **Error Message**

In choosing the pattern vocabulary, we decided to use ordinary names, for example, **Hang** was chosen instead of Response Delay.

Zero Fault Software Diagnostics

Software diagnostics is used whenever there is a fault that triggers some artifact such as a memory dump or a software trace. It is also used proactively in software and network monitoring. We combine all these uses with our pattern-oriented approach to anticipating faults before their occurrence:

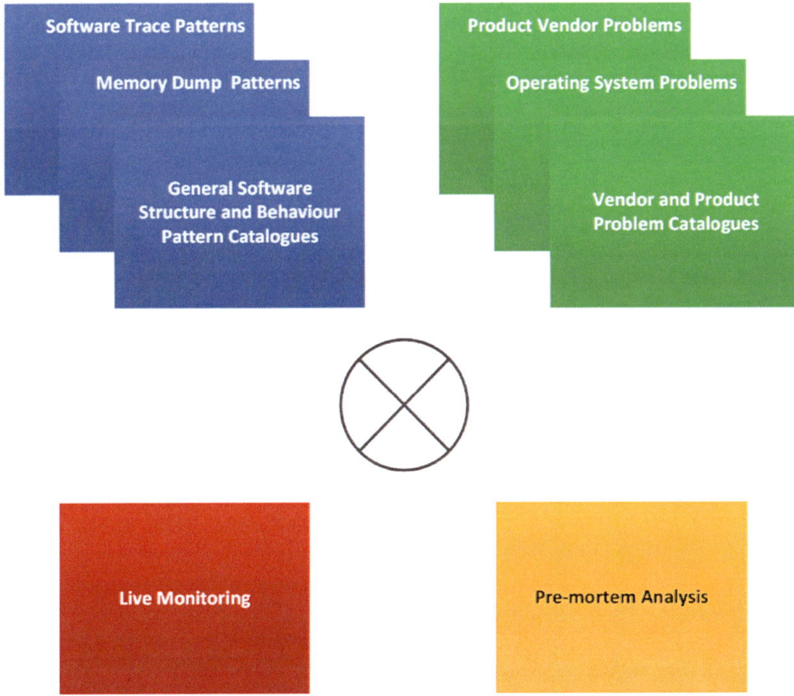

Such preventive software diagnostics consists of 4 interrelated parts:

- General software structure and behavior pattern catalogs;
- Domain, vendor, and product-specific problem catalogs;
- Live monitoring;
- Pre-mortem analysis.

Pre-mortem here means preventive memory dump analysis. It is similar to post-mortem analysis, but artifacts are collected and analyzed proactively before any actual problem. In some sense, the pre-mortem analysis is a part of live monitoring, but we confine the latter to software trace and log analysis.

Zero Fault Software Diagnostics becomes a part of pattern-oriented Software Prognostics discipline.

Agile Software Diagnostics

We introduce this method based on iterative and incremental pattern-oriented diagnostics we founded and developed during the last few years. It is currently based on five principles:

- Patterns are the principal measure of quality;
- Attention to detail through checklists;
- Analysis is done by motivated expertize-driven trusted individuals;
- Customer satisfaction by useful analysis delivered in the shortest possible time;
- Analysis audit as a pair diagnostics.

ADDR Pattern Catalog

In addition to existing pattern catalogs, we introduce patterns (and their schemas) of disassembly (decompilation), reversing, and reconstruction (deconstruction). Here's the current list in the order of their appearance in Accelerated Disassembly, Reconstruction and Reversing training[164]:

- Universal Pointer
- Symbolic Pointer S^2
- Interpreted Pointer S^3
- Context Pyramid
- Potential Functionality
- Function Skeleton
- Function Call
- Call Path
- Local Variable
- Static Variable
- Pointer Dereference
- Function Prologue
- Function Epilogue
- Variable Initialization
- Memory Copy
- Call Prologue
- Call Parameter
- Call Epilogue
- Call Result
- Control Path
- Function Parameter
- Structure Field
- Last Call
- Loop
- Separator Frames
- Virtual Call
- Component Dependencies
- API Trace

Thinking-Based Software Diagnostics

This is a new type of software diagnostics in addition to pattern-oriented and systemic.

It is based on:

- Critical thinking
- Systemic thinking
- Semiotic thinking

Moreover, it uses:

- Inductive reasoning
- Deductive reasoning
- Abductive reasoning

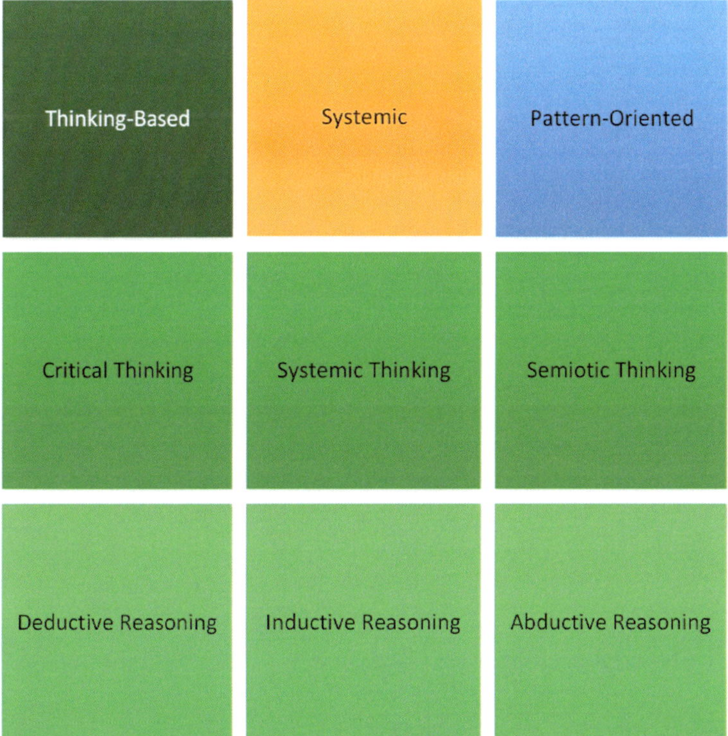

Memory Acquisition Pattern Catalog

Software: the parts of a computer that can be dumped.

In addition to existing pattern catalogs such as for memory analysis, we introduce patterns of memory acquisition as a general platform and product independent, reusable solutions to commonly occurring memory acquisition problems applicable in specific contexts. Here is the current list with their classification:

Structural Space Patterns

- *General*
  - ✓ State Summary Dump
  - ✓ Region Memory Dump
- *Volatile*
  - ✓ Process Memory Dump
  - ✓ Kernel Memory Dump
  - ✓ Physical Memory Dump
  - ✓ Hyper Memory Dump
  - ✓ Fiber Bundle Dump
- *Persistent*
  - ✓ File Memory Dump
  - ✓ Storage Memory Dump

Acquisition Strategy Patterns

- ✓ External Dump
- ✓ Self-Dump
- ✓ Conditional Dump
- ✓ Dump Sequence

Trace Acquisition Pattern Catalog

In addition to existing pattern catalogs such as for trace analysis, we introduce patterns of trace acquisition as a general platform and product independent, reusable solutions to commonly occurring tracing and logging problems applicable in specific contexts. Here's the current list applicable to both software and network tracing:

- ✓ Trace Placing Map
- ✓ Trace Timing Plan
- ✓ Use Case Coverage
- ✓ Supplemental System Tracing
- ✓ Supplemental Network Tracing
- ✓ Supplemental Memory Acquisition
- ✓ Full Capture Tracing
- ✓ Tuned Capture Tracing
- ✓ First Occurrence Tracing
- ✓ Differential Strategy Tracing

Patterns of Software Diagnostics Architecture

In the `Debugging TV`[165] episode 0x1A, we introduced a vision of software diagnostics architecture and its architectural patterns. The latter are the usual patterns of software architecture if we design software diagnostics software. However, if we consider a software diagnostics system architecture in a wider context involving its users and human-assisted pattern-orientation there is a need to devise new patterns such as *Patterns - View - Controller* (PVC) where:

Patterns - represent pattern catalogs from pattern-driven and pattern-based software diagnostics methodology. It corresponds to Model in the traditional Model - View - Controller software architecture pattern.

View - represents pattern catalog(s) view, which might include concrete pattern implementations such as OS and product specifics. A view can also be based on an intersection of several pattern catalogs, for example, memory analysis, malware analysis, and trace analysis. A user diagnostician sees such views. Any updates to underlying pattern catalogs are reflected in pattern views.

Controller - represents software diagnostics tools architecture and is designed using software construction patterns. Such tools may include automated diagnostics or human-assisted debuggers and problem analysis tools. A user diagnostician uses such controllers. Such use may result in updates to underlying pattern catalogs when a new pattern is discovered, for example.

This software diagnostics architecture pattern is illustrated in the following diagram:

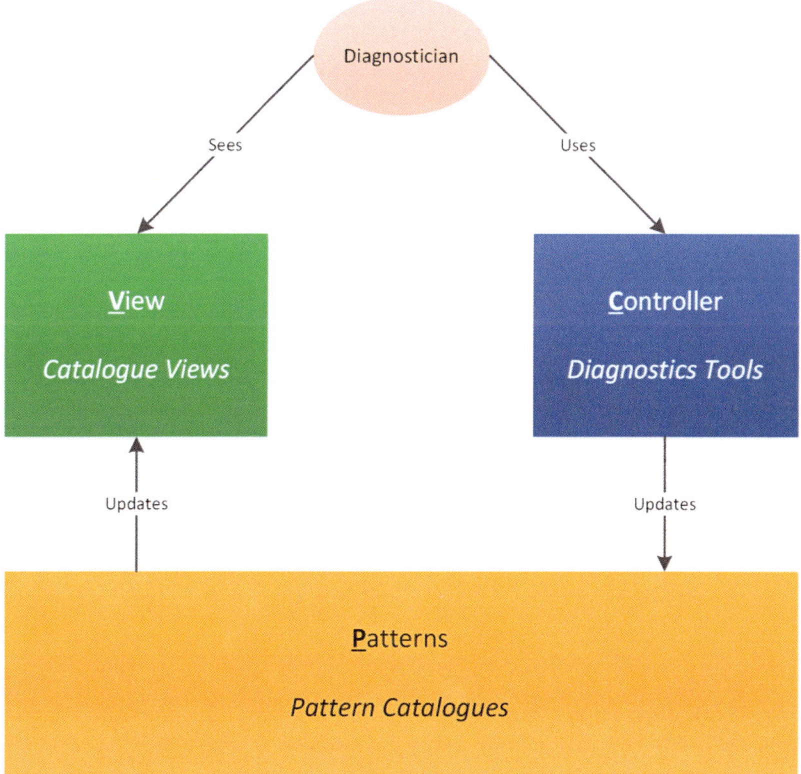

Detecting and Predicting the Unknown

A. The approach of Victimware[166] (which includes abnormal behavior of Malware such as crashes, hangs, resource leaks, CPU spikes) together with memory, malware, and log analysis pattern catalogs allows detecting unknown malware in software diagnostics and digital forensics artifacts such as memory dumps, crash reports, and software traces and logs: pattern-driven software diagnostics[167] and forensics[168].

B. Structural and behavioral patterns found in one operating system and processor architecture can be predicted for another: pattern-based software diagnostics[169] and forensics.

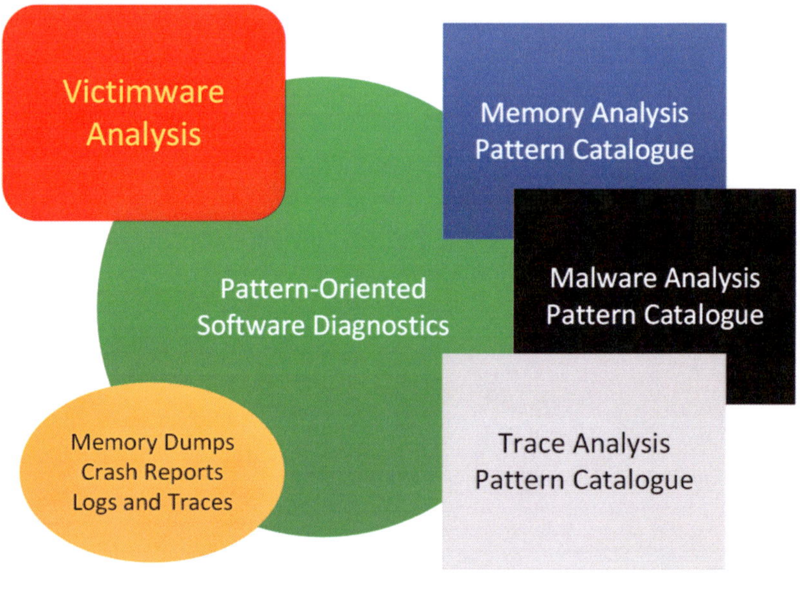

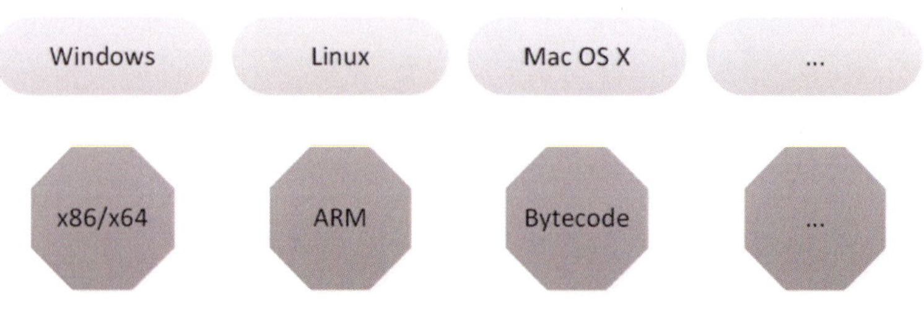

Software Diagnostics as Psychology

Analogy: studying how code construction ideas are executed

- Philosophy - Software Construction
- *Psychology - Software Diagnostics*
- Physiology - Software Execution

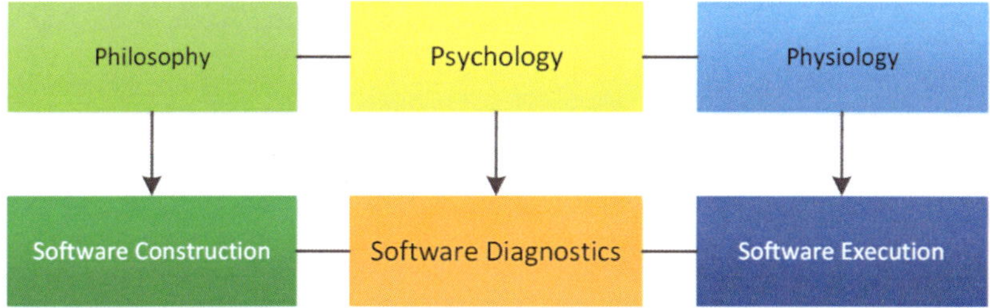

Software Diagnostics as Literary Criticism

Analogy: studying patterns across software execution artifacts such as software narratives (traces and logs) and memory snapshots.

- Writing Fiction - Software Construction
- Reading Fiction - Software Execution
- Reviewing Fiction - Traditional Software Diagnostics
- *Literary Criticism - Pattern-Oriented Software Diagnostics*

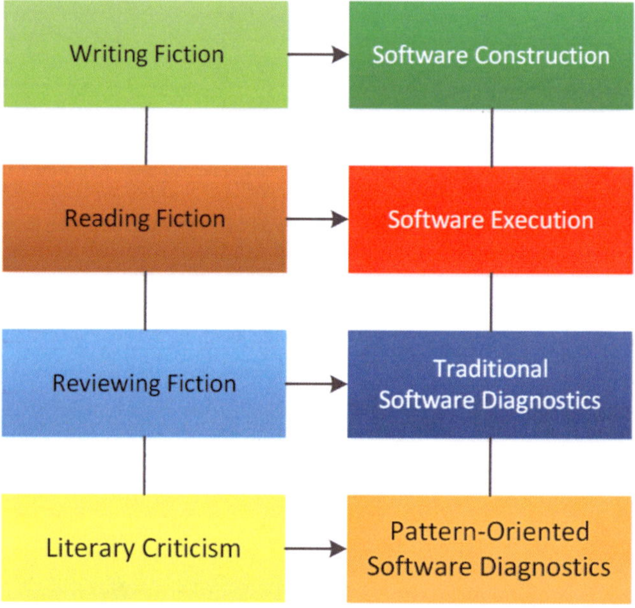

Rapid Software Diagnostics Process (RSDP)

The increased complexity of software incidents and their growing numbers require fast responses. We reviewed and partitioned our pattern catalogs into two tiers. The first tier requires fewer analysis efforts and provides a faster response time than the second tier.

Right First Time Software Diagnosis

It is based on a pattern-oriented diagnostics process and pattern catalogs.

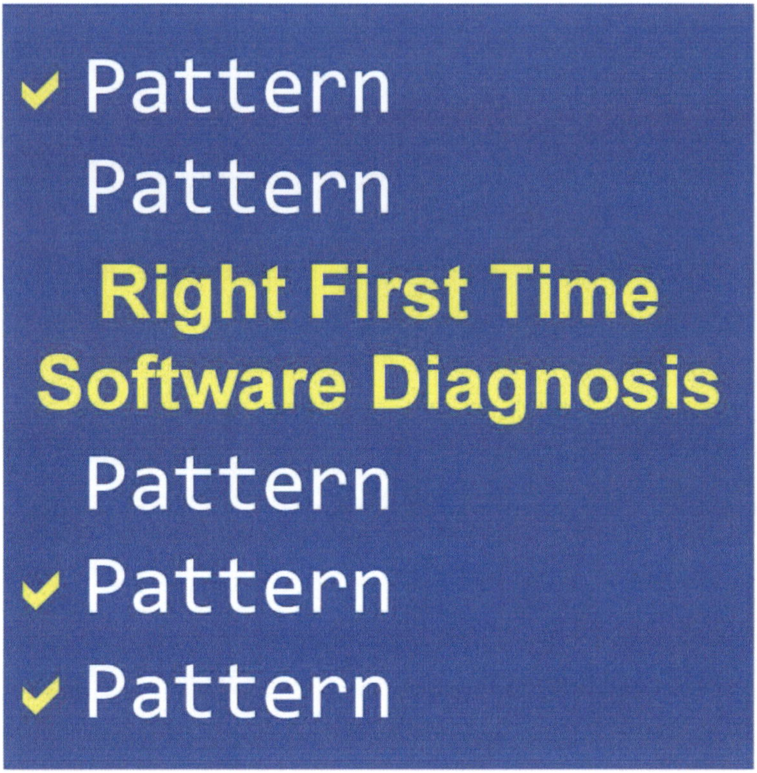

Pattern
Pattern
Right First Time
Software Diagnosis
Pattern
Pattern
Pattern

Software Diagnosis Codes

While working on Diagnostic Manual of Software Problems[170] (DMS), we found the need to introduce software diagnostic codes. The proposed natural candidate schema is based on pattern orientation and pattern catalogs. It consists of major and minor codes. The major code is a combination of a one-letter software artifact type, a 3-letter structural classifier, and a 3-letter behavioral pattern classifier:

Artifact Type - Structural Pattern - Behavioral Pattern

For example:

M-THR-SPK

Memory - Thread - Spike, which corresponds to **Spiking Thread**[171] pattern from the memory analysis catalog.

The optional minor code is not currently specified but may include pattern implementation such as an operating system platform including CPU architecture, for, example: **WIN.X32** or **OSX.X64**. So the final code may look like:

M-THR-SPK.WIN.X64

Vulnerability Analysis Patterns (VAP)

These are general patterns of software vulnerability: synthesis of analysis patterns from these software diagnostics catalogs:

- **MAP** - Memory Analysis Patterns (include behavioral and structural patterns)
- **TAP** - Trace Analysis Patterns
- **CAP** - Code Analysis Patterns (previously introduced as Static Code Analysis Patterns, page 168)
- **ADDR** - Deconstruction, Disassembly, and Reversing (binary equivalent of CAP) Patterns (the current list is available on page 174)

Also:

VEC - Vulnerability, Exploit, and Control of Victimware
Victimware - bugs of software (including bugs of malware) + vulnerabilities (provocative and precipitative victimware)

For victimware classification, please look at the presentation[172].

The following easy to remember diagram combines all these acronyms and terminology:

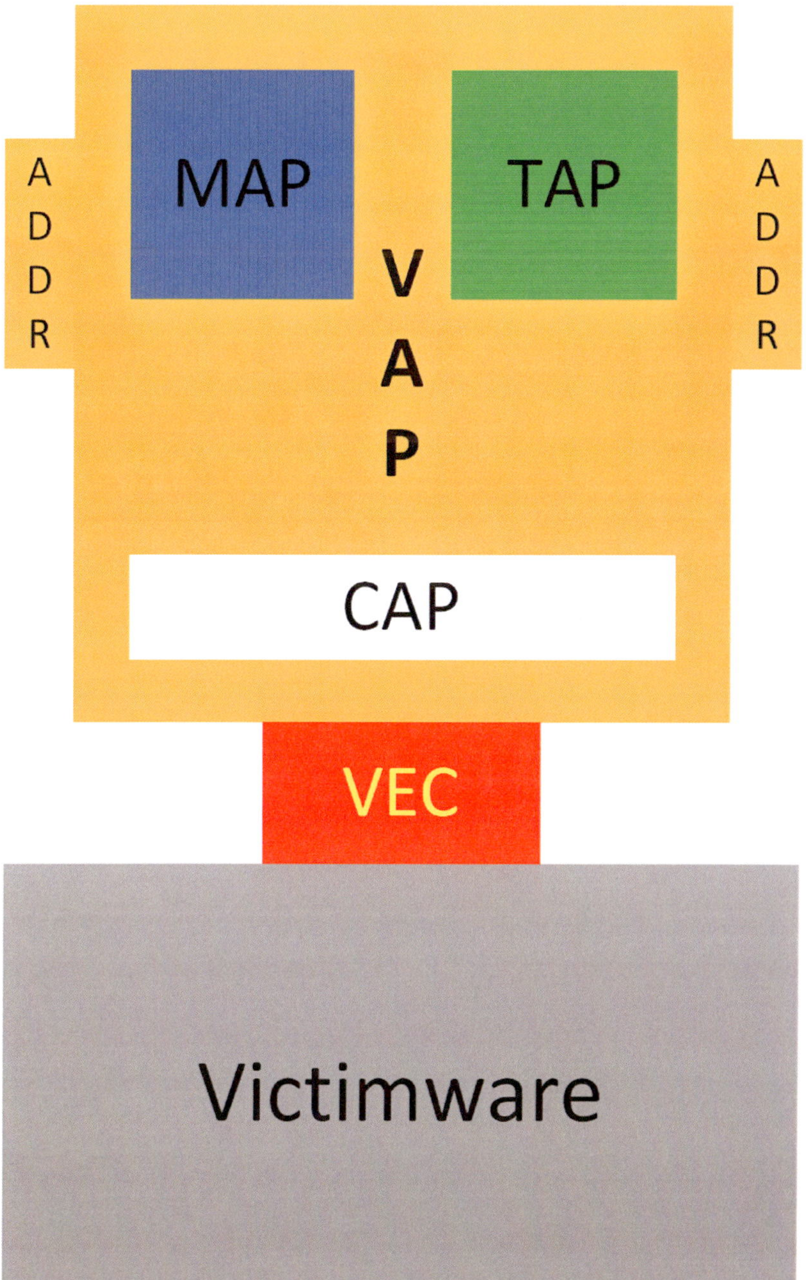

A
D
D
R
MAP
TAP
A
D
D
R
V
A
P
CAP
VEC
Victimware

Analytic Memory Dump - A Mathematical Definition

The previous mathematical definition of a memory dump (page 39) is for raw memory dumps. They are not useful because they require symbol files. Each symbol file entry conceptually is a correspondence between a memory address and a direct sum or product of letters from some alphabet:

```
00000000`76e82c40: kernel32!WaitForMultipleObjectsExImplementation
```

So we propose an analytical definition of a memory dump as a direct sum of disjoint memory areas M_t taken during some time interval (t_0, ..., t_n) where we replace s_{tk} having values from Z_2 with S_{tq} having values from Z_p and cardinality of Z_p depending on a platform (32, 64, ...) plus a symbolic description $\prod D_i$ for each S_{tq} with cardinality of "i" set sufficient enough to accommodate the largest symbolic name:

$$M = \sum M_t \text{ where } M_t = \sum (S_{tq} + \prod D_i)$$

Alternatively, simply:

$$M = \sum \sum (S_{tq} + \prod D_i)$$

This can be visualized as a linear memory space such as a virtual memory space when symbol files are applied to modules one after another. However, all this is not necessary because a symbol from a virtual address can also be mapped to a physical address if necessary. $\prod D_i$ refers to any symbolic description.

General Abnormal Patterns of Structure and Behavior

Memory Analysis Patterns (MAPs), including memory dump, malware, software trace (TAPs), and other patterns and pattern catalogs from Software Diagnostics Institute[173] form the very rich semantic network. Now it is possible (by using a metaphorical bijection, page 83) to create a catalog of General Patterns of Abnormal Structure and Behavior including software, hardware, biological behavior including animal (ethology) and human behavior, sociological and historical behavior including economics, business and finance, ethics and law, and even behavior of chemical and physical systems. Such "GAPs of Structure and Behavior" may include wait chains, spikes, deadlocks. So we are a few steps closer to the realization of our old idea of a parameterized science of universal memory dumps (page 73) by the so-called science files or might even a general diagnostics discipline.

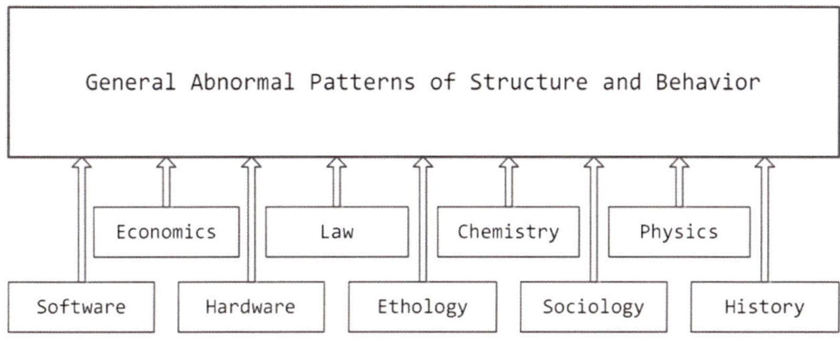

Malware Analysis Patterns

Here we provide a definition of malware that highlights the importance of structural and behavioral patterns:

> *Malware: software that uses planned alteration of structure and behavior of software to serve malicious purposes.*

Notice the recursive character of that definition that includes self-modifying malware and also rootkits where a malicious purpose is to conceal.

Note: These patterns can be found in Memory Dump Analysis Anthology volume 7, and further patterns are planned for publishing.

Software Trace Diagrams (STDiagrams)

When depicting trace analysis patterns, we used two-dimensional diagrams based on ETW traces such as this one for **Bifurcation Point**[174]:

While working on a new pattern, we needed a new expressive way to graphically illustrate the same idea of trace bifurcation points but without too much drawing. Traces from particle chambers and scattering diagrams came to our imagination after drawing the first few diagrams illustrating bifurcation points:

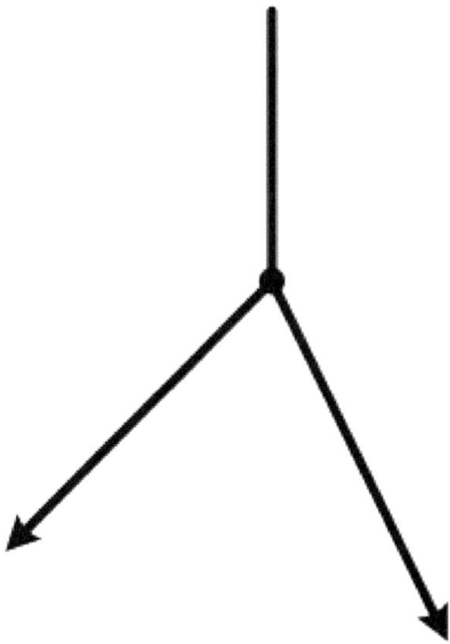

Time directional arrow end can be omitted:

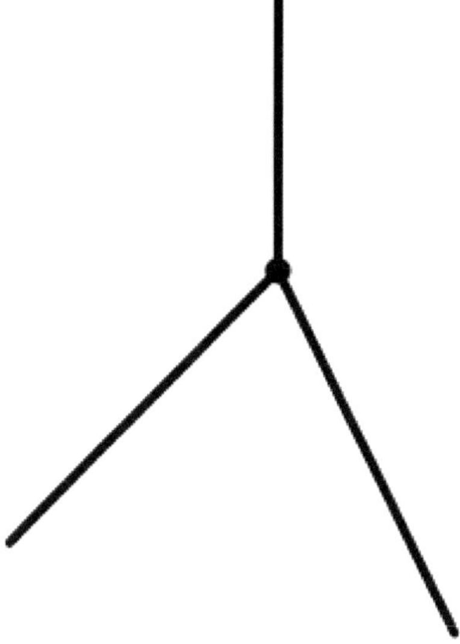

Trace variation after a bifurcation point can be indicated by angle partition:

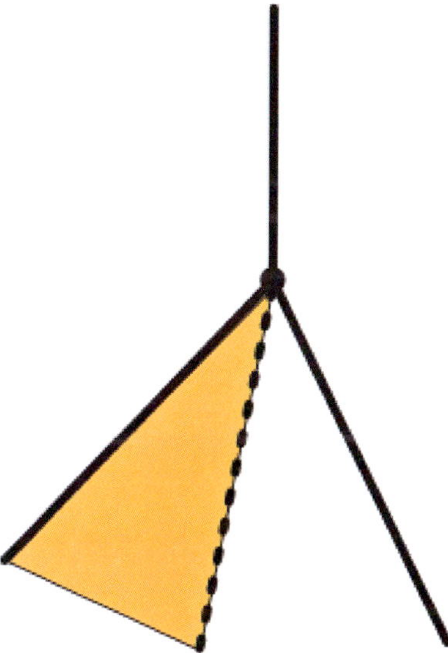

The case when a variation also happens before is illustrated in this diagram:

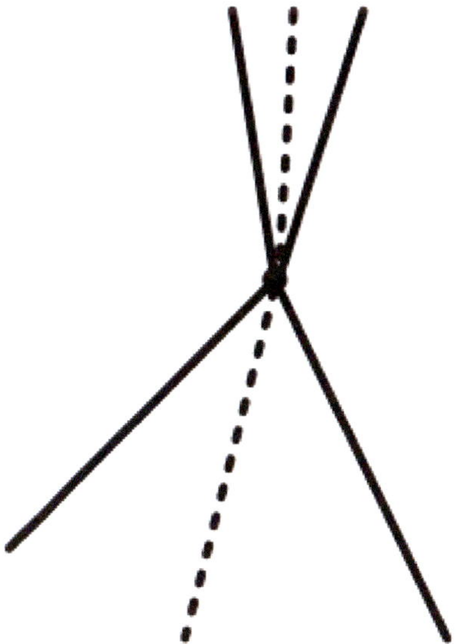

Moreover, the case with several bifurcations:

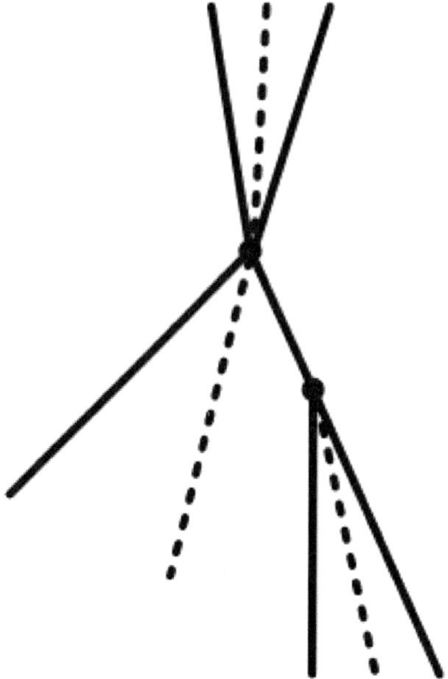

Are N-bifurcations like in the diagram below possible?

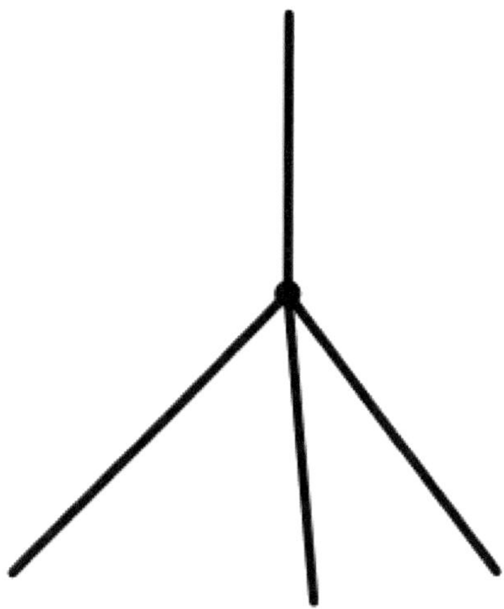

Yes, they are, if the course of execution depends on some non-binary trace message parameter such as a loaded module that implements a required interface differently.

Volume 8

A Pattern Language for Performance Analysis

We introduce a new software diagnostics pattern sub-catalog based on trace and log analysis patterns. It now includes the following performance analysis patterns (with more patterns added soon):

- **Counter Value**[175]
- Global Monotonicity
- Constant Value

Many general log analysis patterns based on software narratology apply to performance monitoring logs because they structure analysis data and corresponding thought process:

- **Adjoint Thread**[176] (can be visualized via different colors on a graph)
- **Focus of Tracing**[177]
- **Characteristic Message Block**[178] (for graphs)
- **Activity Region**[179]
- **Significant Event**[180] and many others

The goal is to discern, describe, and classify general regularities and their interactions in captured performance data, including analysis approaches reused across different operating systems, products, and their performance monitoring and analysis tools. Such **Pattern-Oriented Performance Analysis** as a part of Pattern-Oriented Software Diagnostics includes pattern-driven, pattern-based, and systemic parts.

The Timeless Way of Diagnostics

Paraphrasing two classical books on architecture written by Christopher Alexander et al. "*The Timeless Way of Building*" and "*A Pattern Language: Towns, Buildings, Construction,*" we would like to introduce the complete restructuring of the multivolume Memory Dump Analysis Anthology[181] into the projected ten-volume "**A Pattern Language for Software Diagnostics, Forensics, and Prognostics: Memory, Traces, Deconstruction**." The reference has better browsing and cross-referencing format, additional examples, and case studies. It incorporates comments and new pattern knowledge acquired since we described the first patterns eight years ago. The new edition covers only patterns and does not include additional content found in Memory Dump Analysis Anthology such as philosophy and art. Here's the preliminary front cover based on Software Diagnostics Institute logo:

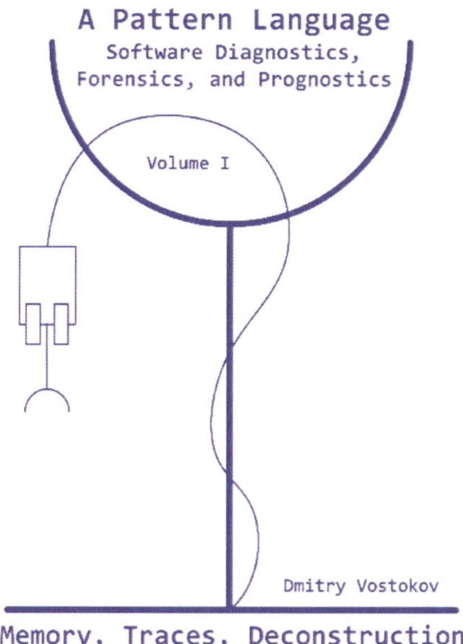

Memory Dump Analysis Anthology continues to be released. It includes up to date research from Software Diagnostics Institute and additional topics not included in "A Pattern Language for Software Diagnostics, Forensics, and Prognostics."

Pattern-Oriented Debugging Process

Modern debugging is complex and usually distributed across organizations involving many persons and teams:

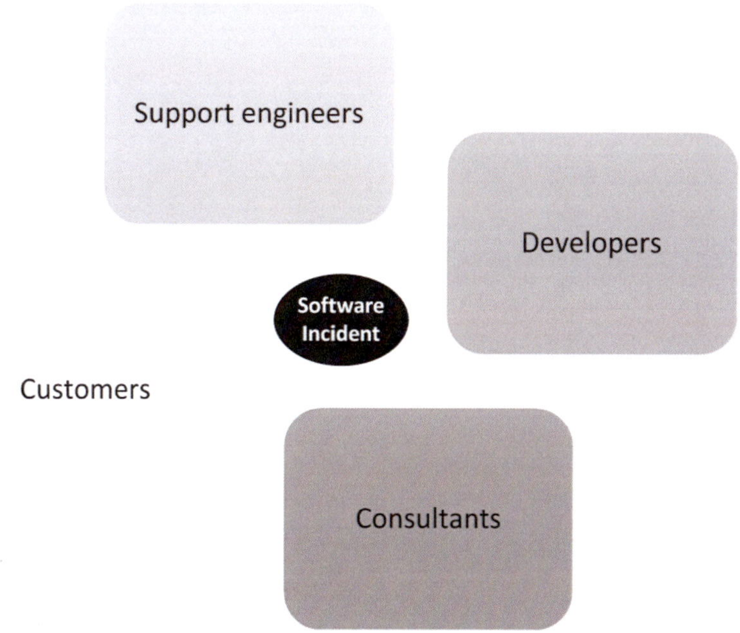

We propose a fully pattern-oriented debugging process that takes into account the integral role of software diagnostics and software construction patterns.

Whenever we have a software incident, we usually start with a small number of **Elementary Software Diagnostics Patterns** (page 170) to identify what kind of software execution artifacts to collect. Such artifacts may include memory dumps and logs for postmortem debugging but can also be running software itself, the so-called live debugging scenario. These patterns can also be called **Software Diagnostics Analysis Patterns,** reflecting the fact that we need to analyze what we further need to do before doing software diagnostics itself.

Based on artifacts, we identify patterns of software behavior such as memory and trace analysis patterns. We call these patterns **Software Diagnostics Usage Patterns**.

Such usage patterns can also be called **Debugging Analysis Patterns** because we need to diagnose the right problem before doing any debugging.

Specific techniques reused across different software diagnostics and debugging scenarios we name **Software Diagnostics** and **Debugging Implementation Patterns**. There can also be **Debugging Usage Patterns** as reusable debugging scenarios.

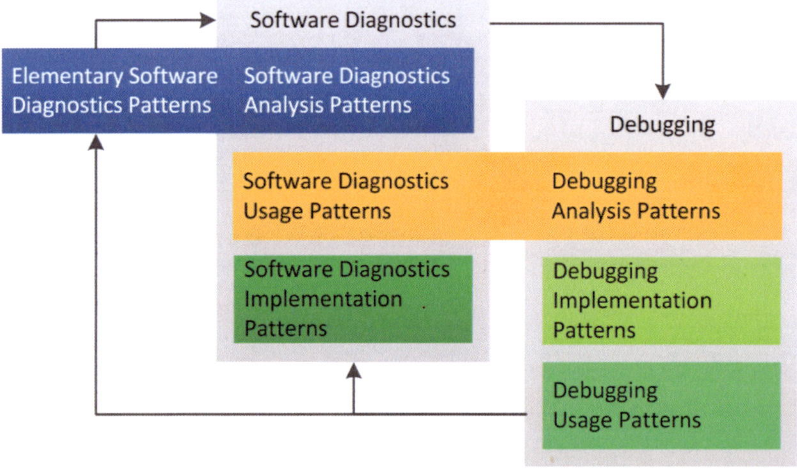

Previously we introduced Unified Debugging Patterns (Analysis, Architecture, Design, Implementation, and Usage, page 129) to which we would like to add **Debugging Presentation Patterns** and similar *pattern stack* for software diagnostics:

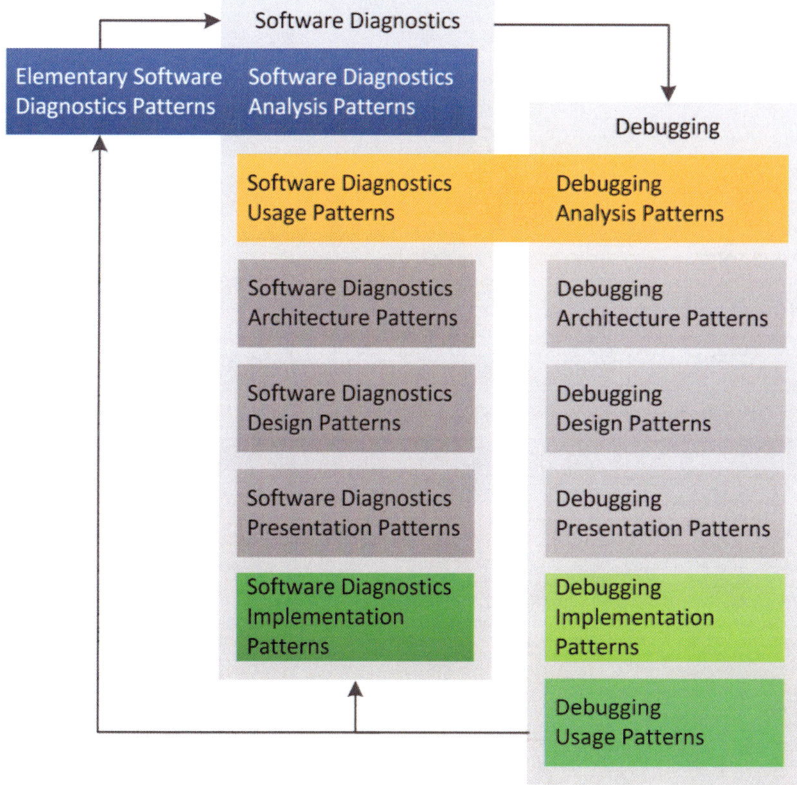

These pattern categories are usually already in existence and are important only when we develop new software diagnostics and debugging infrastructures and tools, for example, the architectural pattern **Patterns-View-Controller** (page 178).

Examples of Elementary Software Diagnostics (Software Diagnostics Analysis) Patterns, Software Diagnostics Usage (Debugging Analysis) Patterns, and Debugging Implementation Patterns can be found in Accelerated Windows Debugging book[182].

Malnarratives

A malnarrative is an intentionally modified narrative for malicious purposes. This word comes from the so-called malware narratives[183] and their patterns. Malware narratives are just software traces and logs (for example, system logs and network traces[184]) that contain diagnostic indicators (signs) pointing to possible or actual malware presence and execution. Therefore, malware narrative analysis patterns are based on general software trace and log analysis patterns[185] as a part of pattern-oriented software diagnostics[186] and forensics[187]. Whereas malware narratives result from planned alteration of structure and behavior of software to serve malicious purposes with resulting narratives incidentally revealing malware, malnarratives are planned alterations of narratives themselves. Because software narratives are based on software narratology[188] (which is an application of general narratology), the extensive trace and log analysis pattern catalog[189] (more than 200 patterns at the time of writing this book edition) can be used to analyze and detect such patterns in non-software narratives. For example, it can be used to analyze cyberspace narratives such as social media narratives (Facebook, Twitter[190], and LinkedIn) and even traditional media narratives such as news, stories, and books. Such a pattern-oriented analysis of malnarratives can be used not only in security but also in intelligence analysis (page 125) and information operations (IO), for example, in information warfare (IW).

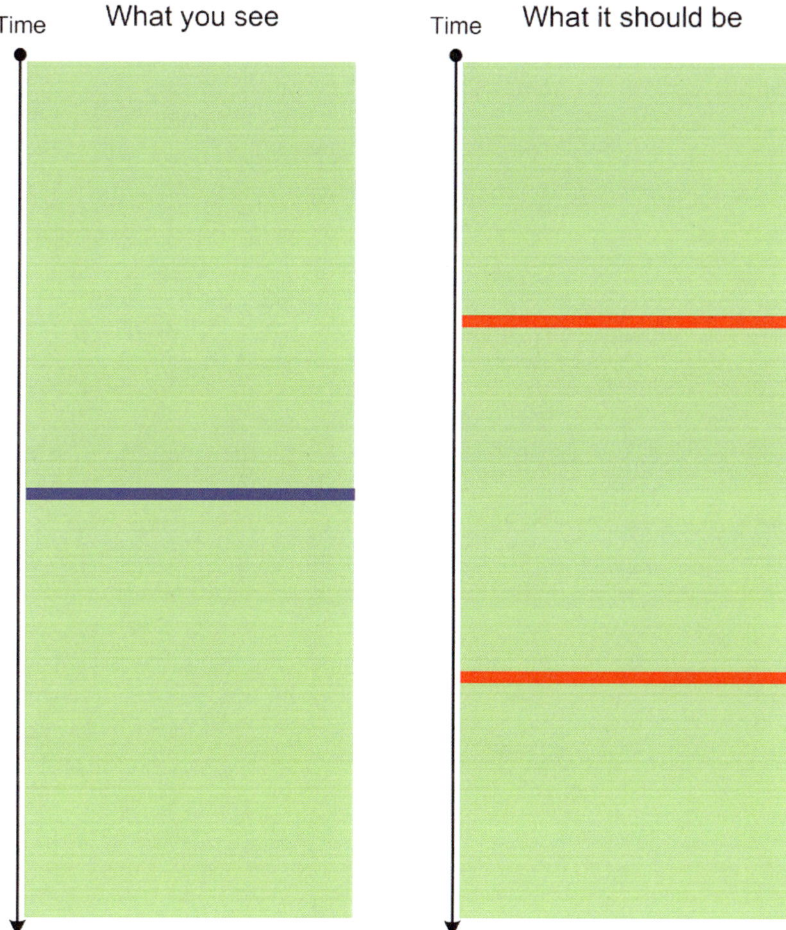
Time
What you see
Time
What it should be

Higher-Order Pattern Narratives (Analyzing Diagnostic Analysis)

A pattern narrative in software narratology means a narrative where messages or log entries are patterns from pattern catalogs. These can be either domain-specific patterns or general trace and log analysis patterns such as **Discontinuity**[191], **Activity Region**[192], **Significant Event**[193], **Macrofunction**[194], and **Back Trace**[195]. The software pattern narrative is a narrative constructed from software execution artifacts such as logs and memory dumps during their analysis. It is different from the usual meaning of a pattern narrative in narratology and literary criticism, where we have a narrative that is a pattern itself like **Master Trace**[196] analysis pattern. So, in our case, it is a narrative of patterns and not a narrative that is a pattern. The following picture illustrates the correspondence between a software trace example and its software pattern narrative:

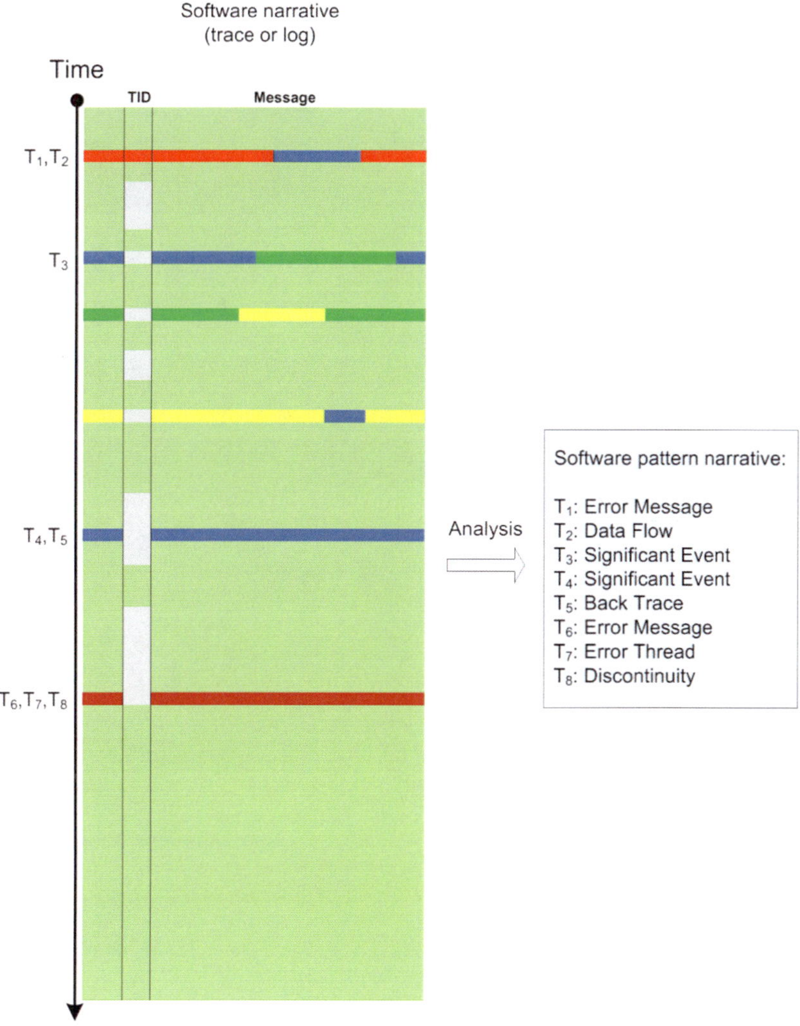

A pattern narrative can be further analyzed for any missing patterns using pattern sequences and schemes.

By a second-order narrative, we mean a narrative about narrative, such as the analysis of the original narrative (a first-order narrative). For example, the transformation of a software log into its pattern narrative equivalent (the so-called analysis narrative) is a second-order narrative. It has its time sequence (called Analysis Time, TA), where certain patterns are diagnosed out-of-order of their appearance in the resulting pattern narrative. In such a narrative, additional patterns may be included that were diagnosed initially but were later replaced or eliminated. The latter property shows that second-order narratives are not simply rearranged plots of the same story (fabula). In the case of generalized memory narratives and hybrid artifacts such as memory dumps, we also have analysis narratives. The following picture shows the analysis narrative used to construct a software pattern narrative from the previous picture example. We see what patterns were found first:

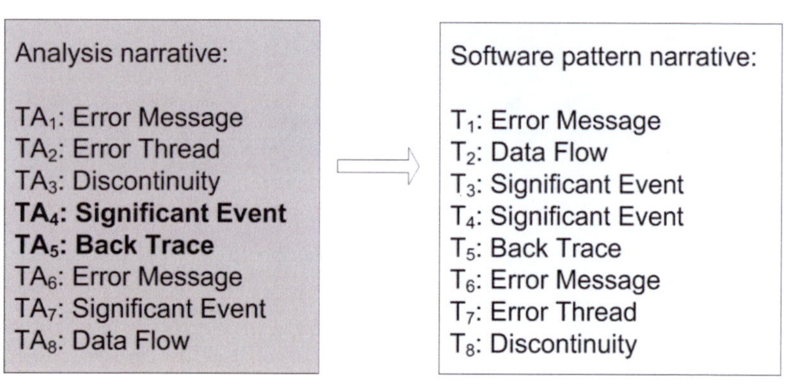

Such second-order narratives can be analyzed further and give rise to third-order narratives and, in general, to higher-order narratives. The following diagram shows the relationship between a software narrative (order N), its pattern narrative (order N), and analysis narrative (order N+1):

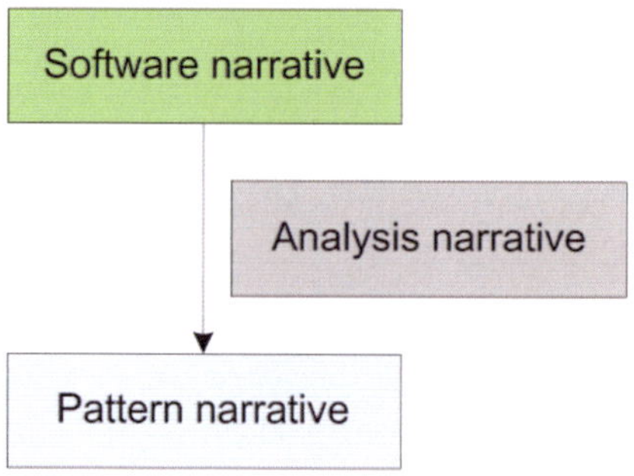

The same principles of software narratology and its analysis patterns can be applied here. **Discontinuities**, **Time Deltas,** and other patterns can be analyzed to find out analysis difficulties that might require further training (such as in domain-specific knowledge) and analysis tool development for subsequent computer assistance. For example, if we compare TAs in the analysis report above, we find out that there was a significant **Time Delta** pattern before the **Back Trace** pattern was found, leading to the first **Error Message**[197] pattern from a different **Thread of Activity**[198]. It took some time for an analyst to get an idea to look for a specific **Data Flow**[199] pattern and construct **Back Trace** (probably by looking at the source code).

For a brief overview of Software Narratology, please read its short introduction book[200].

Special and General Trace and Log Analysis

Most software traces include message timestamps or have an implicit time arrow via sequential ordering. We call such traces **Special**. The analysis is special too because causality is easily seen. Typical examples of analysis patterns here are **Discontinuity**[201], **Time Delta**[202], **Event Sequence Order**[203], **Data Flow**[204] (see also time dependency markers in the training course reference[205]), and more recently added patterns such as **Back Trace**[206], **Timeout**[207], **Milestones**[208], and **Event Sequence Phase**[209]. **Inter-**[210] and **Intra-Correlation**[211] analyses are also easy.

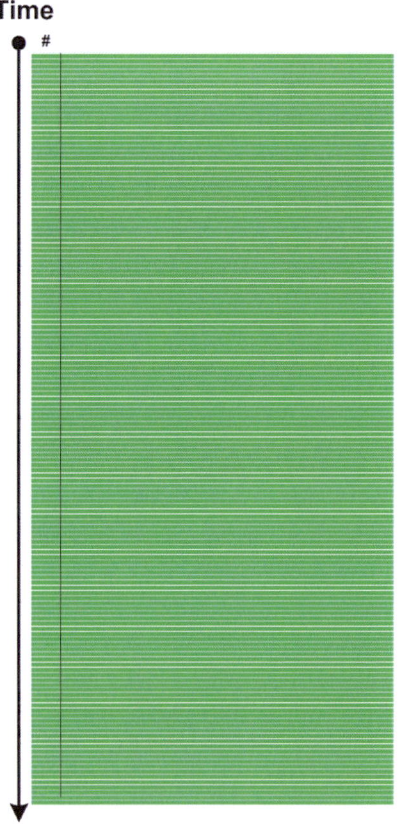

On the other side, there are plenty of software logs or digital media artifacts with "chaotic" records where the time arrow is missing or only partial. Typical examples are debugger logs from WinDbg debugger from

Microsoft Debugging Tools for Windows or logs from debugging sessions on other platforms. Such logs may contain global ordering such as the list of processes and threads (**Last Object** memory analysis pattern[212]) interspaced with local pockets of stack traces that have reversed order. Some logging output may not have any ordering or timing information whatever.

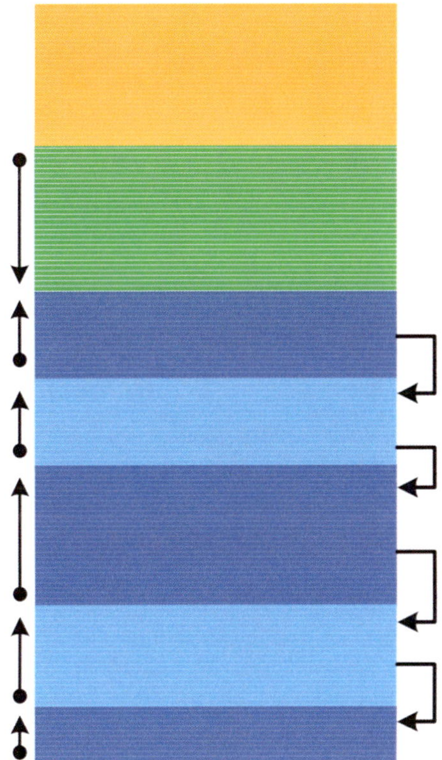

In a more general case, logging may be completely arbitrarily. A typical example is raw stack analysis and its **Rough Stack Trace**[213] and **Past Stack Trace**[214] patterns.

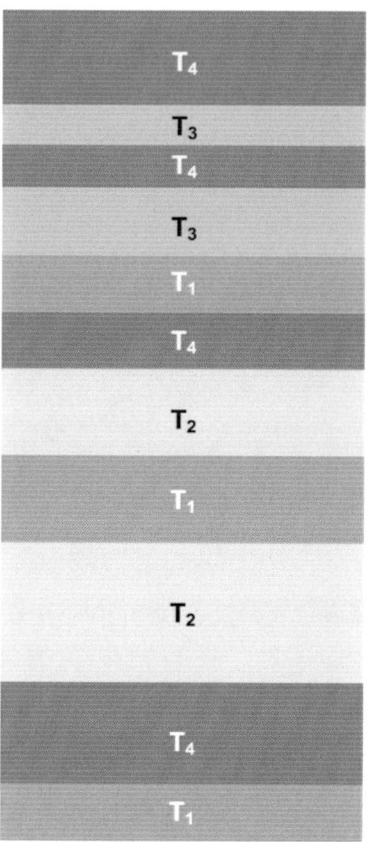

We call such traces **General**. The main task of general trace analysis is to recover causality. It may be possible if another analysis pattern is introduced called **Causality Markers**. The prototypes of such a pattern are various **Wait Chains**[215], **Waiting Thread Time**[216] memory analysis pattern and its process memory dump equivalent[217].

Projective Debugging

Modern software systems and products are hard to debug despite their elaborate tracing and logging facilities. Typical logs may include millions of trace messages from hundreds and thousands of components, processes, and threads. The postmortem diagnostic analysis became more structural after the introduction of **Trace and Log Analysis Patterns**[218] but live debugging requires a lot more effort. Here we introduce **Projective Debugging** as a tool for trace-level debugging. Its main idea is to analyze, diagnose, and debug the so-called "projected" execution of software as seen from the original software execution traces and logs:

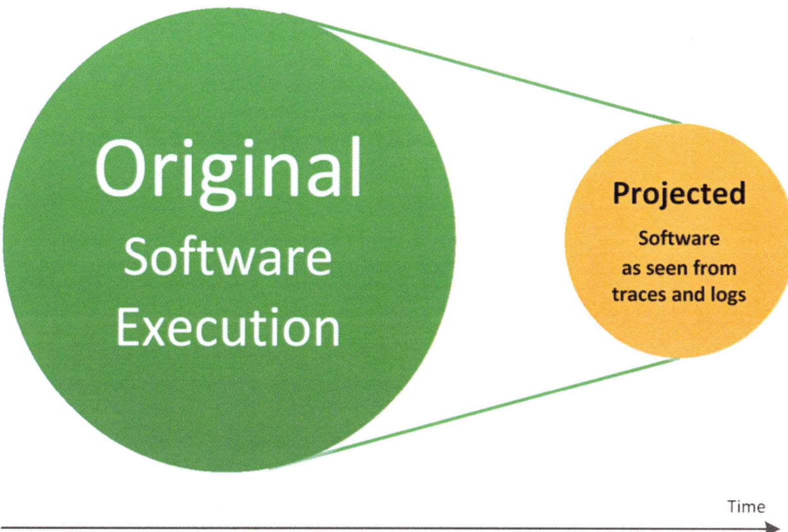

Picture 1. Original software execution is mapped into projected software as seen from traces and logs.

Please notice that **Projective Debugging** is different from the so-called *Prototype Debugging* by creating models after the software product is built (some engineering methodologies prescribe that prototypes should be discarded before building the product):

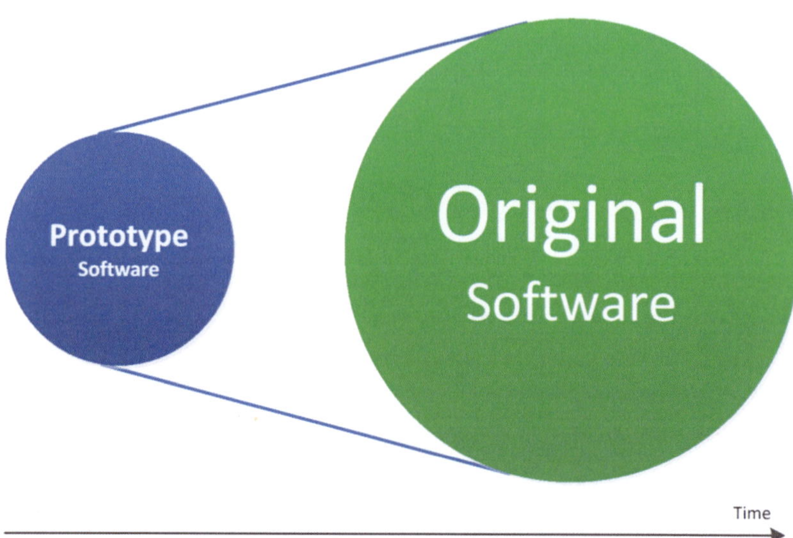

Picture 2. The prototype software is mapped into the product.

The problems diagnosed and solved in the projected system are fed back into the original system:

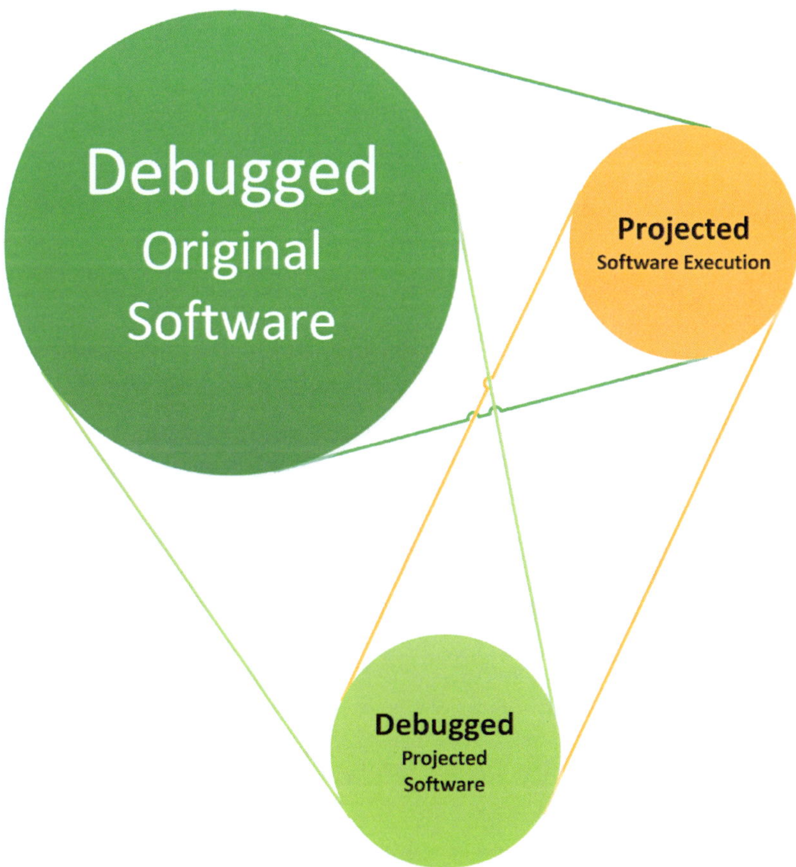

Picture 3. Debugged projected software is mapped into the original software.

The implementation of the main idea of **Projective Debugging** is that: we can take a trace or log, interpret every trace message according to some rules, and translate it into executable code mirroring components and execution entities such as user sessions, processes, and threads. This is a task for the **Projective Debugger**, and it is illustrated in the following diagram where we borrowed notation from UML:

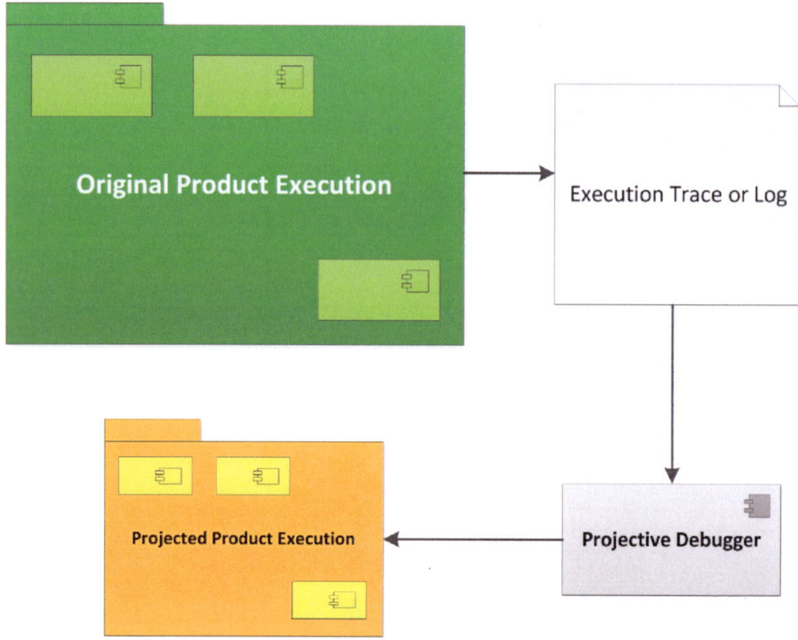

Picture 4. The logs and traces from the original product execution are translated by Projective Debugger.

For example, the **Projective Debugger** (ProjectiveDebugger.exe) interprets these very simple messages below, and creates a process PID220.exe (we have only one thread), and then opens a file "data.txt." After 10 seconds, it closes the file.

```
Time     PID  TID  Message
------------------------------------
11:00:00 220  330  Open "data.txt"
11:00:10 220  330  Close "data.txt"
```

In addition to executing code corresponding to messages using the same time deltas as read from the trace, it may scale execution time proportionally, for example, executing a 2-day log in a matter of minutes. Such scaling may also uncover additional synchronization bugs.

The trace may be pre-processed and all necessary objects created before execution, or it may be interpreted line by line. For complex traces, the projected source code may be generated for later compilation, linking, and execution. Once the projected code is executed, breakpoints may be set on existing traces, and other types of **Debugging Implementation Patterns**[219] may be applied. Moreover, we may re-execute the trace several times and even have some limited form of backward execution.

The resulting code model can be inspected by native debuggers for the presence of **Memory Analysis Patterns**[220] and can even have its own logging instrumentation with traces and logs analyzed by another instance of the **Projective Debugger**:

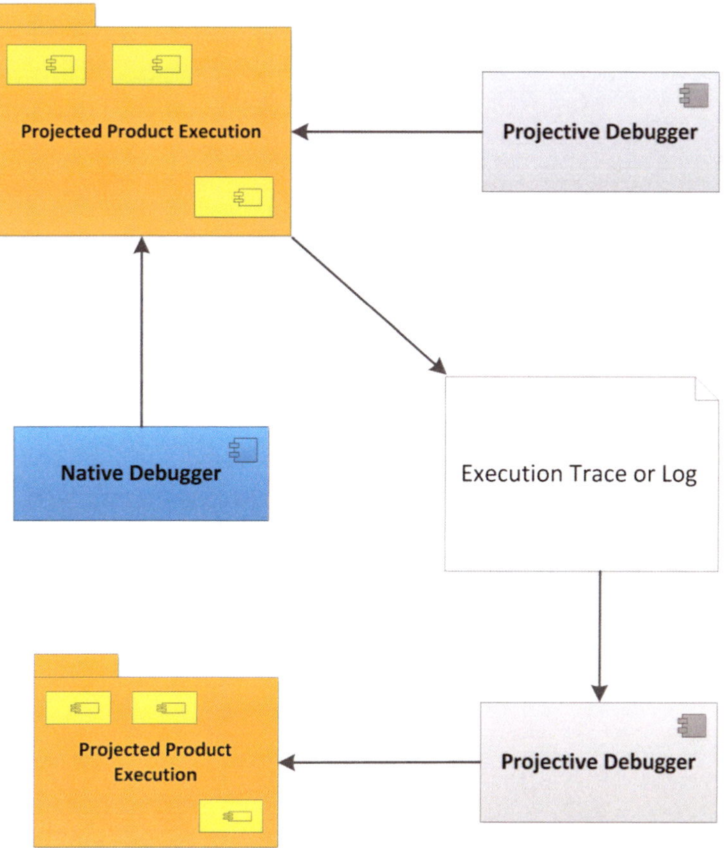

Picture 5. Projected Product Execution is inspected by a native debugger and also generates its own set of traces and logs to be projected to another model by another instance of the Projected Debugger.

We created the first version of the **Projective Debugger** and successfully applied it to a small trace involving synchronization primitives across several threads. The **Projective Debugger** translated it into an executable model with the same number of threads and the same synchronization primitives and logic. The resulting process was hung as expected, and we attached a native debugger (WinDbg for Windows) and found a deadlock.

Since traces are analyzed from a platform-independent **Software Narratology**[221] perspective, it is possible to get a trace from one operating system, and, after applying a set of rules, re-interpret it into an executable model in another operating system. We created the similar multithreading test program on Mac OS X that was hung and reinterpreted its trace into an executable model under Windows:

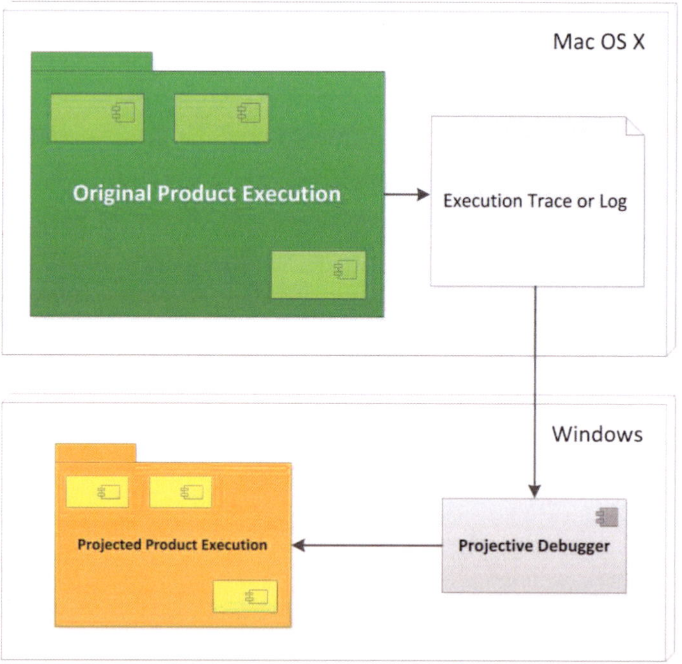

Picture 6. The traces and logs from the original product execution on Mac OS X are projected by a Windows version of Projective Debugger into an executable model for a Windows platform.

Since resultant executable models can also have corresponding logging instrumentation mirroring original tracing, any problems found in executable models can be fixed iteratively, and, once the problem disappears, the resulting fix or configuration may be incorporated into the original product or system.

If tracing involves kernel space and mode, a specialized projected executable can be created to model the operating system and driver level.

The more trace data we have, the more real our projected execution becomes. However, we want to have enough tracing statements but not to complicate the projected model. Then, ideally, we should trace only relevant behavior, for example, corresponding to use cases and architecture.

Projective Debugging may also improve our system or product maintainability by highlighting whether we need more tracing statements and whether we need more accurate and complete tracing statements.

Pattern! What Pattern?

There is confusion about patterns of diagnostics, such as related to crash dump analysis and software trace and log analysis. We are often asked about pattern percentage detection rate or whether it is possible to automate pattern diagnostics. Before asking and answering such questions, it is important to understand what kinds of patterns are meant. Patterns of diagnostics can be subdivided into concrete and general problem patterns, and also into concrete and general analysis patterns.

Problem patterns are simply diagnostic patterns, and they can be defined as (fusing *Diagnostic Pattern* [222] and *Diagnostic Problem* [223] definitions):

> *A common recurrent identifiable set of indicators (signs) together with a set of recommendations and possible solutions to apply in a specific context.*

Concrete Problem Patterns are particular sets of indicators, for example, an exception stack trace showing invalid memory access in the particular function from the particular component/module code loaded and executed on the Windows platform.

However, such indicators can be generalized from different products and OS platforms, giving rise to **General Problem Patterns** forming a pattern language. Our previous example can be generalized as **Exception Stack Trace** [224] showing **Invalid Pointer** [225] and **Exception Module**[226]. **Concrete Problem Patterns** are the implementation of the corresponding **General Problem Patterns**.

Now, it becomes clear why **Memory Analysis Pattern Catalog** does not have any concrete BSOD bugcheck numbers. Most of such numbers are concrete implementations of **Self-Diagnosis**[227] pattern.

Then we have **Concrete Analysis Patterns** as particular techniques to uncover **Concrete Problem Patterns.** For example, thread raw stack analysis for historical information to reconstruct a stack trace. Again, such techniques vary between OS platforms and even between debuggers.

Generalizing again, we have **General Analysis Patterns**, for example, analyzing **Historical Information**[228] in **Execution Residue**[229] to construct **Glued Stack Trace**[230].

General Problem Pattern descriptions may already reference **General Analysis Patterns,** and in some cases, both may coincide. For example, **Hidden Exception**[231] pattern uses **Execution Residue** pattern as a technique to uncover such exceptions.

Most of **Software Trace and Log Analysis Patterns**[232] are **General Analysis Patterns** that were devised and cataloged to structure the analysis of the diverse logs from different products and OS platforms[233]. For example, a specific data value common to both working and problem logs that helps to find out the missing information from the problem description can be generalized to **Inter-Correlation**[234] analysis between the problem trace and **Master Trace**[235] using **Shared Point**[236].

This partitioning is depicted in the following diagram:

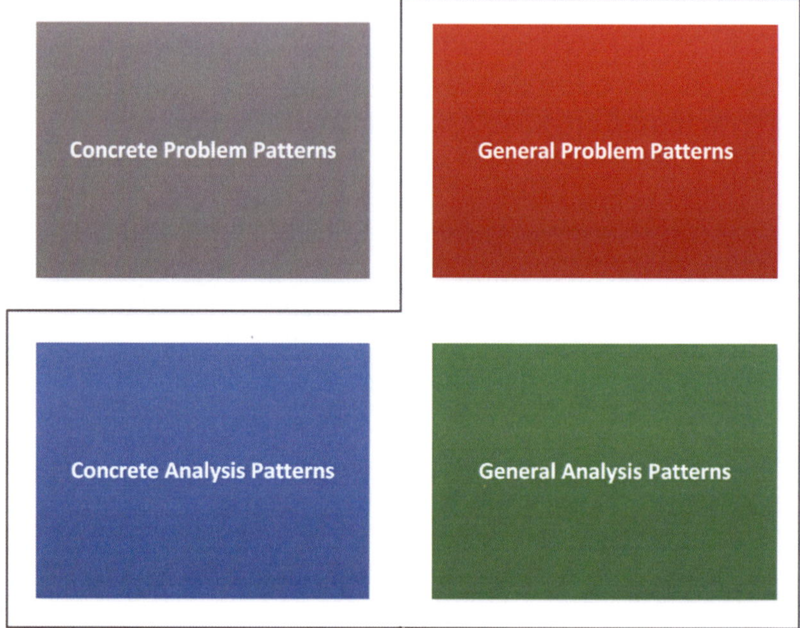

Software Diagnostics Institute[237] innovation involves devising and cataloging general problem and analysis patterns and providing some concrete analysis implementations on specific OS platforms such as Windows and Mac OS X.

We did not See Anything

How often do we hear that back from support departments when we submit our memory dumps and software logs? "Analysis inconclusive", "logs or crash dumps are not good," "we need more," "liaise with another vendor," and many others hide the same response behind the elaborate narrative façade. Based on the audit of memory dump analysis reports submitted to Software Diagnostics Services[238] (former Memory Dump Analysis Services) by its customers over the course of the last few years, we think such responses usually result from support engineers not utilizing the proper software diagnostics methodology, for example, using what they only remembered from their past diagnostics, troubleshooting, and debugging practice. What is the solution to this problem?

Software Diagnostics Institute[239] has been collecting analysis patterns for the past eight years in cooperation with Software Diagnostics Services, providing research funds and software execution artifacts. Patterns are organized into pattern catalogs, and checklists are recommended. The approach is called Pattern-Oriented Diagnostics, which has three parts: pattern-driven, systemic, and pattern-based. Pattern-driven means that we go through the list of patterns and report ones we found and not found. It may be done iteratively. The systemic part means we can apply the same general patterns across different software execution artifacts, products, and operating systems. Pattern-based means we iteratively extend and improve our pattern catalogs and use Pattern-View-Controller diagnostics architecture.

Please find the following presentations for each part:

- Pattern-Driven[240]
- Systemic[241]
- Pattern-Based[242]
- Pattern-View-Controller (page 178)

It is a very flexible approach already applied to malware detection and analysis, digital forensics, debugging, and network trace analysis. There are training courses available[243].

When we hear a similar response from an engineer, we ask to provide the list of patterns not found in memory dumps, traces, and logs.

Coding and Articoding

The analysis of software traces and logs is largely a qualitative activity. We look for specific problem domain patterns using general analysis patterns (page 148). Some methodological aspects of this software defect research are similar to the "qualitative research" method in social sciences[244]. The latter method uses the so-called "coding" techniques for data analysis[245]. Software traces and debugger logs from memory dumps are software execution artifacts we previously called DA+TA (Dump Artifact + Trace Artifact). We propose to use similar "coding" techniques to annotate them with diagnostic indicators, signal and sign mnemonics, and patterns (such as software diagnosis codes, page 185). We, therefore, call this software post-construction "coding" as **articoding** (**artecoding**), from **arti**fact (**arte**fact) + coding, to distinguish it from software construction coding. Such articoding forms a part of software post-construction problem-solving. Articodes form a second-order software narrative (page 202) and can be articoded too.

Many software tools were developed for assisting qualitative research coding, and these can be reused for "coding" debugger logs, for example. In addition to those tools, general word and table processing programs can be used as well for some types of artifacts. Here we show MS Word for a WinDbg log example. The debugger log with stack traces from all processes and threads was loaded into MS Word template table with three columns. The first column is the log itself, the second column is for diagnostic indicators (such as critical section, CPU consumption, ALPC wait), and the third column is for pattern language articodes (here we use pattern names from Memory Analysis Pattern Catalog[246], for traces we can use MS Excel and Trace and Log Analysis Pattern Catalog[247]). Formatting and highlighting creativity here is unlimited. Irrelevant parts from the log can be deleted, and the final analysis log can have only relevant annotated tracing information.

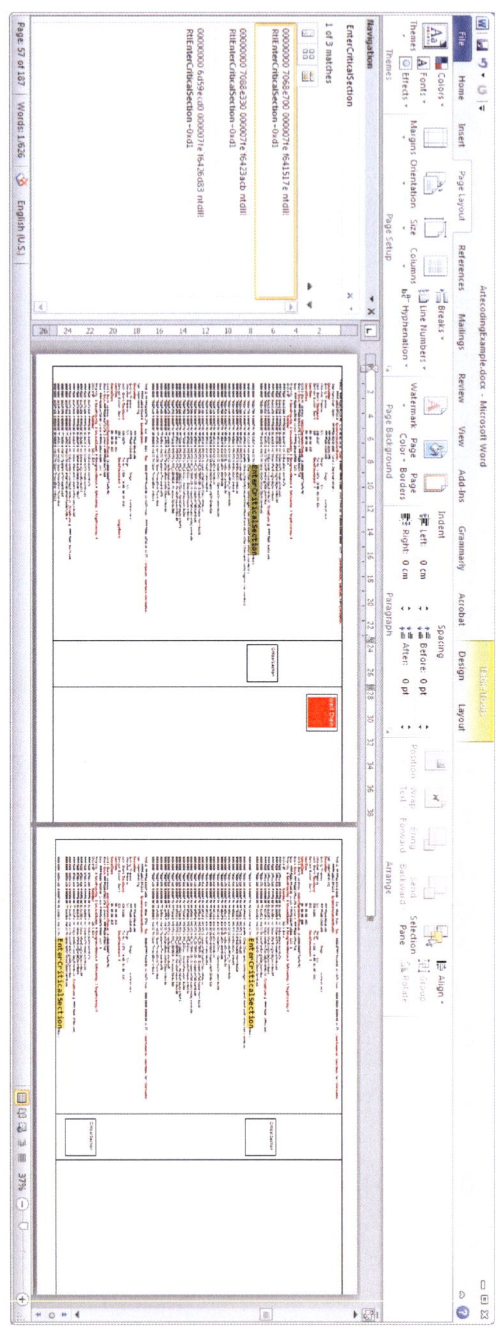

The full-size picture can be found here[248].

Adjoint Space

Sometimes we need memory reference information not available in software traces and logs, for example, to see pointer dereferences, to follow pointers and linked structures. In such cases, memory dumps saved during logging sessions may help. In the case of process memory dumps, we can even have several **Step Dumps**[249]. Complete and kernel memory dumps may be forced after saving a log file. We call such pattern **Adjoint Space**:

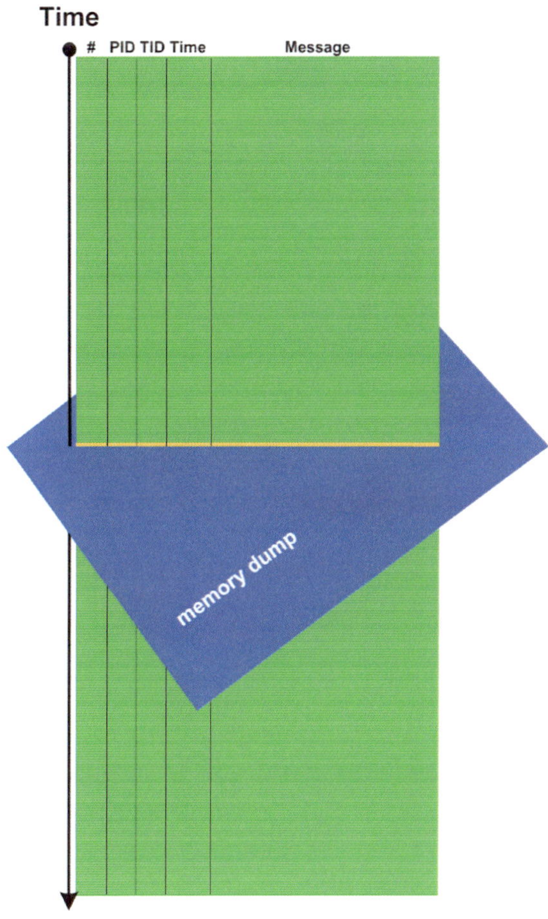

Then we can analyze logs and memory dumps together, for example, to follow pointer data further in memory space:

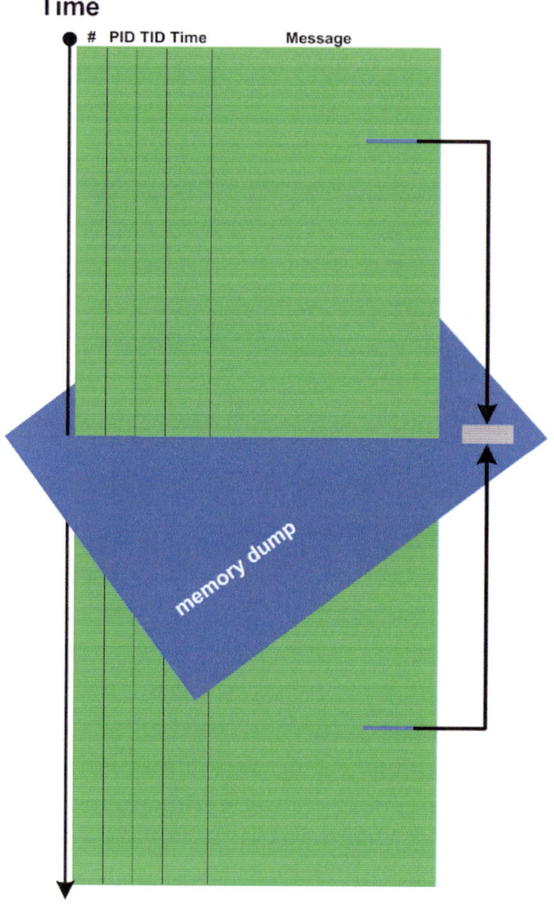

There is also a reverse situation when we use logs to see past data changes before memory snapshot time (**Paratext** memory analysis pattern[250]):

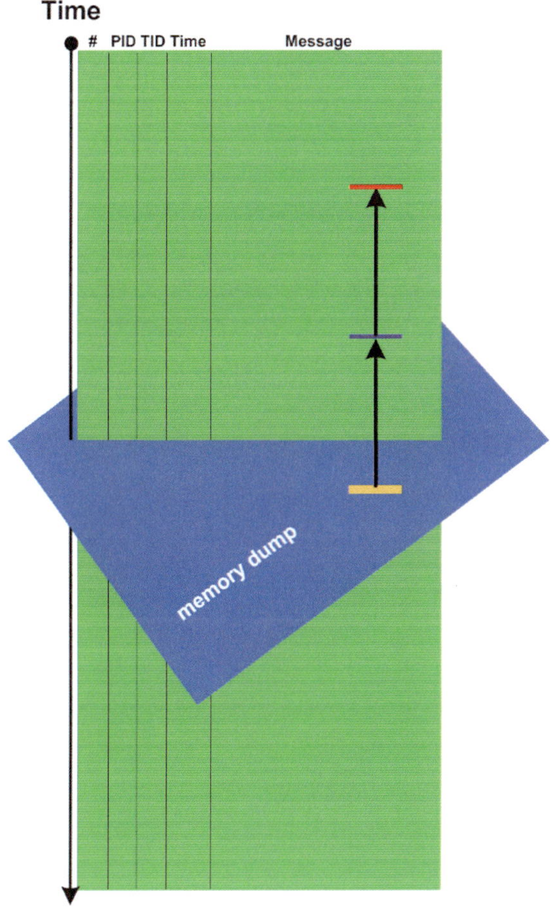

[This page is intentionally left blank]

Volume 9

Diagnostics, Forensics, Prognostics: The Copernican Revolution

Our pattern language system for software diagnostics was originally tool-centric, devised from recurrent analysis problems on Windows platforms when using WinDbg from Microsoft Debugging Tools for Windows. We now call it "Ptolemaic."

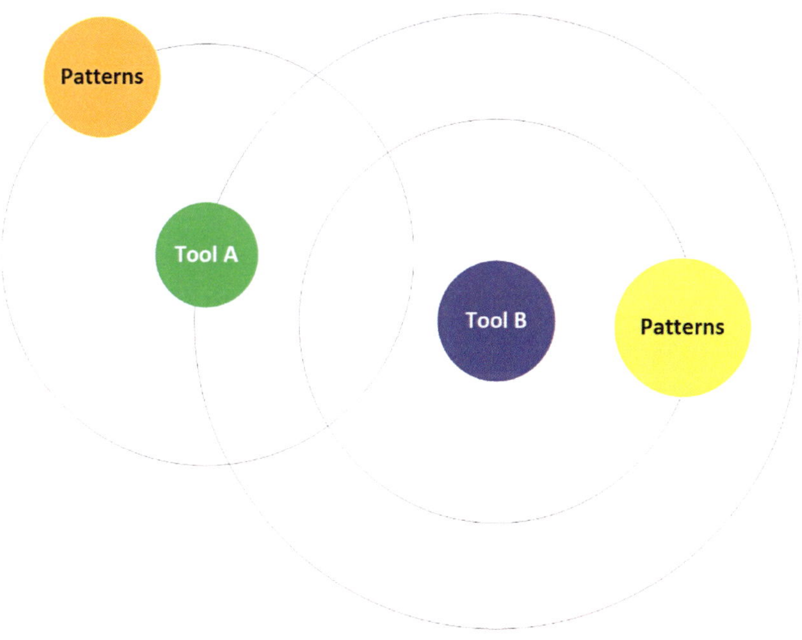

Diagnostics, Forensics, Prognostics: "Ptolemaic" Tool-Centric System

Later we realized that the same system is possible to apply to other platforms and tools, and we proved it with the publication of the book for GDB[251]. When the debugging tool changed on Mac OS X, we ported the same book to different LLDB debugger. With the presenting of a pattern language for memory forensics[252], we extended the same system to other memory analysis tools in principle. Our pattern language system became pattern-centric. We call it "Copernican." In addition, trace and log analysis pattern system[253] was devised as pattern-centric from the ground up based on software narratology[254] and applied to all software execution artifacts, including network traces[255].

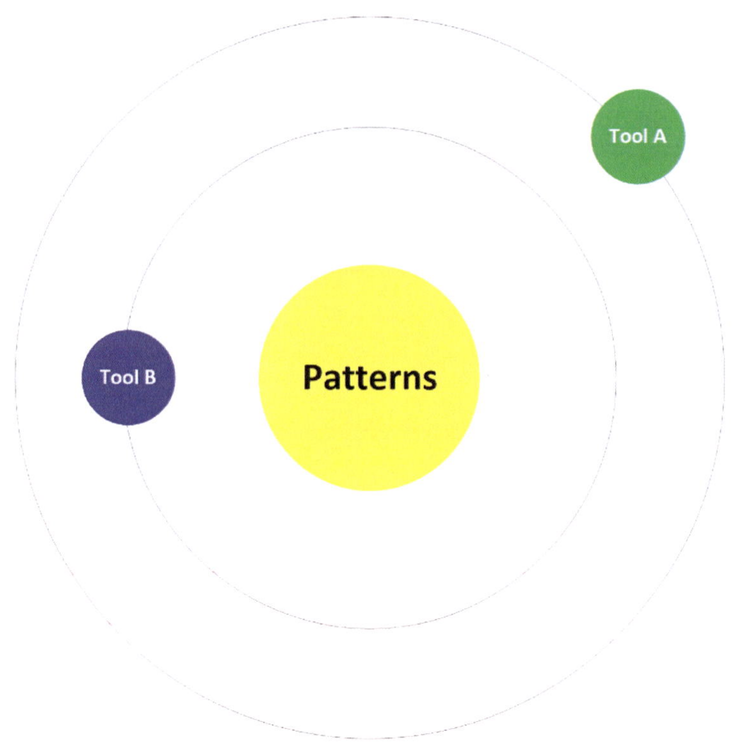

Diagnostics, Forensics, Prognostics: "Copernican" Pattern-Centric System

Although this paradigm shift was evolutionary for us, we call it revolutionary for the whole discipline of software diagnostics, forensics, and prognostics because of previously dominant tool-centric systems.

Pattern Repertoire

When developing, debugging, maintaining, and supporting software, it is important to know general problem analysis patterns (page 216) of abnormal software structure and behavior. As with any language, such a pattern language comes in passive and active usage variants. A passive pattern user knows about a particular analysis pattern but may have difficulty recognizing it in a specific software execution artifact such as a memory dump or log. A passive user may become an active user after training and experience. "Pattern Repertoire" is such user knowledge (or awareness) of a specific set of patterns from pattern catalogs[256] (see the definition of repertoire[257]). An active pattern repertoire of a Windows software engineer first becomes passive when the engineer starts working with Linux, Mac OS X, Android, iOS, z/OS, or any other platform but then becomes active through experience. In any case, the possession of a pattern repertoire and its size (the pattern language vocabulary) is an important asset. What distinguishes the pattern repertoire from a mere set of pattern names is the knowledge of its syntax (analysis pattern combinations), semantics (the meaning of analysis patterns), and pragmatics (active usage in concrete situations and passive knowledge of usage in general situations). Similar to software construction pattern repertoire, which helps with software construction problem analysis, architecture, design, and implementation, software post-construction pattern repertoire[258] helps to perform software post-construction problem diagnostic analysis and debugging more efficiently and effectively. A few words must be told about implicit pattern knowledge. Some patterns may be obvious and used unconsciously. However, their explicit naming helps with communicating analysis decisions, troubleshooting and debugging recommendations, and creating problem-solving case studies.

Here, we would like to show the building of our diagnostic analysis pattern repertoire for memory dumps, software traces, and logs. The following picture illustrates the growth of the number of software diagnostic analysis patterns with each successive volume of Memory Dump Analysis Anthology[259] (excluding malware analysis patterns published in Volume 7, and structural memory patterns published in Volume 5):

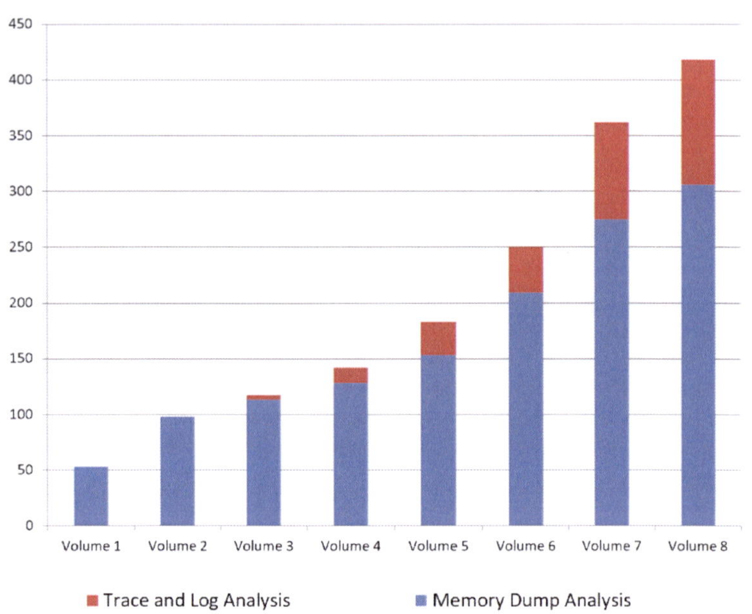

The picture shows, for example, that volumes 6 – 8 introduced more analysis patterns than volumes 1 – 5. Volumes 7 and 8 alone introduced 63% of the current trace and log analysis patterns, and 32% of the current crash and hang memory dump analysis patterns.

Pattern-Oriented Software Internals: Pattern Paradigms and Software Internals Pattern Stack

By software internals, we mean how software works instead of how it was intended to work. Intention and actuality may also coincide, but sometimes, they do not, especially in the cases of victimware[260] and malware. Their discrepancy, therefore, causes various problems. Learning software internals, especially operating system internals, is a necessary step towards better software construction, effective and efficient troubleshooting and debugging, successful forensics, malware and vulnerability research.

There are different approaches to teaching software internals of operating systems and products. Some authors prefer a computer science approach from general software design and architecture principles; some prefer hands-on approaches such as troubleshooting and debugging; some prefer reversing and deconstructive approach. Learners of different backgrounds may find particular approaches difficult to internalize. Here we refer to our own experience learning operating system internals when our main background was in software design, programming, and debugging (before we moved to software support to study software diagnostics).

We think that the ideal way would be to cover all aspects of software construction and post-construction using patterns. However, different phases of software evolution use different pattern paradigms. The software construction phase mainly uses a software construction pattern stack of requirements analysis, architecture, design, and implementation patterns, which are patterns of software construction problem solving. The software construction pattern paradigm considers patterns as solutions to recurrent problems of building software. The software post-construction phase[261] mainly uses diagnostic patterns and debugging pattern stack (page 129). The diagnostic pattern paradigm considers patterns as indicators of software behavior such as signals, symptoms, and signs describing software execution problems[262]. Debugging patterns are similar to software construction patterns in documenting common recurrent problems of fixing software defects (page

197). They provide solutions to recurrent debugging problems. Similar can be said about problem workaround patterns and patterns of building software troubleshooting and debugging tools (Debugware patterns, page 45). There is also a third pattern paradigm: software deconstruction patterns, including reversing (ADDR patterns, page 174) and structural memory patterns (page 104). This paradigm just shows how things are organized before and during software execution, including software/ hardware interface.

In summary, we have three pattern paradigms corresponding to the domain of construction, post-construction, and deconstruction.

All three pattern paradigms are needed to describe software internals, its architecture, implementation, inner workings, and problem-solving. Instead of devising a new set of patterns to describe software internals, we propose a pattern stack of existent patterns. In its rough and simple form, it consists of three stack slots corresponding to three pattern paradigms:

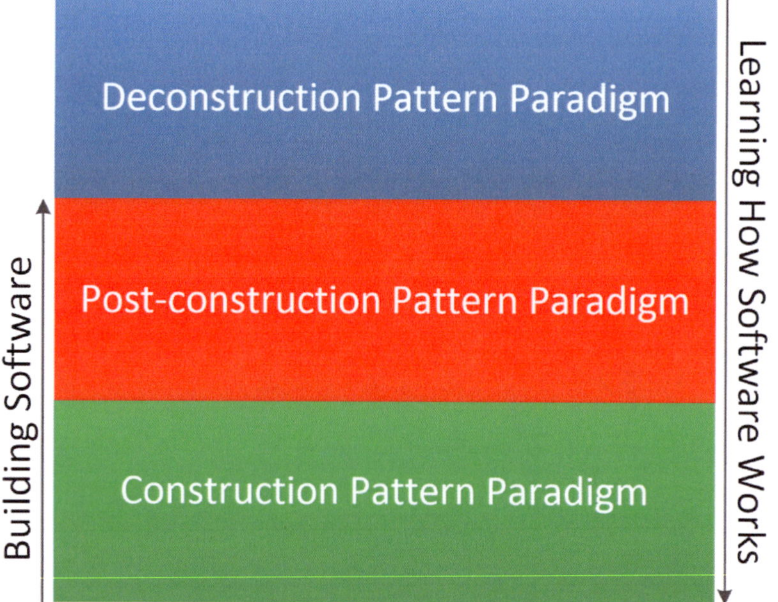

Each pattern paradigm can be expanded into its substack or a collection (when the order is not important) of pattern categories:

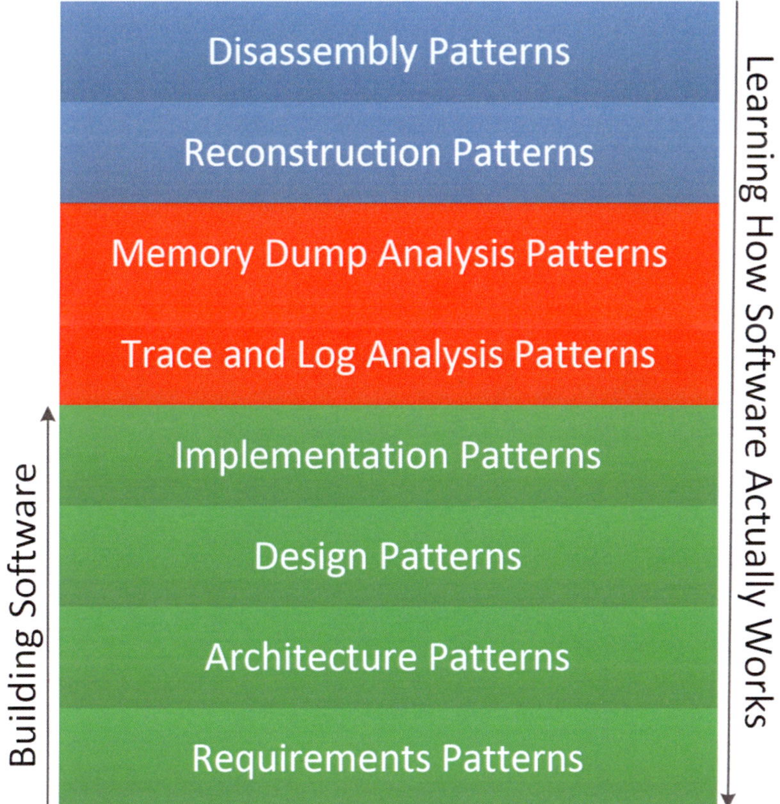

Individual software internal features can be described by a concrete pattern stack of patterns from pattern category subcatalogs[263], for example, software fault processing pattern stack (only a few important conceptual patterns and pattern subcatalogs are listed):

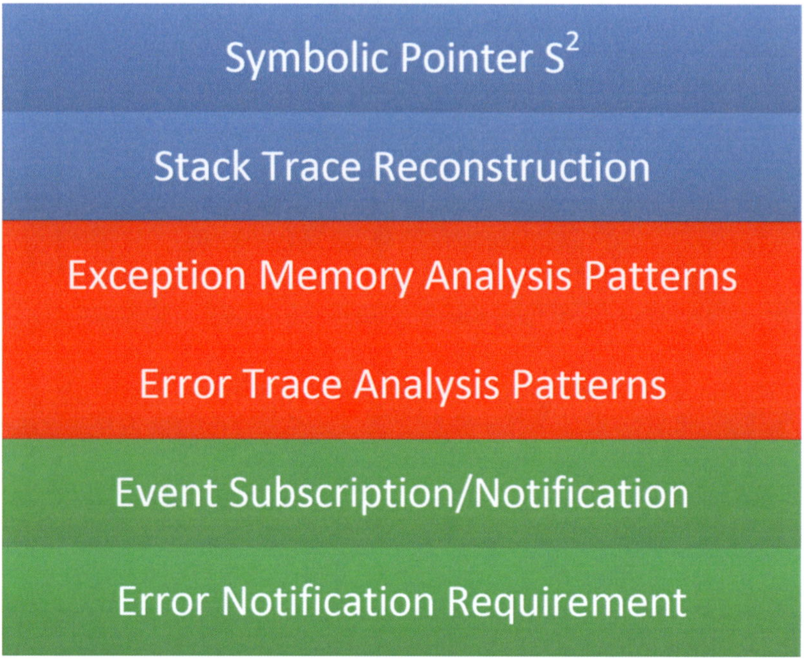

Symbolic Pointer S^2

Stack Trace Reconstruction

Exception Memory Analysis Patterns

Error Trace Analysis Patterns

Event Subscription/Notification

Error Notification Requirement

We believe that teaching software internals, for example, operating system internals, using a pattern stack approach would appeal to all types of learners: software architects, software developers, software support engineers, and software security researchers.

Software Diagnostics Canvas

We introduce canvas for pattern-oriented software diagnostics process to facilitate better diagnostic analysis reports. A piece of paper is divided into three columns: **Input**, **Analysis**, and **Output**.

The **Input** column is divided into two sections: **Problem Description Patterns** and **DA+TA Collection Patterns**. **Problem Description** pattern catalog was introduced earlier (page 154) to help with accurate software problem identification. **DA+TA Collection** pattern catalogs for dump artifacts (DA) and trace artifacts (TA) were also introduced as Memory Acquisition (page 176) and Trace Acquisition (page 177) pattern catalogs.

The **Analysis** column is divided into two sections: **Analysis Patterns** and **Problem Patterns**. The former is about diagnostic analysis techniques, and the latter is about diagnosed software problems. The distinction between them was introduced earlier (page 216). All such patterns can be found in Memory Analysis pattern catalog[264] and Trace and Log Analysis pattern catalog[265].

The **Output** column is also divided into two sections: **Analysis Report Patterns** and **Recommended Action Patterns**. The corresponding pattern catalogs are under development. The former is about patterns for useful and meaningful diagnostic analysis reports, and the latter is about the good workaround, troubleshooting, and debugging recommendations.

Each cell is subdivided into **General** and **Concrete** patterns where the latter are specific product patterns such as a memory access violation in a specific module.

The first version of the canvas template can be downloaded from Software Diagnostics Institute[266].

Input	Analysis	Output
Problem Description Patterns	Analysis Patterns General Concrete	Analysis Report Patterns
DA+TA Collection Patterns	Problem Patterns General Concrete	Recommended Action Patterns

Software Traces and Logs as Proteins

In the past, we introduced structural (page 104) and behavioral memory[267] and software trace[268] analysis patterns as DNA of software behavior (page 135). This metaphor can be illustrated in the following diagram:

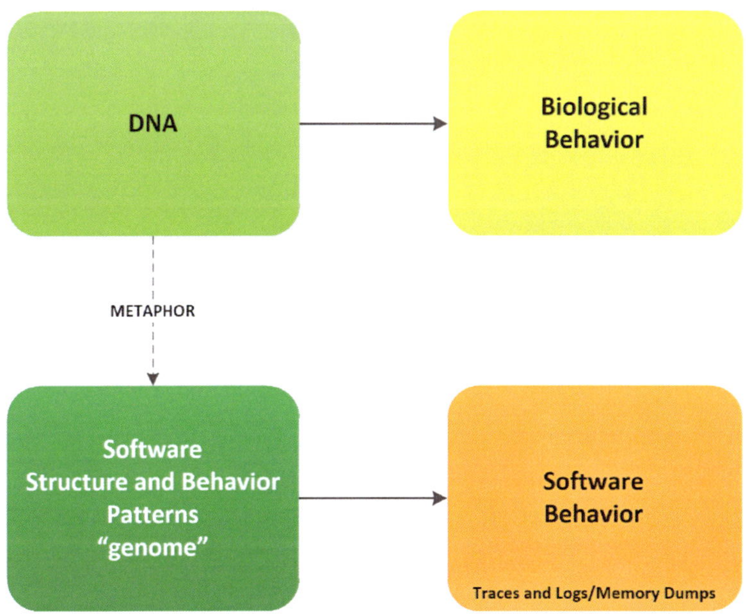

Now, we introduce another metaphor: software traces and logs are "proteins" generated by software code. Such "proteins" are mapped to software functionality:

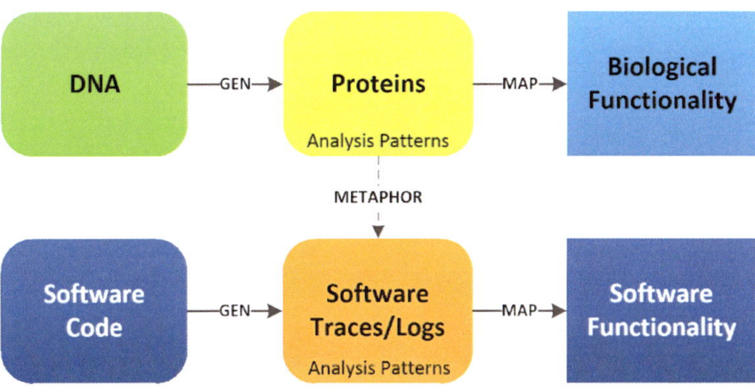

There are many similarities between protein structural analysis and that of traces and logs. For example, sequence motifs[269] are analogous to **Motif** trace analysis pattern[270] (that originally came from motives[271] in mathematics), and structural motifs[272] are possible via **Characteristic Message Blocks**[273] and **Activity Regions**[274] or any other arrangement of structural patterns:

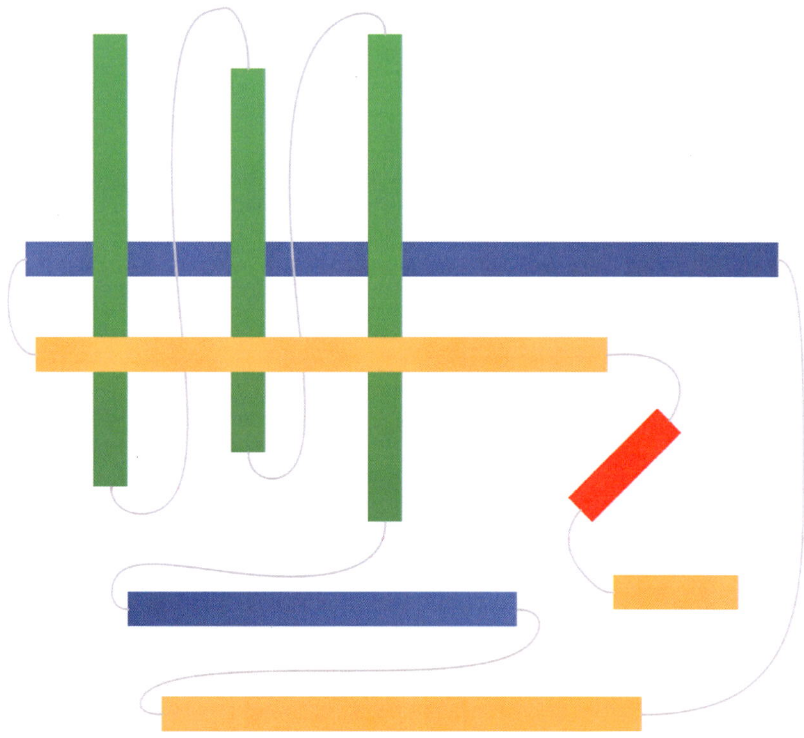

Patterns-Based Root Cause Analysis Methodology

In 2011, we introduced iterative and incremental **A.C.P.** root cause analysis methodology (page 126). Its name is an abbreviation from the three main constituents: artifacts, checklists, and patterns. We get software execution artifacts such as memory dumps and software logs, use checklists to guide us in our problem analysis efforts, recognize patterns of abnormal software structure and behavior, and ultimately find out the root cause(s). Recognized patterns may prompt us to revisit checklists for further guidance and request more software execution artifacts. The process is illustrated in the following diagram:

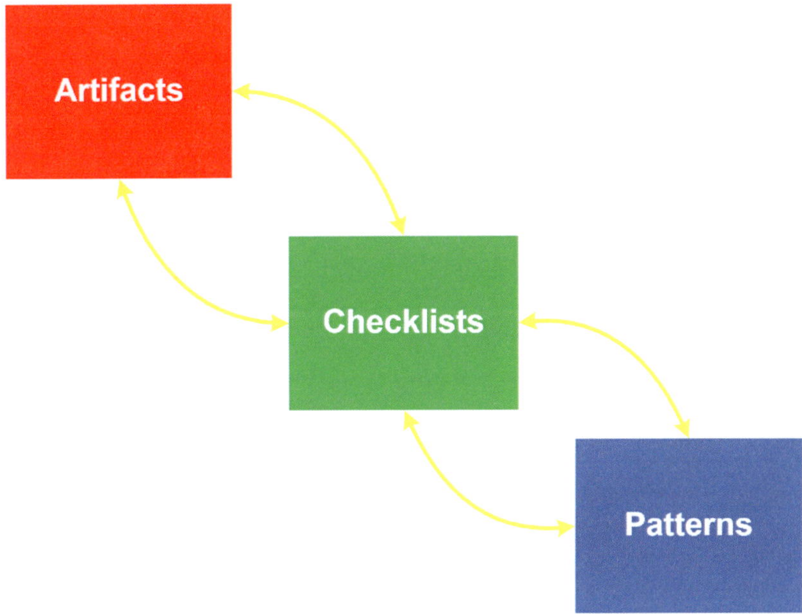

At that time, pattern-oriented software diagnostics was not yet fully developed, so the proposed root cause analysis methodology was primarily debugger commands-based for memory analysis (in the form of checklists[275]) and analysis patterns-based for software trace and log analysis where checklists were patterns-based[276]. Pattern sequences (former pattern succession) help in finding root causes (page 81).

Pattern catalogs as checklists were later introduced for First Time Software Diagnosis methodology (page 184). Patterns were also introduced for memory dump (page 176) and trace collection (page 177).

With the development of pattern-oriented software diagnostics, we realized the centrality of patterns (page 227) and the division of patterns into general and concrete problem patterns and problem analysis patterns (page 216).

This brought the revision of A.C.P methodology where checklists become attributes of artifact collection and pattern catalogs:

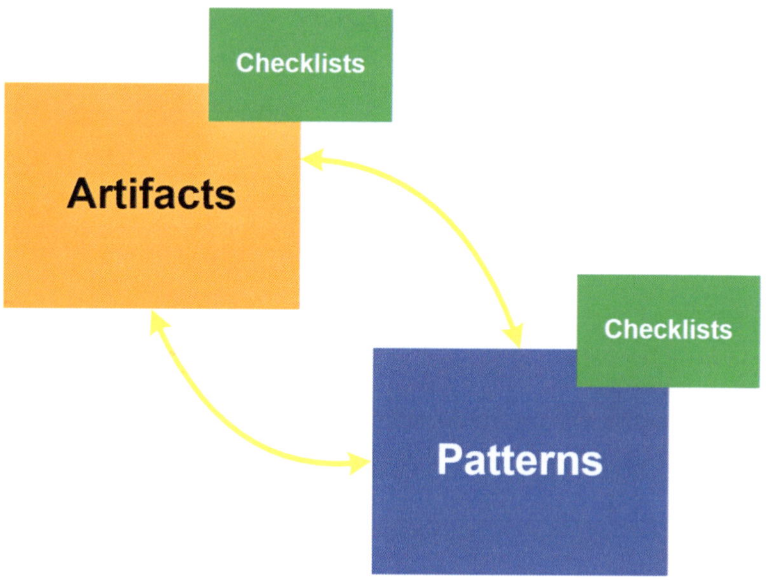

However, the causal nation of root cause analysis is not explicitly mentioned in the process. Many problem patterns can be caused differently; for example, Dynamic Memory Corruption patterns[277] can be caused by buffer overwrites and underwrites, invalid API parameters, double memory releases, and even memory manager defects resulting in similar diagnostic indicators seen in memory snapshots and traces.

Therefore, we introduce the notion of a **Mechanism** to describe the possible cause of a diagnostic pattern. Such mechanisms replace pattern sequences as causal analysis tools. Mechanisms can also be organized into catalogs and have checklists. Mechanisms provide software internal links between software construction, post-construction, and deconstruction pattern paradigms (page 231).

The resulting iterative and incremental **A.P.M.** methodology (Artifacts. Patterns. Mechanisms.) is illustrated in the following diagram:

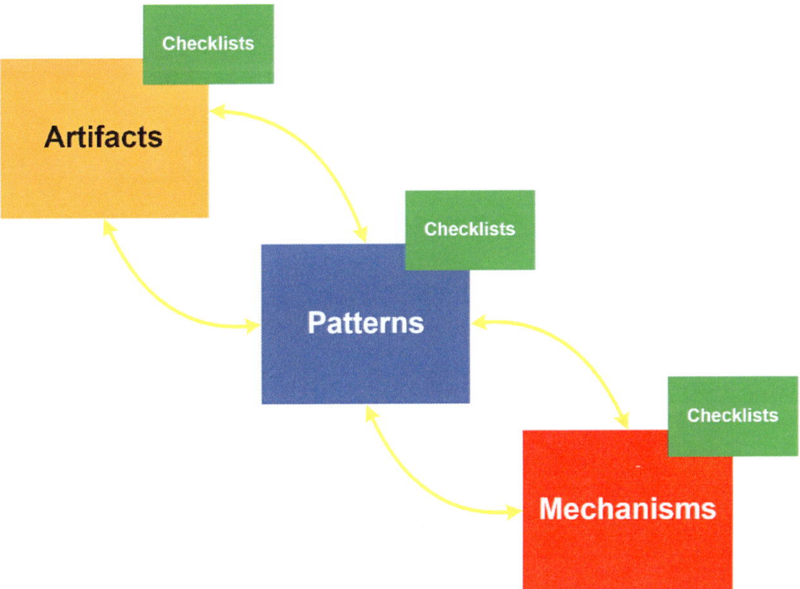

Teaching Complex Diagnostic Scenarios with Artificial Debugger (ArtDbg) and Pseudo-Memory Dumps

One of the problems in teaching software diagnostics and postmortem debugging is a simulation of complex software problem scenarios. There is plenty of real-life memory dumps available, but due to security considerations, they cannot be shared outside of the organization. Here we introduce the Artificial Debugger project (ArtDbg) that simulates the I/O of the real debugger, for example, WinDbg, GDB, or LLDB.

The real memory dump is analyzed in the real debugger, and all debugger input and output is saved in a log file. This log file is then scanned for any potentially sensitive information, and all such information is eliminated[278]. It is then converted into a binary pseudo-memory dump format.

ArtDbg is used to open and analyze such pseudo-memory dumps. It allows using the same real debugger commands that were used to generate the log file. Such commands output the same information that was available from the real debugger. Some real debugger commands that were not used to generate the log file may also be used if possible.

Memory Dump File

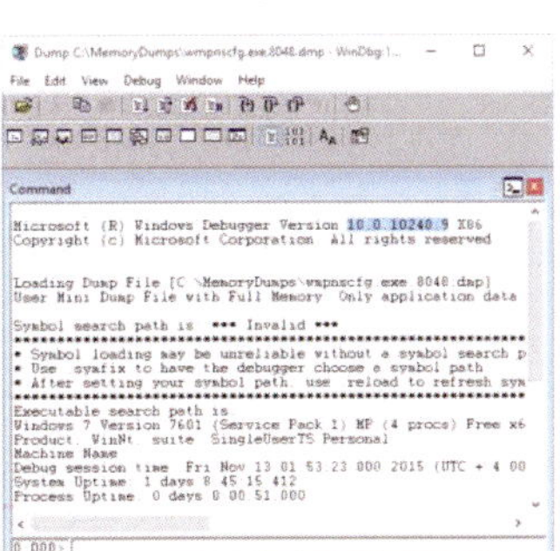

Log File

Pseudo-Memory Dump File

Dump - ArtDbg

```
Microsoft (R) Windows Debugger Version 10.0.10240.9 X86
Copyright (c) Microsoft Corporation. All rights reserved.

Loading Dump File [C:\MemoryDumps\wmpnscfg.exe.8048.dmp]
User Mini Dump File with Full Memory: Only application data

Symbol search path is: *** Invalid ***
****************************************************************
* Symbol loading may be unreliable without a symbol search p
* Use .symfix to have the debugger choose a symbol path.
* After setting your symbol path, use .reload to refresh sym
****************************************************************
Executable search path is:
Windows 7 Version 7601 (Service Pack 1) MP (4 procs) Free x6
Product: WinNt, suite: SingleUserTS Personal
Machine Name:
Debug session time: Fri Nov 13 01:53:23.000 2015 (UTC + 4:00
System Uptime: 1 days 8:45:15.412
Process Uptime: 0 days 0:00:51.000
```

0:000>

The Scope of Software Diagnostics

Should software diagnostics stand alone as a separate, distinct diagnostics or be a part of some other diagnostics? We considered initially three types of diagnostics: medical, technical, and software:

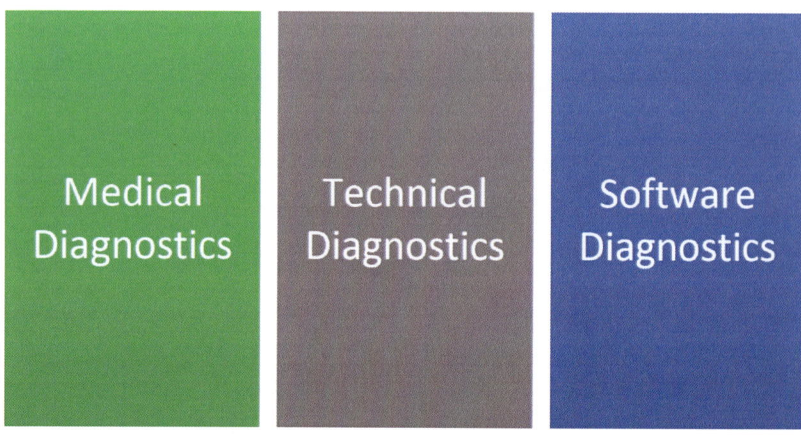

The objects of medical diagnostics are obviously humans and mostly their biological artifacts (we say *mostly* because linguistic and textual artifacts can also be used for diagnosis). The objects of technical diagnostics are structures and systems made from natural and artificial organic and inorganic engineering materials[279]. The objects of software diagnostics are obviously software systems.

We define software diagnostics as "a discipline studying *abnormal* software structure and behavior in software execution artifacts (such as memory dumps, software and network traces and logs)"[280] or, more generally, to include the context of forensics as "a discipline studying signs of software structure and behavior in software execution artifacts (such as memory dumps, software and network traces and logs)."[281]

Although there are many conceptual similarities in general between these diagnostics, there are three features of software that set software diagnostics apart:

- A software system or its artifact can be copied.
- The software can be its own model. This follows from the previous feature since we can copy the software execution state and then study the effects of its execution independently. However, it is possible to have different software models for diagnostics as, for example, in Projective Debugging (page 209).
- Software execution artifacts are both symbolic and digital.

There are also humanistic artifacts[282] such as text (including historical documents), language, literature, and music, which are symbolic and digital (or can be digitized). Diagnostics takes the form of literary criticism and text reconstruction (philology). Many similarities there gave rise to Software Narratology[283] and Systemic Software Diagnostics[284]:

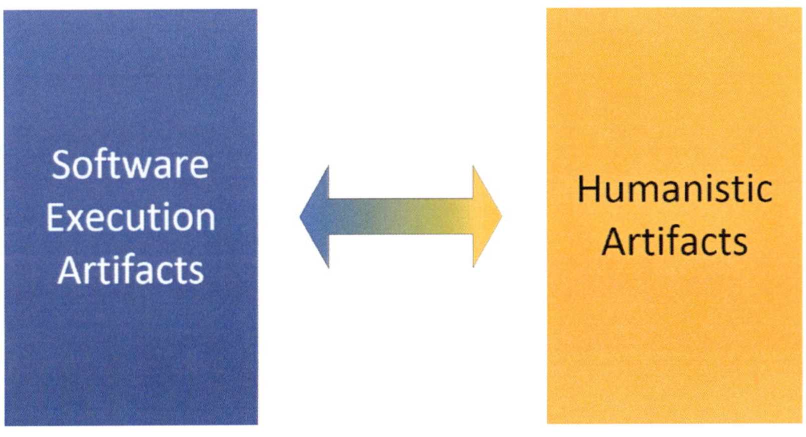

Diagnostics of Things (DoT)

DIAGNOSTICS OF THINGS

We introduced the Narratology of Things as a combination of Software Narratology of Things (page 151) and Hardware Narratology (page 150). Since memory dump analysis may be considered as a part of general trace and log analysis (page 206), we open a new research direction for **Diagnostics of Things** (**DoT**) based on Narratology of Things and Pattern-Oriented Trace and Log Analysis, which also includes software execution artifacts of things and pattern-oriented network trace analysis[285] from IoT.

Riemann Root Cause Analysis Language

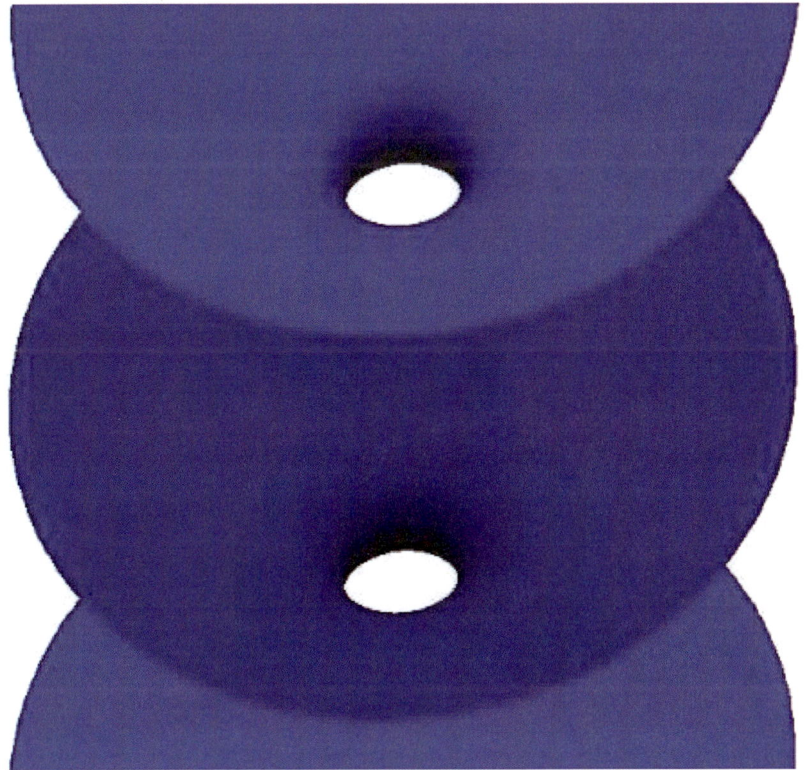

Image generated by 3D-XplorMath[286]

Incepted and named in February 2009 shortly before the first software trace and log analysis pattern[287] (see also page 57) was published in April the same year, Riemann Programming Language[288] (see also page 62) was thought of as a software problem description language (page 153) capable of generating software problem-solving tools (page 143, including TaaS version[289]). A book was planned for publication in 2010[290]. The main motivation at that time for the name was the metaphorical correspondence between multi-valued functions represented by Riemann surfaces[291] and software defects as alternative branches of computation. Since the significant development of pattern-oriented software diagnostics, the introduction of network[292] and performance analysis pattern languages (page 195), and patterns-based root cause analysis methodology (page 239), we now make Riemann Programming Language an optional coding complement to Riemann Root Cause Analysis Pattern Language. The latter includes diagnostic analysis pattern languages for trace analysis [293] and memory analysis [294] developed by Software Diagnostics Institute[295], including structural memory patterns (page 104) in the context of general log analysis (page 206). We can now consider another analogy with multi-valued functions where the same general diagnostic patterns (page 216) in a memory dump or log can be generated by different source code. Riemann RCA Pattern Language facilitates the transformation of software narrative artifacts into much shorter analysis narratives through the process of articoding (page 221). The resulting analysis artifacts can be programmatically processed to generate diagnostic, troubleshooting and debugging configurations, classes and functions, frameworks and plugins, components and nodes. The following diagram describes this process:

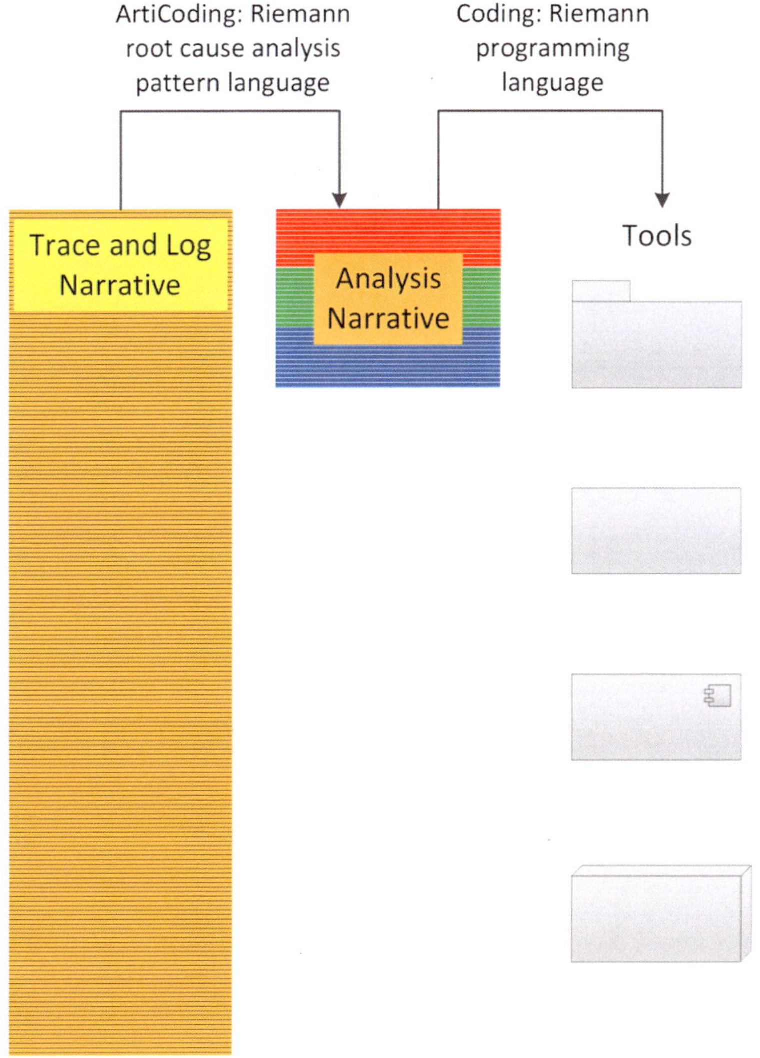

The Riemann programming language should not be confused with the Riemann monitoring system[296], which was named and developed later elsewhere by a different group of people. The latter is about collecting events and not about their collective analysis using pattern-oriented analysis methodology developed by Software Diagnostics Institute. Regarding event monitoring, Software Diagnostics Institute also develops platform-independent software trace and log acquisition patterns (page 177) for better use of various monitoring systems.

Problem Solving as Code

```
// Problem Solving version 1.0

def problemSolving (input: ProblemDescription) : Solution

    Problem = ProblemDescription.analyze()

    Artifacts.collect(Problem)

    foreach Pattern in Patterns
        Report += Pattern.check(Problem, Artifacts)

    Analysis = Report.analyze()

    Solution = Analysis.solve()
```

We introduce **Problem Solving as Code** as a process of developing, managing, and provisioning problem-solving methods and tools. Some problem-solving methodologies, such as pattern-oriented problem-solving developed by Software Diagnostics Institute as a part of Diagnostics Science[297], require constantly evolving pattern catalogs that can be stored in version control systems. For example, pattern-oriented software problem-solving[298] involves pattern-oriented problem description analysis (page 154) and software execution memory (page 176) and trace (page 177) artifact acquisition, pattern-driven[299] and pattern-based[300] software diagnostics (page 160, including forensics[301]), the patterns-based root cause analysis (page 239), and pattern-oriented debugging process (page 197) which introduced design methodology to debugging (page 129). In addition to general problem patterns and problem analysis patterns, there are concrete problem and problem analysis patterns (page 216) where concrete problems are constantly changing (traditional problem repositories). PSaC ("Problem Sack") allows using declarative and imperative problem-solving configurations tailored for specific problem domains or specific systems and products by customizing pattern catalogs. Specific problem artifact types may require specialized tools and configuration so they can also be designed, developed, managed, and provisioned. For example, pattern-oriented problem solving includes DebugWare (page 45) and DiagWare[302] design patterns.

Dia|gram Graphical Diagnostic Analysis Language

One of the current Software Diagnostics Institute[303] projects is the development of Dia|gram graphical language for pattern-oriented software diagnostics, forensics, prognostics, root cause analysis, and debugging. It combines the best features from:

1. Visual Dump Objects: Graphical Notation for Memory Dumps (page 77);
2. STDiagrams: Software Trace Diagrams (page 191);
3. Visual compression of software traces and logs (including "bird's eye view" of software traces), first introduced in **Characteristic Message Block**[304] trace and log analysis pattern;
4. Minimal Trace Graphs, first introduced in **Activity Region**[305] trace and log analysis pattern. Numerous examples can be found in Accelerated Windows Software Trace Analysis training course reference[306] and Software Trace and Log Analysis: A Pattern Reference[307] book;
5. Minimal Stack Trace Diagrams, first introduced in **Constant Subtrace**[308] memory analysis pattern.

The purpose of Dia|gram language is twofold:

- To provide a succinct presentation and visualization of software execution state, artifacts, distribution of problem patterns, problem analysis patterns and their relationship[309];
- To communicate pattern-oriented software diagnostic analysis results.

Additionally, Dia|gram may be used for presentation and analysis of higher-order pattern narratives (page 202).

Software Diagnostics Institute also proposes the UML profile[310] for Software Diagnostics with additional diagram types: artifact acquisition map, activity backtrace, and implementation internals.

Iterative Pattern-Oriented Root Cause Analysis

When we introduced A.P.M. patterns-based root cause analysis methodology (page 239, Artifacts. Patterns. Mechanisms.), it may have made an impression of a waterfall-type process with some iterations between artifact collection and diagnostic analysis when collected artifacts are not good. However, software post-construction problem solving is usually iterative, with memory dumps and software logs collected again and again after the preliminary root cause analysis.

To illustrate the iterative nature of the process, we first name its stages as **Artifact Acquisition** for Artifacts, **Artifact Analysis** for Patterns (diagnostics), and **Analysis** of **Analysis** for Mechanisms (root cause analysis):

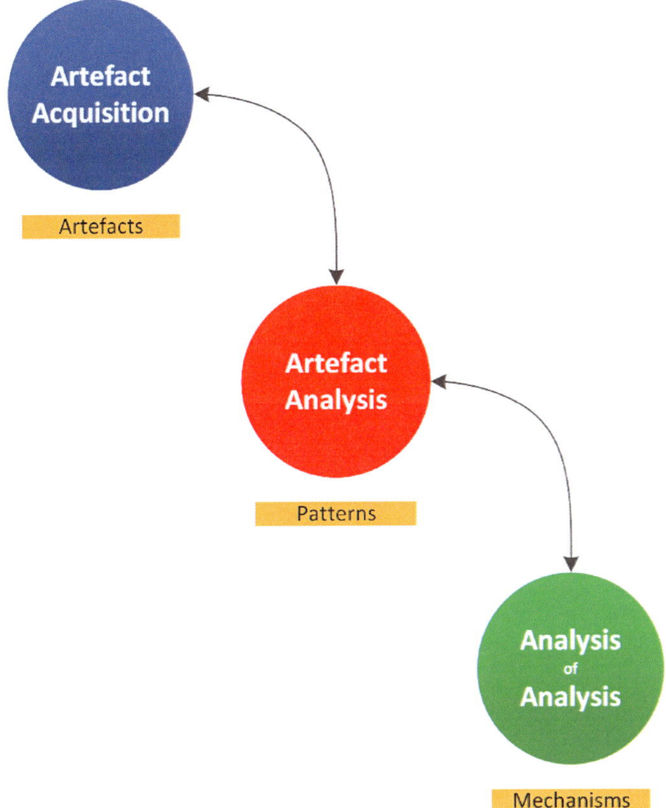

Now we rearrange these **AA** stages:

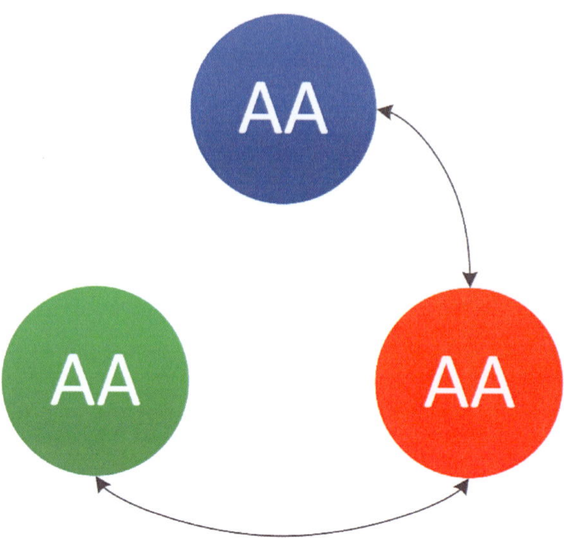

After the preliminary root cause analysis (Analysis of Analysis), we may need to gather more artifacts for further diagnostics and more precise RCA, and this is reflected in more focused stages:

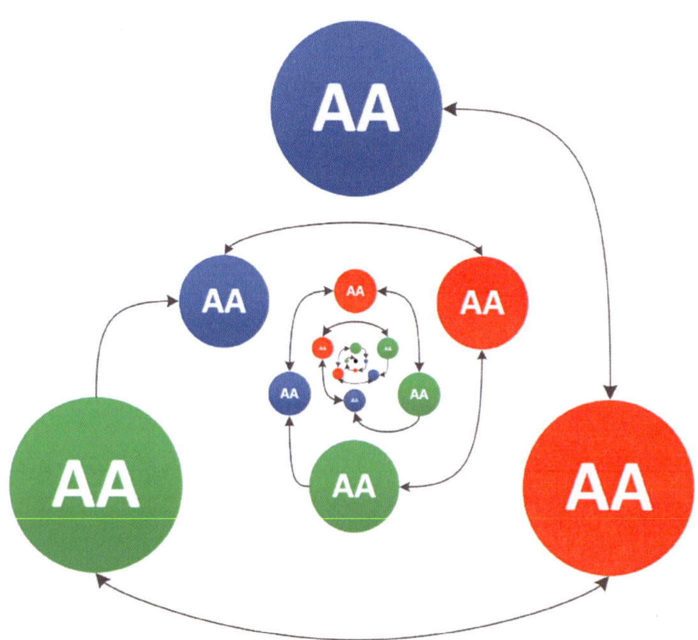

Theoretical Software Diagnostics and Education

After writing so much about software diagnostics, we introduce its abstract generalizing principles of pattern orientation and systems thinking as Theory of Software Diagnostics. We were thinking about the importance of theory[311] for quite some time until we got acquainted with the work of Leo Klejn[312], who coined the term "theoretical archaeology." Then we also decided to coin a similar term for software meta-diagnostics since we compiled two books as guides to software diagnostics principles irrespective of software platforms, vendors, and their software products: Software Diagnostics[313] and Principles of Memory Dump Analysis[314] and planned to publish this book as a compilation of related theoretical articles. Looking for the development of theoretical archaeology as guidance makes sense because it emerged recently in contemporary times and also deals with artifacts, historical reconstruction, and time- and memory-related issues, albeit of a different nature. While working on theoretical foundations and principles for many years, we had to learn theories, ideas, and metaphors of other disciplines used in software diagnostics that we call software para-diagnostic theories by analogy with para-archaeological (coined by Klejn) theories such as history, sociology, linguistics. In his book "Introduction to Theoretical Archaeology: Meta-archaeology,"[315] Klejn made a few remarks on the required theoretical education. We would like to reformulate them in relation to theoretical software diagnostics:

- Very few people do theory because theoretical thinking requires broad education and polymath knowledge across many disciplines. We found that:
    - Computer science and software engineering education helps in the practical side of software diagnostics but is not enough;
    - Knowledge of university-level mathematics and natural science education help in understanding of technical diagnostics but is not enough;
    - Knowledge of the principles of medical diagnostics helps because pattern-oriented facet of theoretical

software diagnostics is partially based on medical metaphors;

- Knowledge of semiotics helps in understanding of the role of signs in theoretical software diagnostics;
- Knowledge of philosophy helps in deeper understanding of foundational aspects of theoretical software diagnostics such as the nature of problems, their phenomenology, meaning, and understanding;

- Humanities education (analysis of human-made artifacts) is very important since software diagnostics is also based on artifact analysis.

- Such education is needed from earlier up and, in addition to computers and coding, should also include history, philology, narratology, and literary theory.

In summary, broad reading is required to get acquainted with diagnostics expertise in various domains of human activity.

Volume 10

Topological Software Trace and Log Analysis

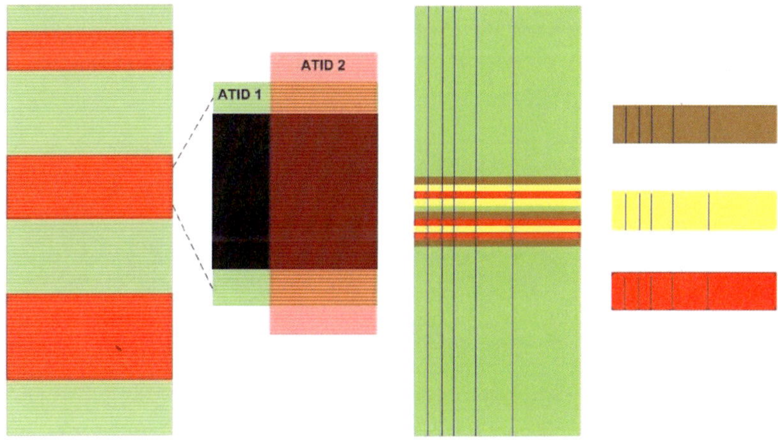

Previously we based software trace and log analysis on software narratology[316]. While continuing further research and development in that direction, we are now constructing a new software trace and log analysis system called **TopoLog** based on ideas and techniques from topology[317] (originally called *analysis situs* in Latin: analysis of the situation) as a part of theoretical software diagnostics (page 255). Over the years, we described a few trace and log analysis patterns based on topological metaphors: **Quotient Trace**[318], **Message Cover**[319], **Fiber Bundle**[320], **Sheaf of Activities**[321], and **Adjoint Space**[322]. Before starting our pattern work on software trace analysis, we considered threads as braids in abstract space (page 41), and, after the first analysis patterns, we considered multithreading as multibraiding (page 98). For general software traces and logs (page 206), including memory snapshots, we propose topological state analysis, for example, analysis of the covering space via open and closed **Memory Regions**[323] and **Region Strata**[324].

Software Diagnostic Space as a General Graph of Software Narratives

By connecting various memory spaces (user, kernel, physical, virtual, orbifold [page 132], manifold [page 96], fiber bundle [page 93], adjoint [page 223]), trace and log spaces, and problem description narratives, we introduce **Software Diagnostics Space** as a search space for finding problem patterns using general and concrete analysis patterns (page 216). Using mathematical metaphors, we view it as a general graph[325] of statements from **Software Problem Narrative** (graph vertices) and various software narratives such as logs, traces and memory spaces (edges). Software problem narratives may be different from software problem descriptions (which we get from software users and which have their own analysis patterns, page 154) because they are controlled narratives of actor interactions while working with software (top right corner of software narratology square, page 147). For completeness, every software narrative edge has vertices by default as start and stop vertices.

We consider **Software Diagnostic Space** as **Trace Mask**[326] of **Software Problem Narrative** with **Special and General Traces and Logs** (page 206). Let's look at one example depicted in the following diagram:

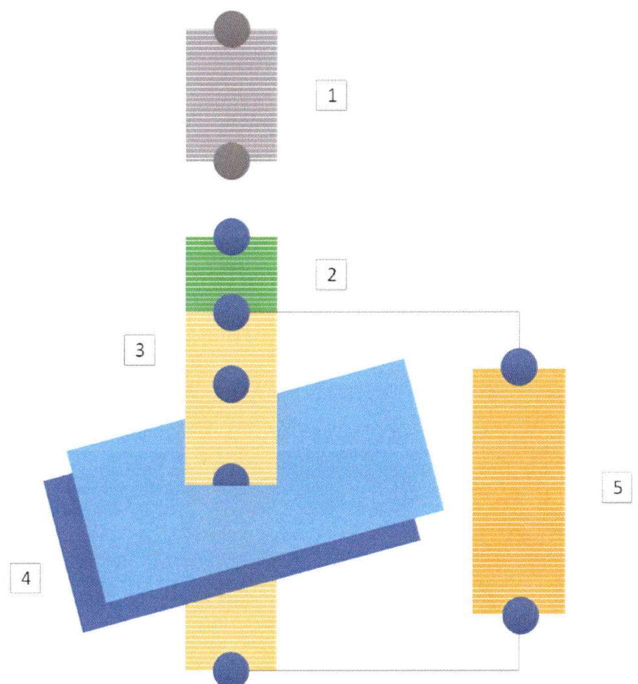

We have the problem description from a user who could not exercise some software functionality unless some service was restarted. This is a problem description narrative (no. 1). A software support person constructed the problem reproduction setup narrative (no. 2) and recorded problem narrative no. 3 – 5 with tracing the client and server software and taking memory snapshots (**Adjoint Space** trace and log analysis pattern, page 223) of the corresponding service and another **Coupled Process**[327] (memory analysis pattern).

This can all be depicted in the following general graph (multigraph) diagram where loops show adjoint spaces ("instantaneous" artifact snapshots like memory, data):

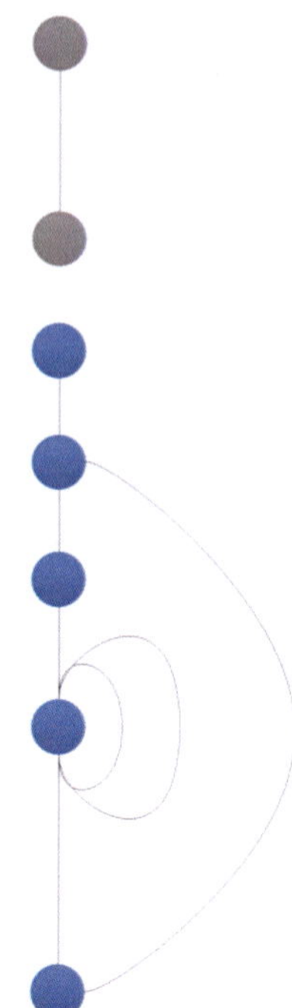

Such graphs may not be connected, and additional multiple edges with extra vertices may replace loops.

The practical usage of such graphs can be demonstrated by their construction during problem analysis. Suppose that we have a problem description:

After its analysis, we construct a problem narrative:

During its trace analysis, we identify needed software trace edges:

We add multiple edges if tracing involves several software systems or different trace varieties:

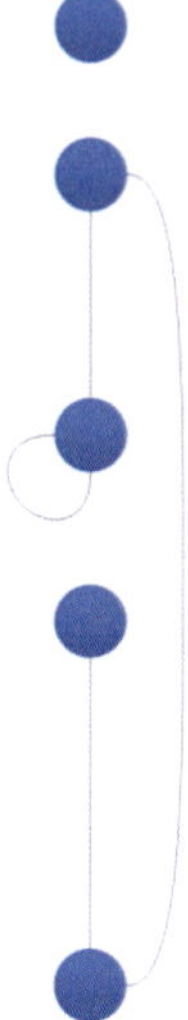

Software Diagnostics as Archaeology

Analogy: studying software execution artifacts and traces left in artifacts by software execution. Traces themselves may have undergone aging, e.g., memory overwrites. Root Cause Analysis (page 239) uses mechanisms from Software Internals (page 231) to understand causal connections and reconstruct original software execution context.

- Sociology - Software Internals
- Archeology - Software Diagnostics
- History - Root Cause Analysis

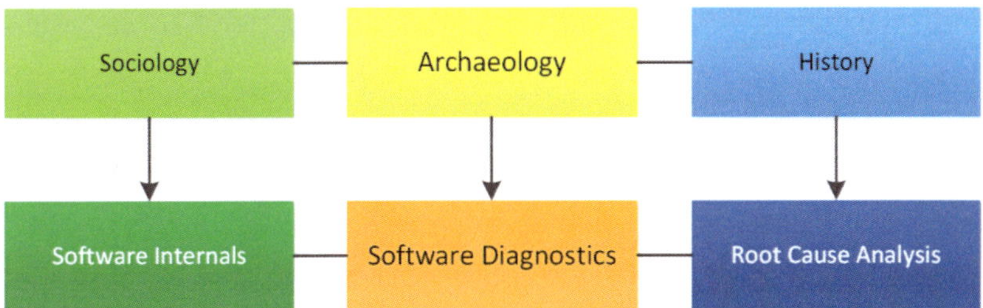

Pattern-Oriented Diagnostic Analysis Process

Previously we introduced Pattern-Oriented Debugging Process (page 197), where software diagnostics played the major role as a part of debugging. However, in the case of a separate software diagnostic process (page 166), we introduce **Pattern-Oriented Diagnostic Analysis Process**, which incorporates diagnostic analysis requirements elicitation from problem description analysis and diagnostic report construction. Both new additions require separate pattern catalogs. The problem description analysis pattern catalog is already being extended (page 154), and the new catalog for diagnostic report construction is under development and will be published soon. The central process part, diagnostic artifact analysis, already has two extensive analysis pattern catalogs for software log analysis[328] and memory analysis[329]. The process is illustrated in the following diagram:

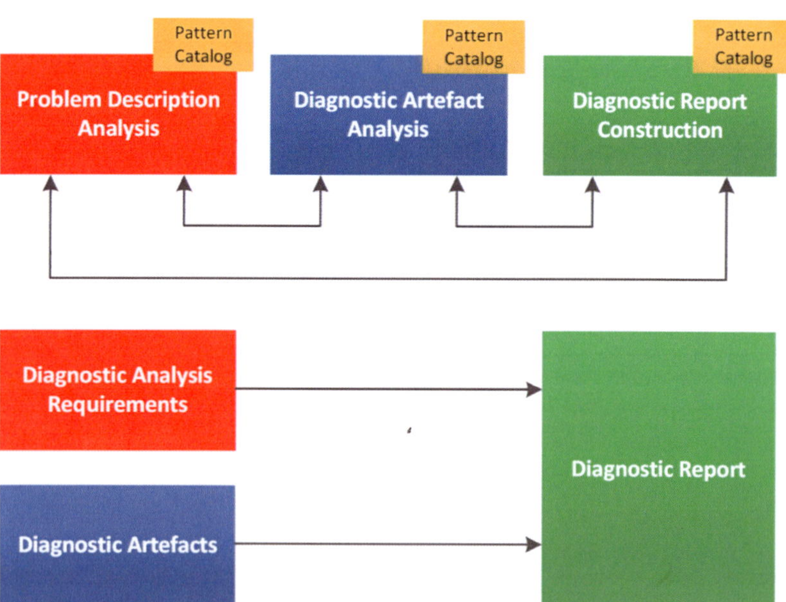

Principles of Pattern-Oriented Software Data Analysis

For 2017 we look forward to applying software diagnostics and software post-construction problem-solving[330] insights gained over the ten years of Software Diagnostics Institute[331] research to software data analysis in general. In addition to memory snapshots (Dump Artefacts) and logs (Trace Artefacts) and their analysis that we abbreviated as DA+TA, we extend our pattern-oriented approach to additional artifacts as security data, source code, configuration data, telemetry, revision repositories, and stores. We consider all additional software data types as examples of generalized software narratives (page 149) and traces (page 206) and abbreviate as simply DATA.

It is time to bring together the principles of pattern-oriented data analysis:

1. Patterns-based

Data patterns and data analysis patterns are classified into catalogs and named to form pattern languages. Every major kind of software data and activity associated with its data analysis can have its pattern language and catalog. Pattern catalogs are dynamic structures. New patterns are added, old are revised. New catalogs are refined, added, or combined. Pattern names change if necessary to accommodate new data meta-analysis insights[332]. Patterns can be reused across different data domains.

2. Patterns-driven

Data patterns that are diagnosed using data analysis patterns that are guided by meta-patterns trigger appropriate actionable decisions[333].

3. Systemic-based

Data analysis is a multidisciplinary activity incorporating insights from natural and medical sciences, humanities, and social sciences[334].

4. Mechanisms-based

The pattern-oriented data analysis may lead to data root cause analysis when coupled with mechanisms (page 239).

5. Narrative-based

Software data is a form of a software narrative (page 147), including data analysis itself (the higher-order narrative analysis, page 202).

6. Pattern square-based

There are special and general data patterns and special and general data analysis patterns (page 216).

7. Patterns-assisted

Since software usage is a human activity, software data analysis should be human-assisted[335]. Data analysis patterns facilitate data analysis verifiability, elimination of data analysis errors, and provide independence of data analysis reporting from idiosyncratic data analysis habits[336]. Software data and data analysis patterns and their languages assist humans in achieving and maintaining software data analysis quality.

Abstract Debugging Commands (ADC) Initiative

This short article was originally published in Software Diagnostics Library in November 2008.

While working on WinDbg command cards[337] and even before that, when compiling a comparison table[338] for both WinDbg and GDB, we came to an idea of abstract debugging commands that correspond to common debugging tasks, have clear syntax and semantics and serve metaphorically as a basis for conversion of analog thinking to digital debugger assistance (see analog-to-digital conversion[339] for ADC abbreviation). Here a WinDbg extension can help, but now we think about using a tree-based approach similar to CMDTREE.TXT for CDA Checklist[340].

Reducing Analysis Pattern Complexity via Elementary Analysis Patterns

There are hundreds of debugger commands, such as commands from WinDbg, GDB, LLDB, and other debuggers. A typical diagnostic analysis pattern, for example, a memory dump analysis pattern, may involve many commands[341]. In November 2008, we proposed abstract debugging commands for common diagnostic, forensic, and debugging tasks (page 267). After the introduction of pattern-oriented diagnostic thinking, we propose another analysis pattern abstraction level of **Elementary Analysis Patterns** that groups either real or abstract debugging commands and allows chaining analysis activities to describe diagnostic analysis patterns uniformly:

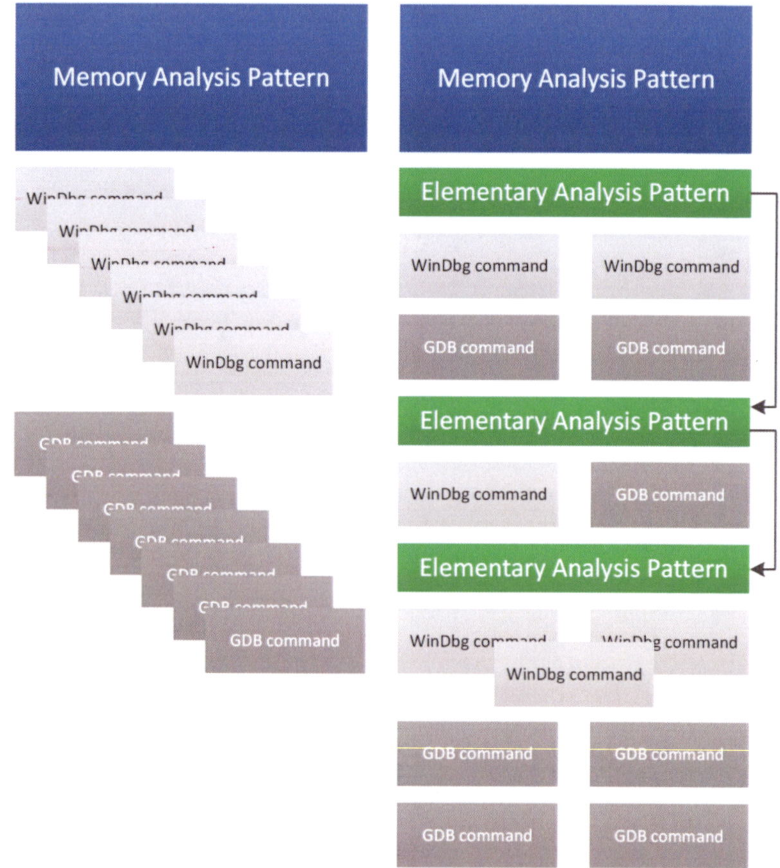

Typical candidates include the following draft elementary analysis patterns for the new analysis pattern catalog:

- Setting Symbolic Information
- Listing Processes
- Setting Processes
- Listing Threads
- Setting Threads
- Listing Modules
- Listing Memory Regions
- Dumping Memory
- Listing Object Names
- Counting Objects
- Dumping Object State
- Checking Instrumentation
- Listing Heaps
- Listing Heap Entries
- Listing Stack Traces
- Listing CPUs
- Dumping Thread State
- Searching Memory
- ...

Some Elementary Analysis Patterns may correspond to a single WinDbg command, and some may group several debugger commands. The exact names are incrementally added and incrementally refined over the course of the catalog building process.

Some Elementary Analysis Patterns may be reused across different analysis pattern catalogs, for example, **Setting Symbolic Information** is also applicable to trace and log analysis, for example, Windows ETW traces (see **No Trace Metafile** analysis pattern[342]), and **Fiber Bundle**[343] analysis pattern where symbols are needed for associated stack traces, or **Adjoint Space**[344] where symbols are needed for associated memory snapshots.

Such analysis patterns are different from *Elementary Software Diagnostics Patterns* (page 170) since the latter are about observed behavioral signs, but the former is about the analysis process.

Let's look at one example. We observe increasing memory **Counter Values**[345] for one Windows server process and look at its memory snapshots. The process does not use .NET, so we use the process heap **Memory Leak** analysis pattern[346], which can be split into the following sequentially applied **Elementary Analysis Patterns** that group appropriate WinDbg commands:

1. Setting Symbols (**.symfix**, **.sympath+**)
2. Checking Instrumentation (**!gflag**)
3. Listing Heaps (**!heap -s**)
4. Listing Heap Entries (**!heap -k -h**)

In the case of missing user mode stack trace database or before asking for it, we can also use the following Elementary Analysis Patterns for symbolic hints such as **Module Hint** analysis pattern[347], ASCII, and UNICODE data:

5. Dumping Memory (**dc**, **dps**, **dpS**, **dpa**, **dpu**) for heap entries
6. Searching Memory (**s-sa**, **s-su**) for heap entries

All these provide a better description of analysis patterns. The same approach can be applied to trace and log analysis, including network trace analysis, memory forensics, reversing and malware analysis.

Categorical Foundations of Software Diagnostics

Since extracting information about behavior from states is a coalgebra[348] (in our case, we have a behavior functor from software execution artifacts such as memory snapshots and logs to diagnostic indicators that form concrete problem patterns, page 216), we decided to recast pattern-oriented software diagnostics in category theory[349] language terms.

We introduce the following categories:

- ***Concrete Execution Artefacts***: Category **CArtefacts**

Example: 3 memory dumps of a Windows process with monotonically increasing size. Three objects from **CArtefacts** category.

- ***Concrete Problem Patterns***: Category **CProblemPatterns**

Example: 3 instances of monotonically increased Windows process heap allocations from specific modules.

- ***Concrete Analysis Pattern***: Functor **FAnalysisPattern**

Example: Memory Leak (Process Heap)[350] specifies the analysis process.

- ***Concrete Analysis Patterns***: Category **CAnalysisPatterns** with natural transformations between functors.

Some functors may be similar, for example, Memory Leaks from different platforms. There exists a natural transformation between them. Such natural transformations are called ***General Analysis Patterns***. They form a 2-category[351].

Some objects from **CProblemPatterns** may be similar. There exist "generalizing" arrows between them. The collection of such arrows forms a 2-category of ***General Problem Patterns***.

This is a bottom-up approach. A top-down approach is possible when we start with general categories and select concrete subcategories inside. However, we think in the bottom-up approach, general categories arise naturally and correspond to principles of pattern-based part[352] of pattern-oriented diagnostics.

The following diagram illustrated concrete software diagnostics categories:

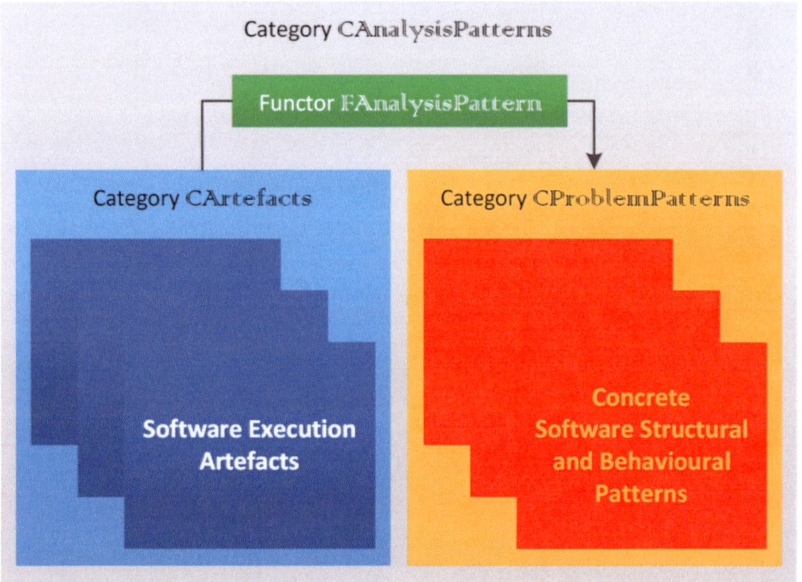

Existential Prognostics: Periodic Table of Diagnostic Patterns

One of the features of the Periodic Table of Elements[353] was the prediction of missing elements. In November 2010, we announced the discovery of the Periodic Table of Software Defects as *"rules that make it possible to devise a memory dump and software trace analysis equivalent of the Periodic Table of Elements in Chemistry. It allows prediction of abnormal software behavior and structural defects and what patterns to look for after deploying software and collecting its artifacts"* (page 138).

The publication of the second edition of Encyclopedia of Crash Dump Analysis Patterns[354] makes it possible to see what patterns are expected in our favorite operating system and software product even if they have not been observed or cataloged yet (see its Table of Contents[355]). This is why we call this type of prognostics *existential* as affirming or implying the existence of a diagnostic pattern, whether it is a problem pattern or problem analysis pattern (page 216).

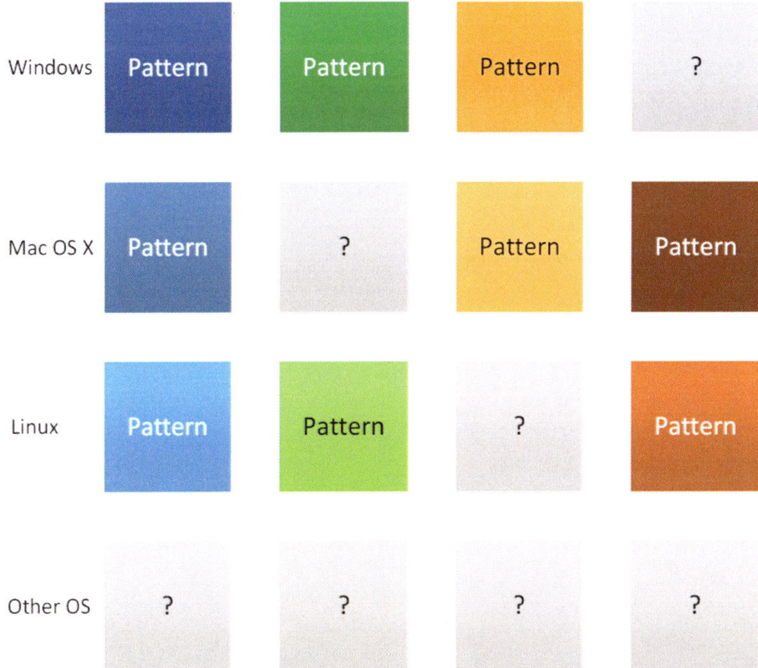

As an example, we can tell the story of pattern prediction and discovery. An engineer expressed the doubt about the existence of **Lateral Damage**[356] crash dump analysis pattern for Linux systems since he had never observed it during his diagnostic practice. Years passed, and it was recently observed and cataloged when analyzing Linux process core dumps[357].

Software Codiagnostics

Software diagnostics is rarely a straightforward process of extracting the list of diagnostic indicators from software execution artifacts. Usually, it involves artifact transformation through trace and log analysis patterns[358].

Consider a very large software log. Simple inspection if its trace messages may point to some problem patterns:

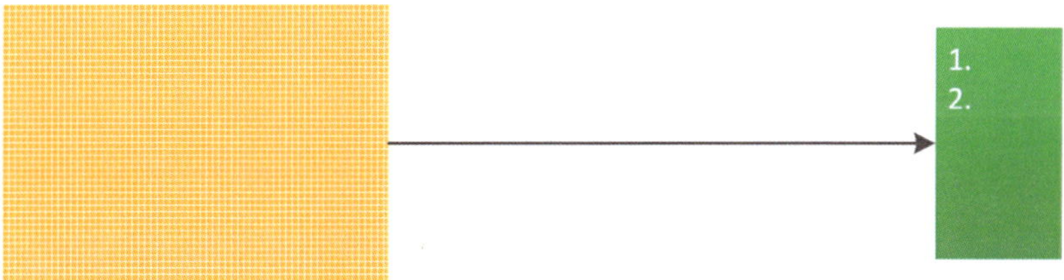

However, different log transformations via trace analysis patterns may reveal additional problem patterns:

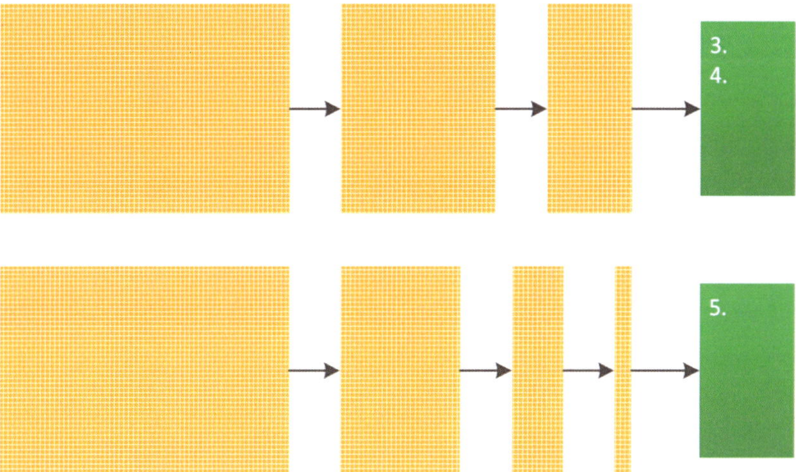

We call such transformations **Software Codiagnostics** or **Data Codiagnostics** in general for pattern-oriented data analysis (page 265). The prefix **co-** signifies cooperative processes and also the fact that such transformations are dual (by analogy with dual categories [359] in mathematics) to diagnostic processes (page 271), especially when such transformations are reversible (or partially reversible):

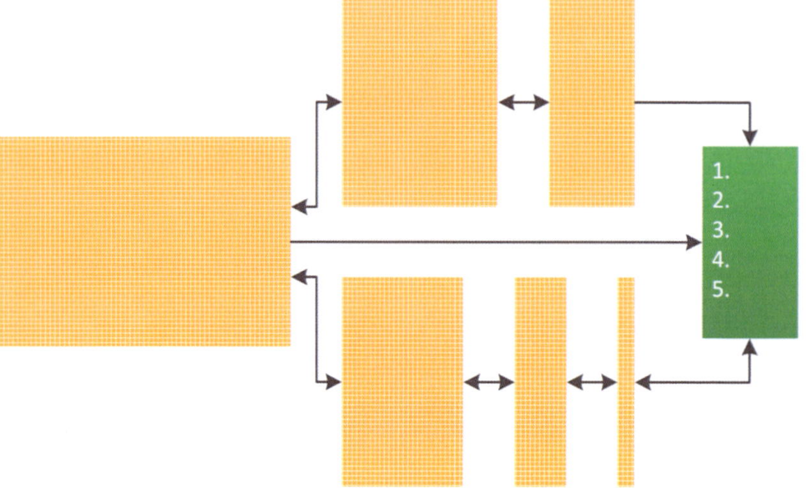

Volume 11

The Most Important Skill in Software Diagnostics

Browsing through the pile of the "old" unread Communications of the ACM magazines, we found an article *"A Closer Look at Attention to Detail"* about "another non-technical skill fundamental to success in IT beyond communications, interpersonal, and leadership skills."[360]

The reason why it caught our attention was that we already thought about it in the context of software diagnostics (page 173), initially as various common mistakes[361], anti-patterns[362], and style[363]. Some of these can be considered as attention to detail patterns (ATDP), and we are working on attention to the detail pattern catalog.

Although according to the article, some view this skill as a personal quality and some as a skill that can be improved, we view it as a general skill everyone has but with varying domain-dependent levels. It can be taught if its level is very low and improved if already present. Individuals have degrees of this skill depending on a domain of activity: for example, a person may be good at business or people management attention to detail but somewhat lack that skill when it comes to technical matters and vice versa. So domain-specific facets of that skill may be improved over time through training and self-education and reinforced via auditing feedback. This is especially true in software support environments that require a different skill set than software engineering.

Analysis pattern orientation facilitates this attention to detail through various pattern catalogs and checklists (page 239) from software execution artifact collection to writing diagnostic analysis reports (page 235), including analysis audits.

The ACM article also lists various definitions and views of attention to detail from quality, accuracy, correctness, "not overlooking anything," and conscientiousness to "a firm grasp of what's going on." Here, for the latter, pattern orientation applied to software internals (page 231) may help too.

Regarding the importance of attention to detail (ATD), we would like to quote the referenced ACM article: “ATD is most important in the analyst role where ‘the details’ are analyzed and evaluated. The challenge is frequently putting details in context and knowing what needs to be analyzed and when enough analysis has been completed”.

We also think that organizations that don’t emphasize this skill are not good at attention to detail.

Diagnostic Operads

When introducing software data codiagnostics (page 275), we mentioned artifact transformations through data analysis patterns. Such analysis patterns were devised for human-assisted data diagnostics (for example, software log analysis[364]) and maybe too coarse and high-level for formalization and software implementation. Some of them may be split into more elementary transformations, which are composable in an associative way. Some may have multiple artifact inputs and additional parameters. All these suggested a name for such transformations based on the analogy with operads in mathematics[365]: a diagnostic operad. However, this name is a different portmanteau of "**opera**tions" and "**d**iagnostics". "Historically, the theoretical study of compositions of operations appeared in the 1950s in the work of Michel Lazard as *analyseurs*"[366].

The preliminary definition for our purposes is:

A diagnostic operad is a sequence of diagnostic operations required to extract diagnostic indicators in a diagnostic process described by diagnostic analysis patterns.

Such a sequence may involve operations from different analysis patterns. This is illustrated in the following diagram:

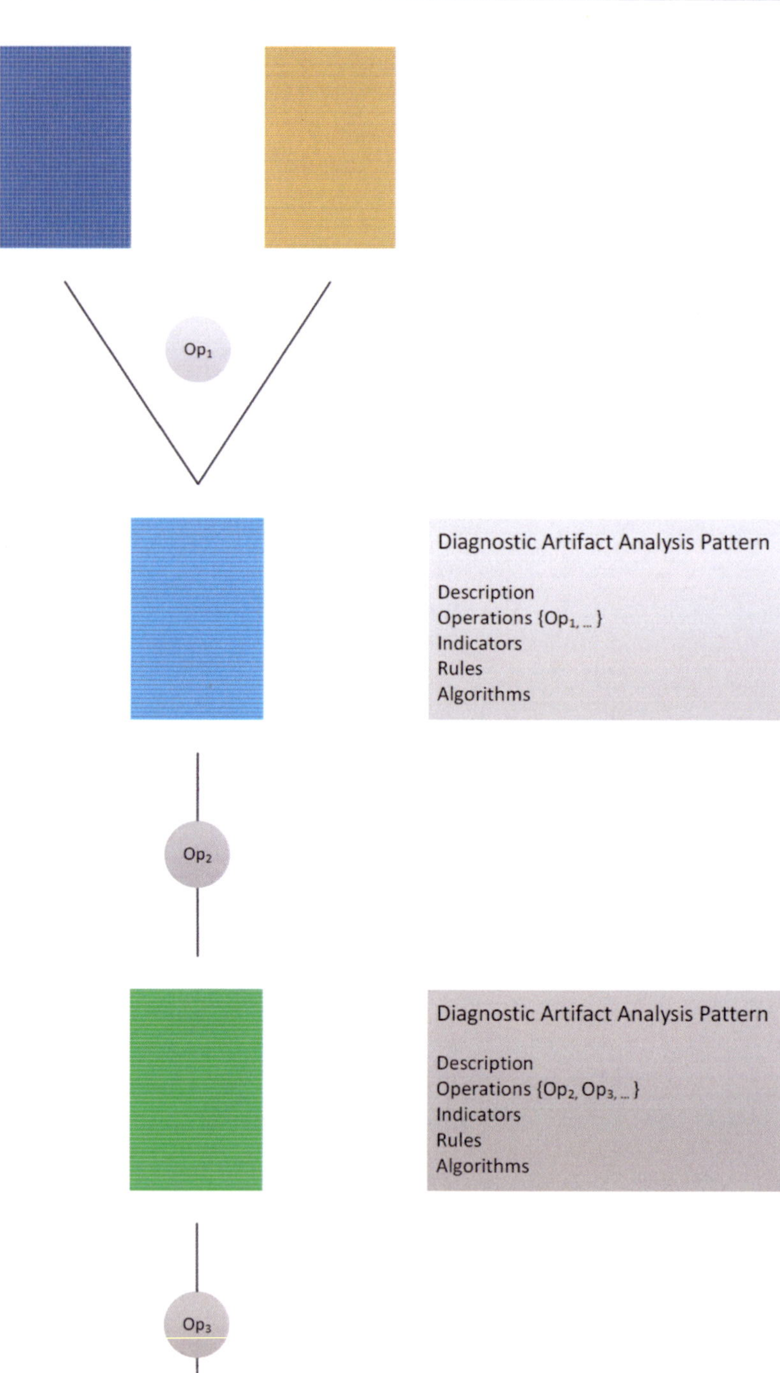

Op1
Diagnostic Artifact Analysis Pattern
Description
Operations {Op1, … }
Indicators
Rules
Algorithms
Op2
Diagnostic Artifact Analysis Pattern
Description
Operations {Op2, Op3, … }
Indicators
Rules
Algorithms
Op3

The operadic approach resembles Elementary Analysis Patterns (page 268) introduced earlier for memory artifact analysis, but the latter include operations that do not transform or query artifacts. Perhaps diagnostic operads should include some of such operations formalized in a way to make them applicable to other types of artifacts such as logs.

Mathematical Concepts in Software Diagnostics and Software Data Analysis

Various mathematical analogies and metaphors inspired memory and log analysis patterns and some concepts of software diagnostics and software data analysis. We list them in alphabetical order:

- 2-categories (page 361)
- Adjoints[367] (see also page 98)
- Braid groups[368]
- Braids[369] (see also page 41)
- Cartesian Product[370]
- Categories (page 88)
- Causal sets[371, 372, 373]
- Coalgebras, functors, 2-categories (page 271)
- Cones[374]
- Continuous and discontinuous functions[375]
- Cover[376]
- Critical points, Morse theory[377]
- Curves[378]
- Defect group of a block[379]
- Derivatives, partial derivatives[380, 381]
- Dessin d'enfant[382]
- Direct sums and products of sets (pages 39, 188)
- Divergence[383]
- Dual categories (page 275)
- Duality[384]
- Dynamical systems (page 37)
- Edge contraction[385]
- Equivalence relation[386]
- Fiber bundles[387] (see also page 93)
- Fibrations[388]
- Fixed points[389]
- Flag, filtration[390]
- Foliation[391]
- Fourier series[392]

- Functor[393]
- Fuzzy sets[394]
- Galois connections[395]
- Graphs (page 258)
- Hasse diagrams[396]
- Homotopy[397, 398]
- Injections, surjections, bijections (page 83)
- Intervals[399]
- Jaccard index[400]
- Lattices (page 94)
- Manifolds (page 96), gluing[401]
- Maps (pages 60, 149)
- Minimal surface[402]
- Moduli space[403]
- Monoids (page 361)
- Motives[404, 405]
- Motivic integration[406]
- Nerve complex[407]
- Open and closed sets[408]
- Operads (page 279)
- Orbifolds (page 132)
- Order duality (page 313)
- Ordinals[409]
- Phase[410]
- Piecewise linear functions[411]
- Poincaré map, Poincaré section[412]
- Posets[413]
- Powerset[414]
- Presheaves[415]
- Projective spaces[416]
- Quotient groups[417]
- Quotient space[418]
- Retraction[419]
- Riemann surfaces, multivalued functions (page 62)
- Rough sets[420]
- Scalar field[421]

- Semigroups (page 361)
- Sheaves[422]
- Significant digits[423]
- Simplicial complex[424]
- Step functions[425]
- Structure Sheaf[426]
- Surfaces[427]
- Tensors[428]
- Topology (page 257)
- Ultrametric spaces, p-adic numbers[429]
- Variadic functions[430]
- Whiskering[431] (page 361)

The links to their definitions and examples can be found in the corresponding references. We give the original references to Memory Dump Analysis Anthology[432] where possible, but most of them can also be found in Pattern-Oriented Software Diagnostics Reference books[433].

Software Diagnostics Engineering

When analyzing best practices for cloud architectures and corresponding software design and implementation, we realized that telemetry and logging patterns were completely detached from their analysis activities, which were not even mentioned when expected. Some unification is needed there for software construction and software post-construction phases related to software diagnostics solutions. We propose to name the unified discipline **Software Diagnostics Engineering** which has a solid foundation in Theoretical Software Diagnostics we introduced earlier (page 255). This discipline is not limited to the cloud and site engineering but encompasses software technologies vertically (the full-stack software diagnostics) as well as horizontally (IoT devices[434], mobile[435] and desktop applications, individual servers, clusters, clouds[436], and fogs). The difference between other diagnostic engineering disciplines is that in software diagnostics we know software internals (page 231) and can perform operations not possible in technical and medical diagnostics (page 244). We use the definition of software diagnostics introduced in the latest seminar[437] as *a discipline studying signs of software structure and behavior in software execution artifacts (such as memory dumps, software and network traces and logs) using systemic*[438] *and pattern-oriented analysis methodologies*.

Software diagnostics engineering includes specialized patterns for software diagnostics architecture (page 178) in addition to software engineering best practices and patterns used to construct software diagnostics components and systems. However, it also includes software post-construction best practices and patterns[439], for example, software data analysis patterns (page 265) for software execution artifacts such as memory dumps and machine-generated logs[440], as well as security-related analysis of network traces[441], logs[442] and memory[443]. We depict software diagnostics engineering and its theoretical and engineering foundations in the following diagram:

Theoretical Software Diagnostics

Mathematical, Computer Science, and Humanities Foundations

Software Diagnostics Engineering

Software
Construction

Architecture, Design,
Implementation

Best Practices and Patterns

Software
Post-Construction

Software
Data Analysis

Best Practices and Patterns

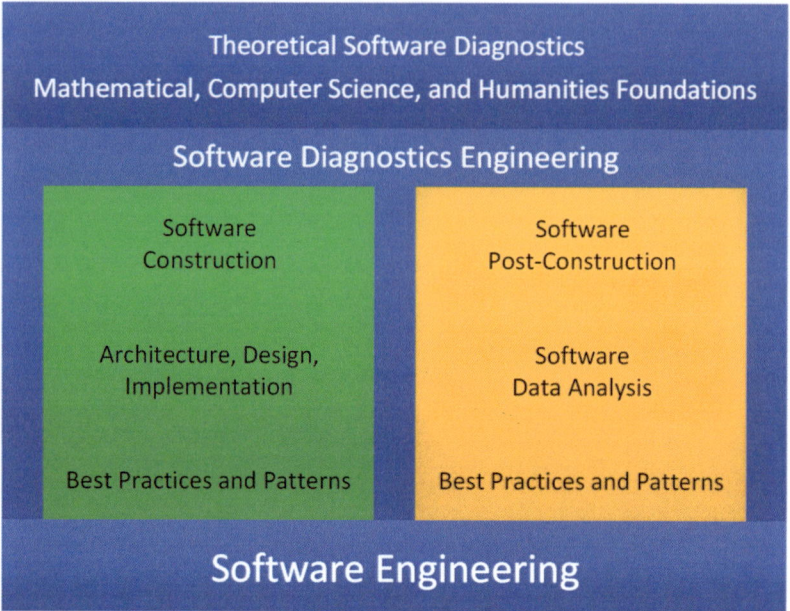

Software Engineering

Narrachain

Narrachain is an application of blockchain technology[444] to software narratives[445], stories of computation, such as traces and logs, including generalized traces (page 149) such as memory dumps. Based on Software Narratology Square (page 147), it also covers software construction narratives and, more generally, graphs (trees) of software narratives (page 258).

In the case of software traces and logs, a blockchain-based software narrative may be implemented by adding a distributed trace that records the hash of a message block together with the hash of a previous block (a hash chain[446]). This is depicted in the following diagram where **Palimpsest Message**[447] appeared after the software narrative was growing for some time:

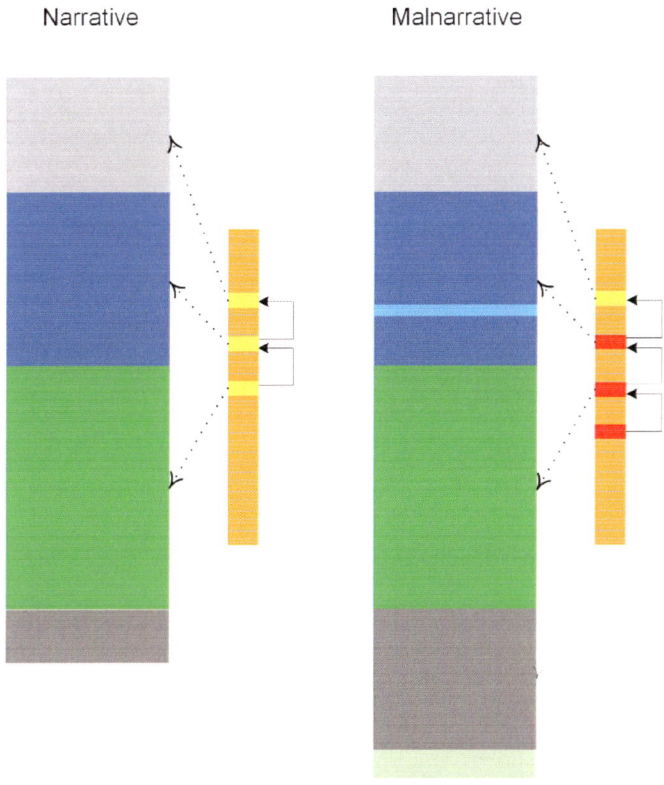

Performance considerations may affect the size of message blocks.

Narrachains can be used to prevent malnarratives (page 200) and prove the integrity of software execution artifacts. The novel approach here is an integration of such technology into a system of diagnostic analysis patterns (for example, problem description analysis patterns, trace and log analysis patterns, memory analysis patterns, unified debugging patterns). Narrascope, a narrative debugger, developed by Software Diagnostics Services[448], includes the support for NarraChain trace and log analysis pattern as well.

Narrachains can also be used for maintaining the integrity of software support workflows by tracking problem information and its changes. For example, changes in problem description or newly found diagnostic indicators trigger invalidation of diagnostic analysis reports and re-evaluation of troubleshooting suggestions.

Diagnostics-Driven Development

Bugs are inevitable in software during its construction. Even if good coding practices such as test-driven development, checklists for writing effective code, and using well-tested standards-based libraries instead of crafting our own, eliminate non-functional defects such as resource leaks and crashes, functional defects are there to stay. On the other hand, if test cases show that functional requirements are met, some non-functional defects such as leaks may evade detection and manifest themselves during later phases of development. Therefore, it is vital to start diagnosing all kinds of software defects as earlier as possible. Here, pattern-oriented software diagnostics may help by providing problem patterns (what to look for), and analysis patterns (how to look for) for different types of software execution artifacts such as memory dumps and software logs. The following two best practices we found useful during the development of various software over the last 15 years:

- ✓ Periodic memory dump analysis of processes. Such analysis can be done offline after a process finished its execution or just-in-time by attaching a debugger to it.
- ✓ Adding trace statements as earlier as possible for checking various conditions, the correct order of execution, and the state. Such **Declarative Trace**[449] allows the earlier application of pattern-oriented trace and log analysis. Typical analysis patterns at this stage of software construction include **Significant Events**[450], **Event Sequence Order**[451], **Data Flow**[452], **State Dump**[453], and **Counter Value**[454].

We plan to explain this proposed software development process further and provide practical examples (with source code).

Integral Diamathics – Tracing the Road to Root Cause

Recently we noticed a published book about biology and mathematics (with some emphasis on category theory[455]) called "Integral Biomathics: Tracing the Road to Reality" (ISBN: 978-3642429606). We liked that naming idea because we are interested in applying category theory to software diagnostics (and diagnostics in general). Our road started more than a decade ago after reading "Life Itself: A Comprehensive Inquiry Into the Nature, Origin, and Fabrication of Life" by Robert Rosen (ISBN: 978-0231075657) recommended in "Categories for Software Engineering" by Jose Luiz Fiadeiro (ISBN: 978-3540373469). We also read "Memory Evolutive Systems: Hierarchy, Emergence, Cognition" book (ISBN: 978-0444522443) written by one of the editors and contributors to "Integral Biomathics" (Andrée C. Ehresmann) and the semi-popular overview of contemporary physics "The Road to Reality" (ISBN: 978-0679454434) by Roger Penrose. Certainly, the editors of "Integral Biomathics" wanted to combine biology, mathematics, and physics into one integral whole. Something we also wanted to do for memory analysis and forensics intelligence (unpublished "Memory Analysis Forensics and Intelligence: An Integral Approach" ISBN: 978-1906717056) planned before we started our work on software trace analysis patterns[456] and software narratology[457]. Our subsequent research borrowed a lot of terminology and concepts from contemporary mathematics (page 282).

As a result, we recognized the need to name diagnostic mathematics as **Diamathics**, and its **Integral Diamathics** version subtitled as "The Road to Root Cause" since we believe that diagnostics is an integral part of root cause analysis (page 239) as analysis of analysis (page 253). To mark the birth of **Diamathics,** we created a logo for it:

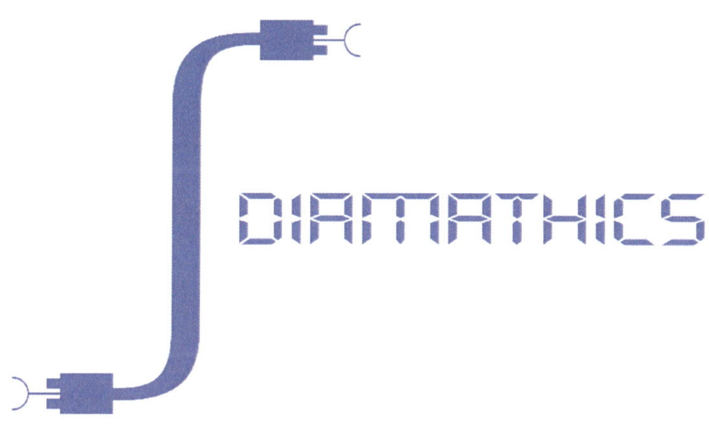

In its design, we used the sign of an indefinite integral and diagnostic components from Software Diagnostics Institute logo[458] (also featured on this book front cover). The orientation of UML components points to past (forensics) and future (prognostics) and reflects our motto: Pattern-Oriented Software Diagnostics, Forensics, Prognostics[459] (with subsequent Root Cause Analysis and Debugging).

Meso-problem Solving using Meso-patterns

Meso-problems are software design and development problems that require short hard-limited time to solve satisfactorily with good quality. The time limit is usually not more than an hour. The prefix **meso-** means *intermediate*. These meso-problems are distinct from normal software design problems (macro-problems), which require much more time to solve, and implementation idioms (micro-problems) that are usually implementation language-specific. In contrast to macro-problems, where final solutions are accompanied by software documentation and micro-problems solved without any documentation except brief source code comments, meso-problem solutions include a specific narrative outlining the solution process with elements of theatrical performance. In a satisfactory meso-problem solution, such a narrative dominates an actual technical solution, for example, code.

Meso-problems are solved with the help of **Meso-patterns**: general solutions with accompanying narrative applied in specific contexts to common recurrent meso-problems. Since problem-solving time is limited, the solutions may not be optimal, extendable, and maintainable as real-world solutions for similar (macro-)problems. The accompanying narrative should mention such differences.

We should not confuse meso-patterns with elemental design patterns[460], elementary building blocks of conventional design patterns. Such patterns and their building blocks can be a part of meso-patterns' solutions and narratives.

Typically, meso-problem solving occurs during technical interviews. However, it can also be a part of code and design reviews, mentoring, and coaching.

Whereas general patterns and specific idioms address the questions of *What* and *How,* meso-patterns also address the *Why* question.

Because the *Why* narrative is an integral part of Meso-patterns, they can be applied to homework interview programming problems as well (even when they are not Meso-problems). In such a case, it is recommended to embed *Why* narratives in source code comments. Such narratives are not necessary for programming contests and online coding sessions when solutions are checked automatically. However, it is advised to duplicate essential narrative parts in code comments in case the code is forwarded to other team members for their assessment, even if an interviewer is present during the online coding session.

The first general Meso-pattern we propose is called **Dilemma**[461]. Dilemma problems arise at almost every point of a technical interview and need to be solved. They also happen in software design and development, but their solutions are not usually accompanied by explicitly articulated narratives outlining various alternatives and their pro and contra arguments (except in good books teaching computer science and software engineering problem solving). Time constraints are not overly fixed and can be adjusted if necessary. The documentation contains only final decisions. In contrast, during technical interviews, when we have dilemmas, we need to articulate them aloud, outline alternative solutions considering various hints from interviewers while asking questions during the problem-solving process. The dilemma problem-solving narrative is as much important as the written diagram, code, or pseudo-code, and can compensate for the incomplete solution code if it is obvious from the narrative that an interviewee would have finished writing solution code if given more time.

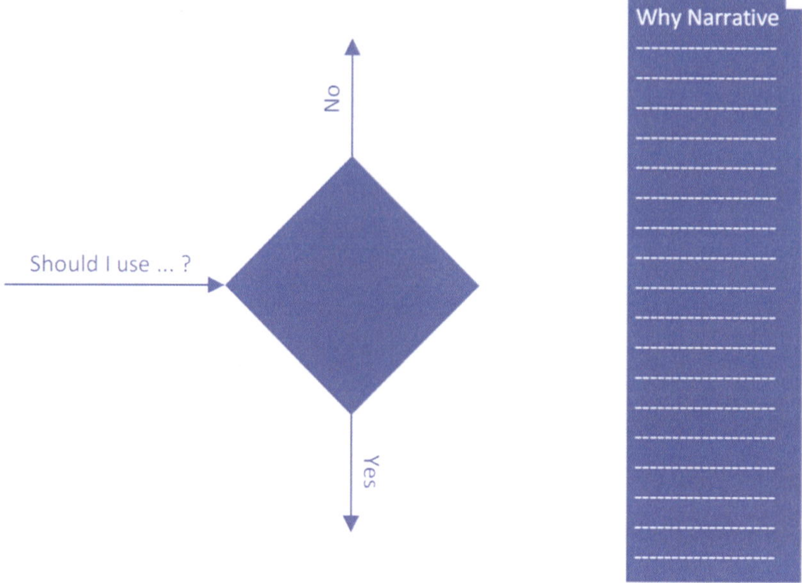

Dilemma meso-problems also happen during design and code review discussions as stakeholders must defend their decisions.

It is important to narrate every Dilemma as the failure to do so may result in a wrong perception, downgraded, and even rejected solution. For example, even the simple act of choosing a particular naming convention needs to be articulated, making an interviewer aware of an interviewee's knowledge of coding standards and experience with programming styles dominant on various platforms.

Lego Log Analysis

In addition to **Dia|gram** graphical diagnostic analysis language (page 251) that we use to illustrate trace and log analysis patterns, we introduce a Lego-block approach. A typical software log is illustrated in this picture with Lego blocks of different colors corresponding to different trace message types, **Motifs**[462], activities, components, processes, or threads depending on an analysis pattern:

For a starter, we illustrate 3 very common error message patterns (red blocks). The illustration of **Error Message**[463] shows different types of error data visualizations:

The two illustrations of **Periodic Error**[464] pattern show typical **Error Distribution**[465] patterns:

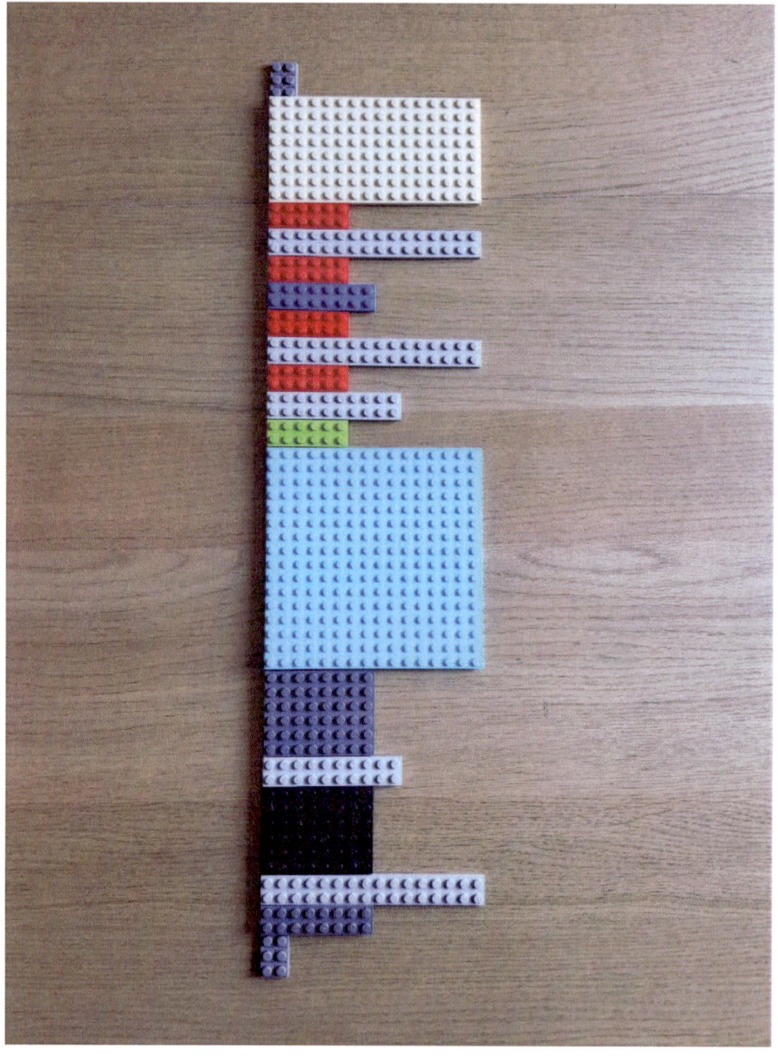

Artificial Chemistry Approach to Software Trace and Log Analysis

In the past, we proposed two metaphors (page 237) regarding software trace and log analysis patterns[466] (we abbreviate them as TAP):

- TAP as the "genes" of software structure and behavior.
- Logs as "proteins" generated by code with TAP as patterns of "protein" structure.

We now introduce a third metaphor with strong modeling and implementation potential we are currently working on: **Artificial Chemistry**[467] (AC) approach where logs are "DNA" and log analysis is a set of reactions between logs and TAP, which are individual "molecules."

In addition to trace and logs as "macro-molecules", we also have different molecule families of general patterns (P) and concrete patterns (C). General patterns, general analysis (L), and concrete analysis (A) patterns are also molecules (that may also be composed of patterns and analysis patterns) that may serve the role of enzymes[468]. Here we follow the division of patterns into four types (page 216). During the reaction, a trace T is usually transformed into T' (having a different "energy") molecule (with a marked site to necessitate further elastic collisions to avoid duplicate analysis).

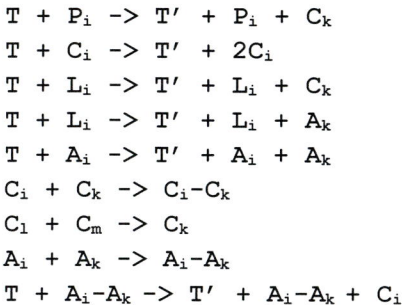

$$T + P_i \rightarrow T' + P_i + C_k$$
$$T + C_i \rightarrow T' + 2C_i$$
$$T + L_i \rightarrow T' + L_i + C_k$$
$$T + L_i \rightarrow T' + L_i + A_k$$
$$T + A_i \rightarrow T' + A_i + A_k$$
$$C_i + C_k \rightarrow C_i\text{-}C_k$$
$$C_l + C_m \rightarrow C_k$$
$$A_i + A_k \rightarrow A_i\text{-}A_k$$
$$T + A_i\text{-}A_k \rightarrow T' + A_i\text{-}A_k + C_i$$

...

Different reactions can be dynamically specified according to a reactor algorithm. The following diagram shows a few elementary reactions:

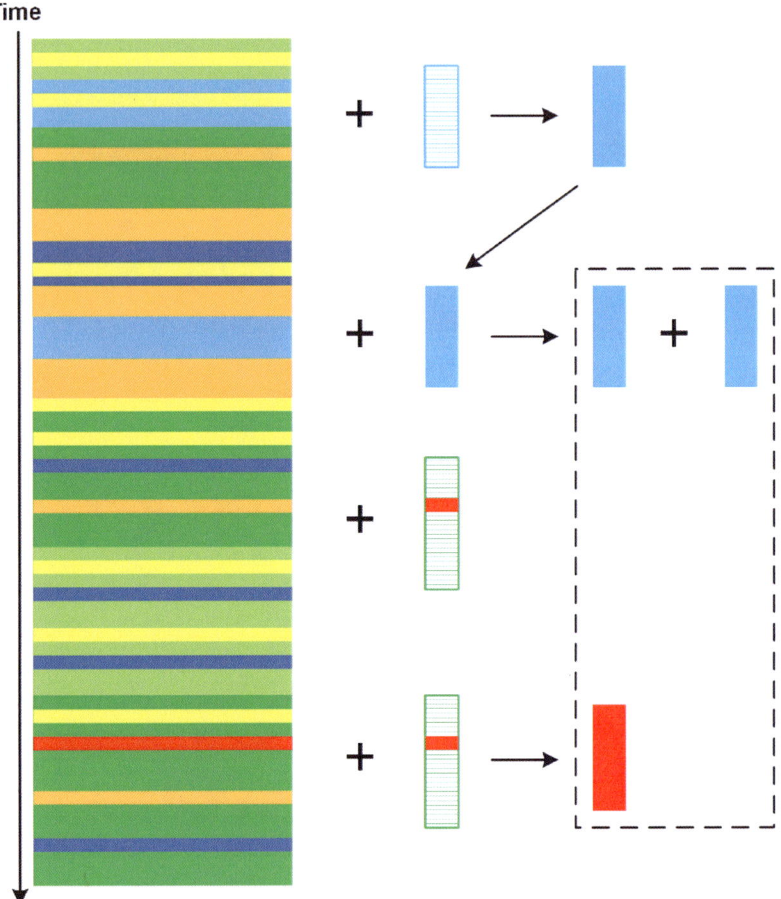

The concentration of patterns (reaction educts) increases the chances of producing reaction products according to the corresponding reaction "mass action."[469] We can also introduce pattern consuming reactions such as $T + L_i \rightarrow T' + C_k$, but this requires the constant supply of analysis pattern molecules. Intermediate molecules may react with a log as well, and be a part of analysis construction (second-order trace and log, page 202).

Since traces and logs can be enormous, such reactions can occur randomly according to the Brownian motion of molecules. The reactor algorithm can also use **Trace Sharding**[470].

Some reactions may catalyze log transformation into a secondary structure with certain TAP molecules now binding to log sites. Alternatively, we can use different types of reactors, for example, well stirred or topologically arranged. We visualize a reactor for the reactions shown in the diagram above:

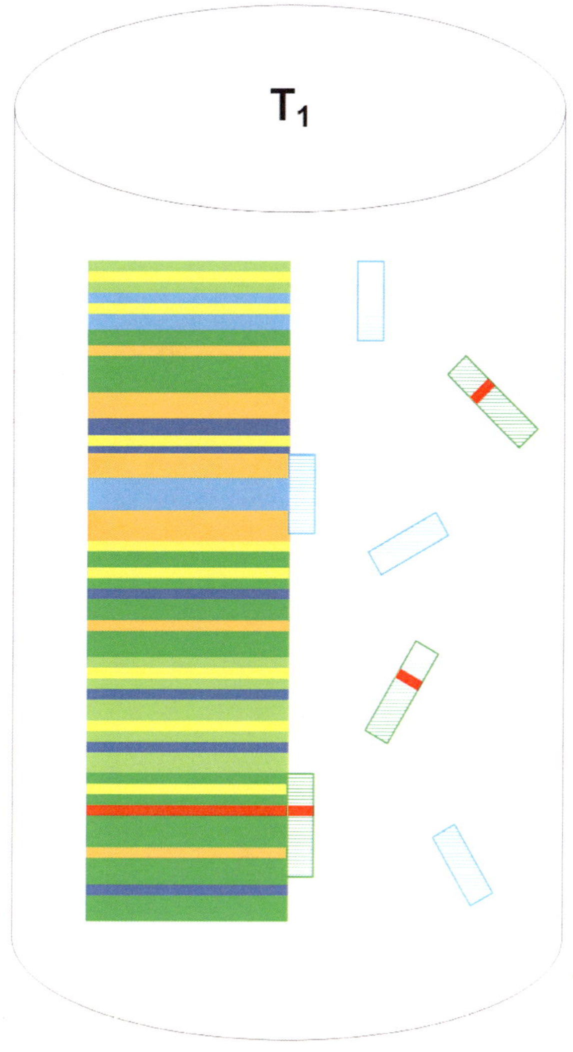

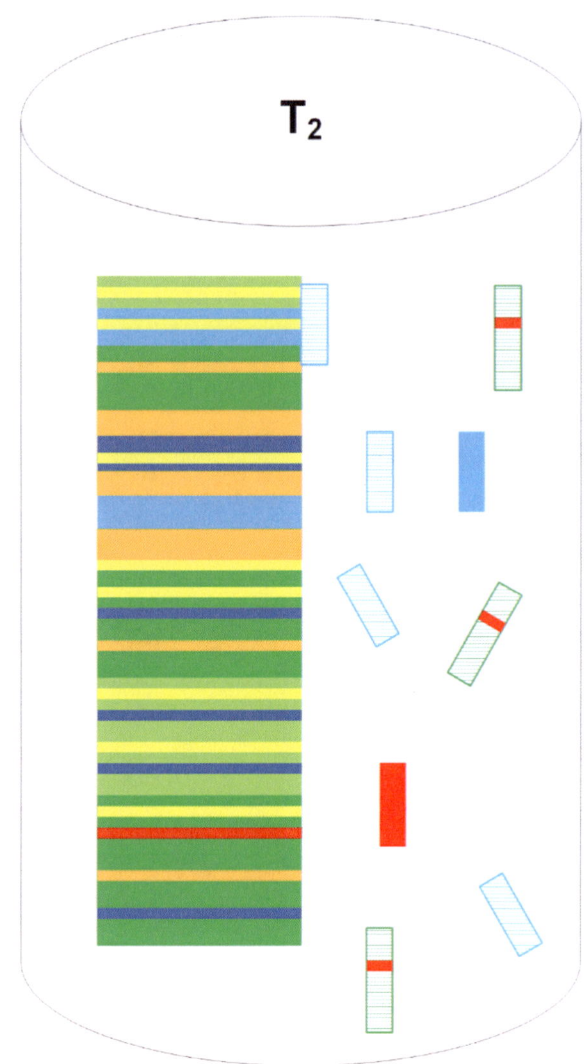

We can also add reactions that split and concatenate traces based on collision with certain patterns and reactions between different logs.

Many AC reactions are unpredictable and may uncover emergent novelty that can be missed during the traditional pattern matching and rule-based techniques.

The AC approach also allows simulations of various pattern and reaction sets independently of concrete traces and logs to find the best analysis approaches.

In addition to software trace and log analysis of traditional software execution artifacts, the same AC approach can be applied to malware analysis[471], network trace analysis[472], and pattern-oriented software data analysis in general (page 265).

[This page is intentionally left blank]

Volume 12

Introducing Software Pathology

Some time ago, we introduced Iterative Pattern-Oriented Root Cause Analysis (page 239), where we added mechanisms in addition to diagnostic checklists. Such mechanisms became the additional feature of Pattern-Oriented Software Data Analysis principles (page 265). Since medical diagnostics influenced some features of pattern-oriented software diagnostics, we found further extending medical metaphors useful. Since Pathology is the study of causes and effects,[473] we introduce its systemic software correspondence[474] as **Software Pathology**. The parts of the name "**path**-o-**log**-y" incorporate logs as artifacts and paths as certain trace and log analysis patterns such as **Back Trace**[475]. We depict this relationship in the following logo:

Please also note a possible alternative category theory [476] interpretation of "**path**-**olog**-y" using an **olog** approach[477] to paths.

We, therefore, are happy to add Software Pathology as a discipline that studies mechanisms of abnormal software structure and behavior. It uses software traces and logs (and other types of software narratives[478]) and memory snapshots (as a generalized software narrative, page 149) as investigation media. Regarding the traditional computer graphics and visualization part of medical pathology, there is certain correspondence with software pathology as we demonstrated earlier that certain software defects could be visualized using native computer memory visualization techniques[479] (the details can be found in several Memory Dump Analysis Anthology volumes).

The software pathology logo also prompted us to introduce a similar logo for Software Narratology as a “**narra**tion **to log**” metaphor:

SOFTWARE NARRATLOG✓

Moving “y” from “Narratolog**y**” results in a true interpretation of software tracing: N-arra**y**-to-log (page 59).

Please note that the log icon in the “narratology” logo part does not have any abnormality indicator because a software log can be perfectly normal.

The last note to mention is that Software Pathology is different from pathology software; the same distinction applies to Software Narratology vs. narratology software, Software Diagnostics vs. diagnostics software, Software Forensics vs. forensics software, and Software Prognostics vs. prognostics software.

Log's Loxels and Trace Message's Mexels Graphical Representation of Software Traces and Logs

Our system and method stem from *texels*[480], *voxels*[481], and *pixels*[482] as elements of textures, 3D and 2D picture representation grids, and the way we depict traces and logs in **Dia|gram** graphical diagnostic analysis language (page 251):

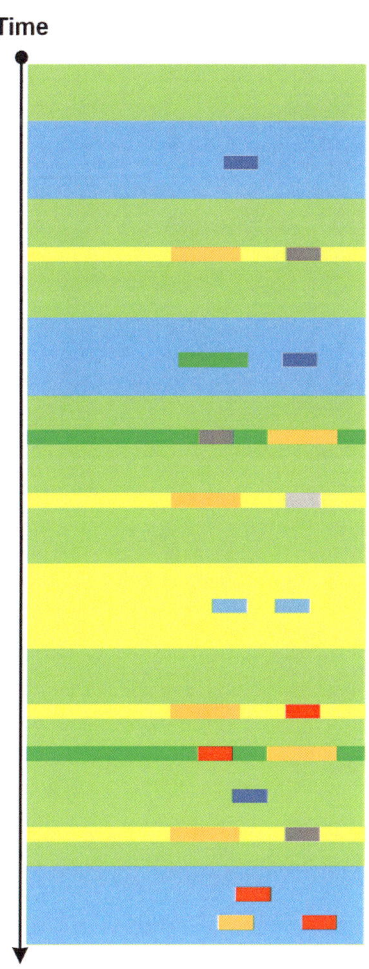

Loxel is an element of a log or software trace. It is usually a log or trace message. Usually, such messages are generated from specific code points, and, therefore, may have unique identifiers. Such UIDs can be mapped to specific colors:

For visualization purposes and 2D processing, we can collapse 1D picture into a 2D loxel image using top-to-down and left-to-right direction:

We can also include **Silent Messages**[483] in the picture by imposing a fixed time resolution grid:

We apply the same procedure to get 1D and 2D images:

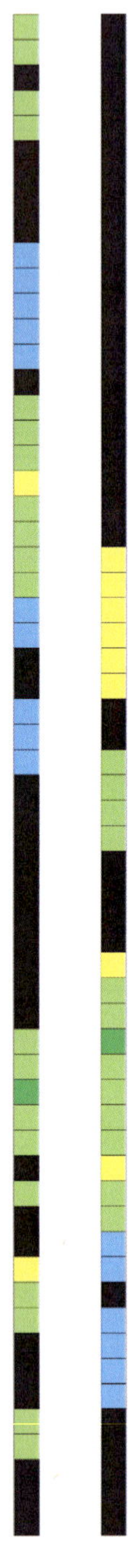

Each loxel may contain **Message Invariant**[484] and variable parts such as **Trace Constants**[485] and other data values such as handles, pointers, **Counter Values**[486], and other **Random Data**[487] in general. We call a variable parts **mexel**, and mexels form layers in order of their appearance in loxels:

Therefore, for this modeling example, after loxelation and mexelation, we got 3 layers that we can use for anomaly detection via digital image processing and machine learning:

In conclusion, we would like to note that this is an artificial representation compared with the natural representation where trace memory content is used for pixel data[488].

Analysis Pattern Duality

Some of our memory analysis patterns are parameterized by structural constraints (such as a particular type of space or dump, or a memory region) or objects (for example, synchronization). We recently worked on a few analysis patterns and discovered the type of duality between them when the parameter itself could have related problems:

ProblemPattern(*Parameter*) <-> *Parameter*Problem(**ProblemPattern**)

For example, **Insufficient Memory** (*Stack*)[489] vs. *Stack* Overflow (**Insufficient Memory**)[490]. In the first analysis pattern variant, insufficient memory may be reported because of the full stack region, and in the second analysis pattern variant, stack overflow is reported because there is not enough memory to expand the stack region.

This duality can aid in new pattern discoveries and especially in analyzing possible root causes and their causal mechanisms (software pathology) given the multiplicity of diagnostic indicators when we consider parameters as analysis patterns themselves. Let's look at another example: **Invalid Pointer** (Insufficient Memory). It is a common sequence when a memory leak fails memory allocation, and then certain pointers remain uninitialized or NULL. Consider its dual Insufficient Memory (**Invalid Pointer**) when, for example, memory is not released because some pointer becomes invalid. The latter can happen when memory is overwritten with NULL values, or access violation is handled and ignored.

The closest mathematical analogy here is order duality[491]. It is different from the duality of software artifacts (**De Broglie Trace Duality**[492]), such as logs and memory dumps, and memory space dualities (**Dual Stack Trace**[493]).

Application of Trace and Log Analysis Patterns to Image Analysis: Introducing Space-like Narratology

A while ago, we introduced special and general trace and log analysis (page 206) with the emphasis on causality. However, both types are still time-like, based on explicit or implicit time ordering. We now extend the same pattern-oriented analysis approach to image analysis where the ordering of "messages," "events," or simply some "data" is space-like, or even metric-like (with the additional direction if necessary). In the initial step, we replace *Time* coordinate with some metric based on the nature of data; for example, the case of **Periodic Error**[494] is shown in this simplified spatial picture:

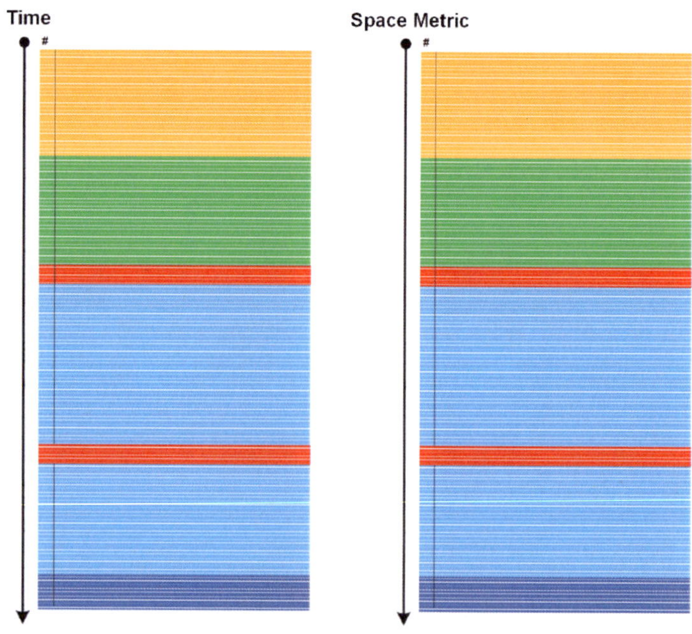

Similar replacement can be done in the case of **Time Delta**[495] -> **Space Delta** -> **Metric Delta** and **Discontinuity**[496]. We are now assessing the current 200 analysis patterns[497] (where most of them are time-like) in terms of their applicability to image analysis and submit analysis pattern extensions.

Machine Learning Square and Software Diagnostics Institute Roadmap

When researching ML from the point of view of sociology and humanities,[498] we came upon an idea of Machine Learning Machine Learning ... sequence. Then we realized that there is a distinction between Machine-Machine Learning (Machine Learning of Machine structure and behavior) and Machine-Human Learning (Machine Learning of Human state and behavior, ML approaches to medical diagnostics). This naturally extends to a learning square where we add Human-Machine Learning (Human Learning of machine diagnostics) and Human-Human learning (Human Learning of Human state and behavior, medicine, humanities, and sociology):

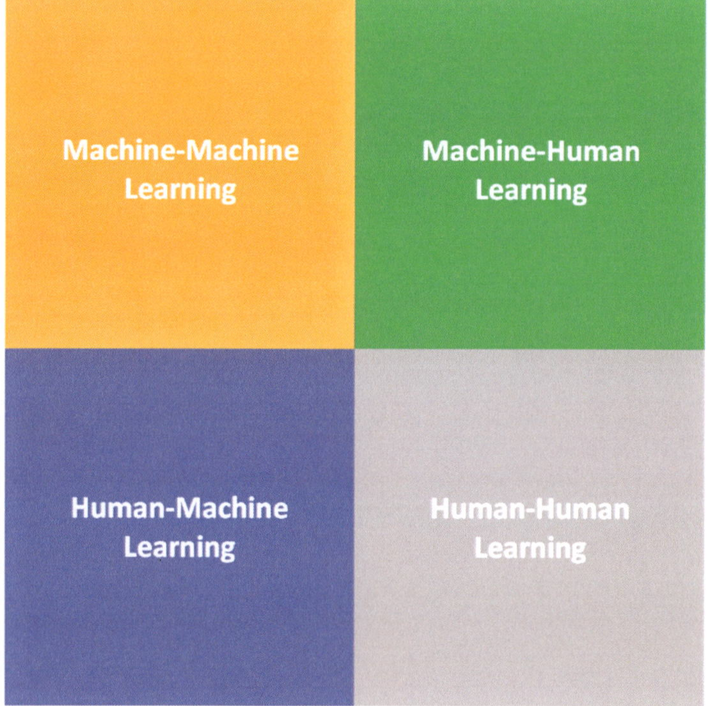

We did not find whether this was explicitly proposed before. In any case, we would like to elaborate on the applicability of this diagram to past, current, and future Software Diagnostics Institute activities.

What we were mainly doing before 2018 is devising a set of Human-Machine Learning pattern languages. Recently we moved towards ML approaches, and this activity occupies the Machine-Machine Learning quadrant. Since analysis patterns developed for Human-Machine Learning are sufficiently rich to be used in other domains than software, results can be applied to Human-Human Learning (for example, narratology), and together with additional results from Machine-Machine Learning can be applied to Machine-Human Learning (for example, space-like narratology for image analysis, page 314):

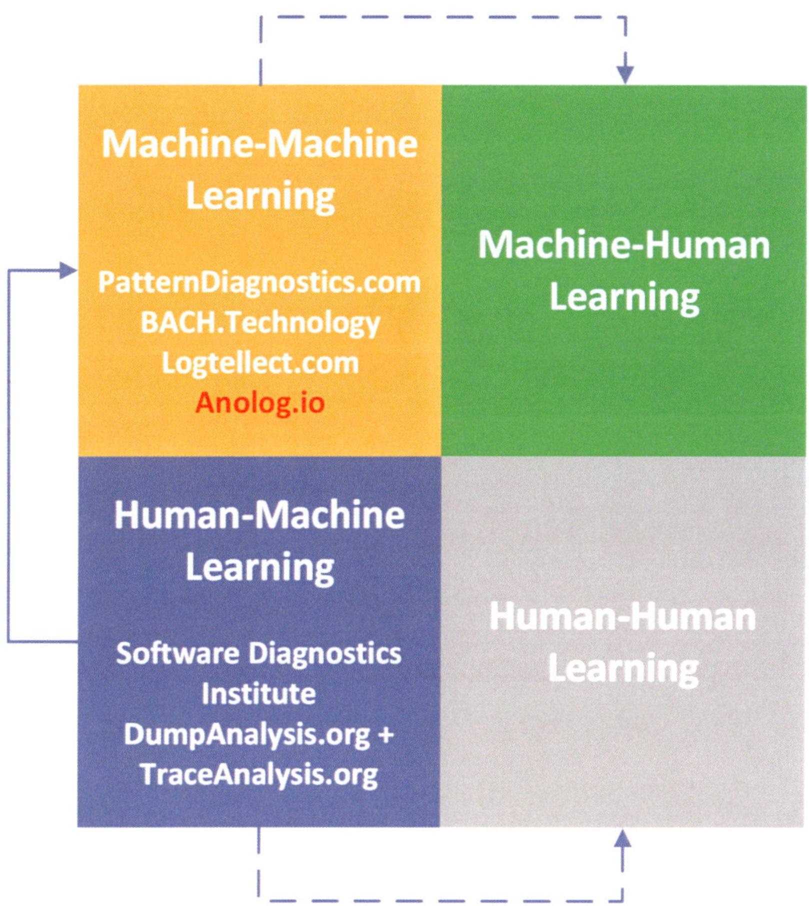

[This page is intentionally left blank]

Debugging and Category Theory

$$Debugging : \boldsymbol{T} \rightarrow \boldsymbol{Sets}_{\boldsymbol{DA+TA}}$$

What is debugging? There are many definitions out there, including analogies with forensic science, victimology, and criminology. There are also definitions involving set theory. They focus on the content of debugging artifacts such as source code and its execution paths and values. We give a different definition based on debugging actions and using category theory. We also do not use mathematical notation in what follows.

What is category theory? We do not give a precise mathematical definition based on axioms but provide a conceptual one as a worldview while omitting many details. A category is a collection of objects and associated arrows between them. Every pair of objects has a collection of arrows between them, which can be empty. So an arrow must have a source and a target object. Several sequential arrows can be composed into one arrow. We can even consider arrows as objects themselves, but this is another category with its new arrows between arrows as objects. If we consider categories as objects and arrows between these categories as objects, we have another category. So we can quickly build complex models out of that.

Can we build a conceptual model of debugging using objects and arrows? Yes, and it even has a particular name in category theory: a presheaf. So, debugging is a presheaf. To answer a question, what is a presheaf, we start constructing our debugging model focusing on objects and arrows. To avoid using mathematical language that may obscure debugging concepts, we use LEGO® bricks because we can feel the objects and arrows, and most importantly, arrows as objects[499]. This hands-on activity also reminds us that debugging is a construction process.

Debugging activity involves time. We, therefore, construct a time arrow that represents software execution:

We pick two **Time** objects representing different execution times:

In our **Time** category, an arrow means the flow of time. It can also be some indexing scheme for time events or other objects (a different category) that represents some repeated activity. Please note that an arrow has specific object indicators assigned to it. Different object pairs have different arrows. It is not apparent when we use black and white mathematical notation and diagrams.

We can associate with **Time** objects some external objects, for example, memory snapshots, or some other software execution states, variables, execution artifacts, or even parts of the same artifact:

Therefore, we have a possible mapping from the **Time** category to a possible category of software execution artifacts that we name **DA+TA** (abbreviated [memory] dump artifacts + trace [log] artifacts). **DA+TA** objects are simply some sets useful for debugging. The mapping between different categories is usually called a functor in category theory. It maps objects from the source category to objects in the target category. It is itself an arrow in the category that includes source and target categories as objects:

However, we forgot to designate arrows in the target **DA+TA** category. Of course, a different choice of arrows makes different categories. We choose arrows that represent debugging activities such as going back in time when trying to find the root cause, such as walking a stack trace. It is a reverse activity:

A functor that maps arrows to reversed arrows is called a contravariant functor in category theory:

Such a contravariant functor from a category to the category of some sets is called a presheaf. Now we look at debugging using software traces and logs as another target category of sets. With our **Time** category objects, we associate different log messages:

When we use log and trace files for debugging, we also go back in time trying to find the root cause message (or a set of messages) or some other clues:

Again, we have a presheaf, a contravariant functor that maps our **Time** category objects to sets of messages:

So, we see again that debugging is a presheaf, a contravariant functor that maps software execution categories such as a category of time instants to sets of software execution artifacts.

Trace and log analysis pattern catalog includes another example of the source and target categories candidates for a debugging presheaf, **Trace Presheaf** analysis pattern[500] that maps trace messages to memory snapshots (sets of memory cells or some other state information).

Presheaves can be mapped to each other, for example, from a presheaf of logs to a presheaf of associated source code fragments or stack traces, and this is called a natural transformation in category theory. It also fits with natural debugging when we go back in logs and, at the same time, browse source code or some other associated information sets.

Introducing Diags: Diagnostic Analysis Gestures and Logues

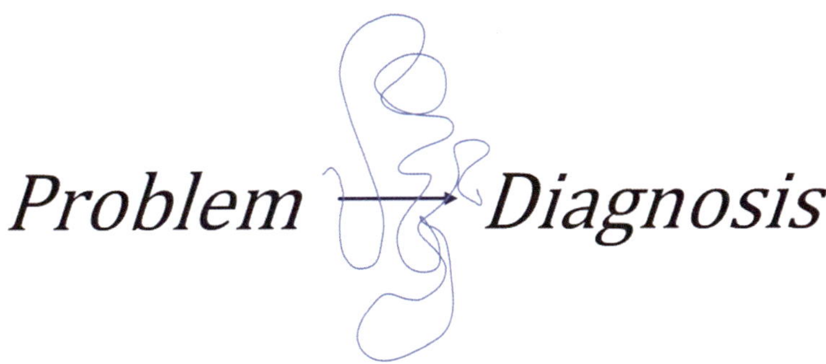

First, we introduce some definitions:

- A *diagnostic action* is a user interface action, a command, a technique, a diagnostic algorithm, a diagnostic analysis pattern.
- A *space of tools* is a collection of physical and virtual (mental, imaginary) tools at some physical or virtual (mathematical) distance from each other.
- A *configuration of diagnostic actions* is a directed graph (**di**graph) in a topological space of tools or a diagram in a category theory sense[501].
- A *diagnostic analysis gesture* (diag) is a configuration of diagnostic actions across the space of tools and time, resulting in a workflow of diagnostic analysis actions.
- A *diagnostic analysis hypergesture* is a gesture of diagnostic analysis gestures, a transformation of one gesture into another, between sets of tools, similar to porting diagnostic analysis patterns from one platform to another, for example, from Windows to Linux, or from one domain to another, for example, from logs to texts. We can view diagnostic hypergestures as diagnostic gesture patterns.

The "gesture" metaphor stems from the fact that despite recent automation efforts, the diagnostic analysis process is still manual when it requires substantial domain expertise. We still use various tools, graphical and command line (hand movements), and move in cyberspace. So, it is natural to combine all these physical and virtual movements into some abstract space path. There is also a question of diagnostic performance (in terms of achieving diagnostic goals) and repertoire (page 229). Diagnostic gestures also include tool improvisation, data exploration, action experimentation, and aesthetics as well (coolness, for example). Some gestures can be used to discover analysis patterns.

Different mathematical approaches can be used to formalize Diags and HyperDiags; for example, category theory like it was done for musical gestures [502] and homotopy theory for hypergestures [503]. For various perspectives on general gestures, please also refer to the opening chapters of The Topos of Music III[504].

Initially, years ago, we proposed thinking of diagnostic tools as arrows in a category of troubleshooting where objects are diagnostic artifact states (page 109). Diags approach considers tools as objects.

Second, diagnostic gestures (and gestures in general) may be described using narrative forms, and we propose some new terminology here.

A **log**ue is a narrative of diagnostic actions which that can be viewed as a langue[505] from theoretical linguistics. It is similar to logs in their structure and allows the application of the whole apparatus of software narratology[506] and trace analysis patterns[507] similar to higher-order pattern narratives, page 202.

The idea stems from viewing catalogs of analysis patterns as **cat-a-logs**, a category of logs (and other categories of diagnostic artifacts and their analysis patterns in general, page 271), and the difference in cata**log** and cata**logue** spellings.

Finally, we also have dia-logs and dia-logues, dialogic actions between diagnostic actors and logs (logues).

Volume 14

Introducing Methodology and System of Cloud Analysis Patterns (CAPS)

We wrote a short post about the added complexities of virtualization almost 15 years ago[508] and then about orbifold memory space (named cloud memory space initially) 10 years ago (page 132), reflecting cloud internals as a multi-VM/bare metal or multi-process distributed system.

At that time, memory dump analysis patterns[509] were added for several types of memory space, including fiber bundle (page 93) and manifold (page 96) memory spaces, and we also held a webinar on cloud memory dump analysis[510]:

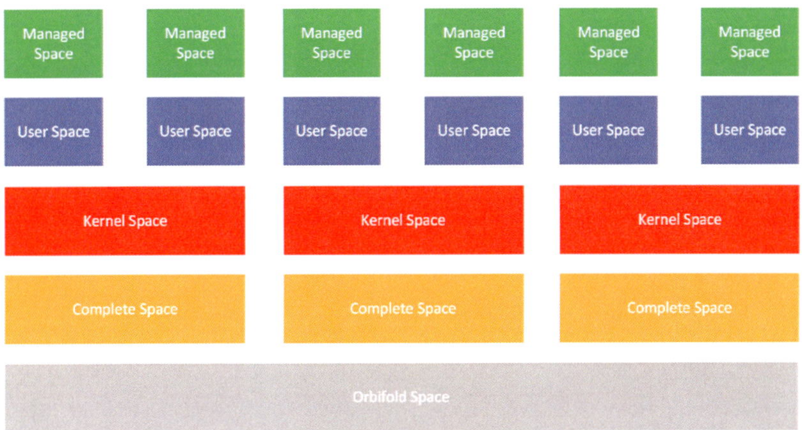

In addition to the process/kernel dichotomy, managed space abstracts runtime environments such as .NET CLR.

This picture of complete and cloud spaces is somewhat simplified as it does not reflect the complexities of hypervisor types and some nested spaces, as in Hyperdumps[511].

Also, at that time, trace and log analysis patterns[512] were being extensively developed and later split into general and special analysis patterns (page 206), resulting in the current overall picture:

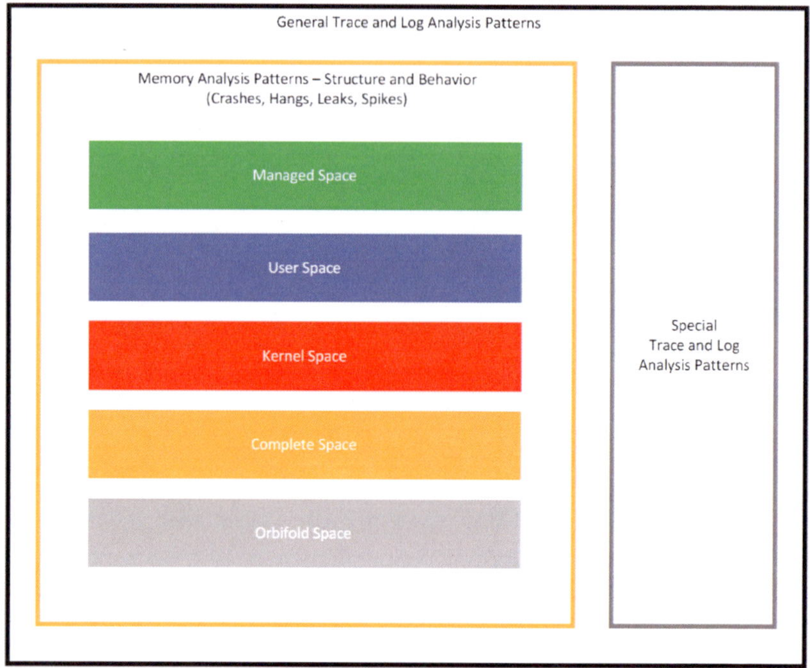

Memory dump types we can get from VM and traditional OS concepts such as threads and processes that span memory spaces are shown in this picture (spanning means that information about them can be found in all those memory dumps and associated spaces):

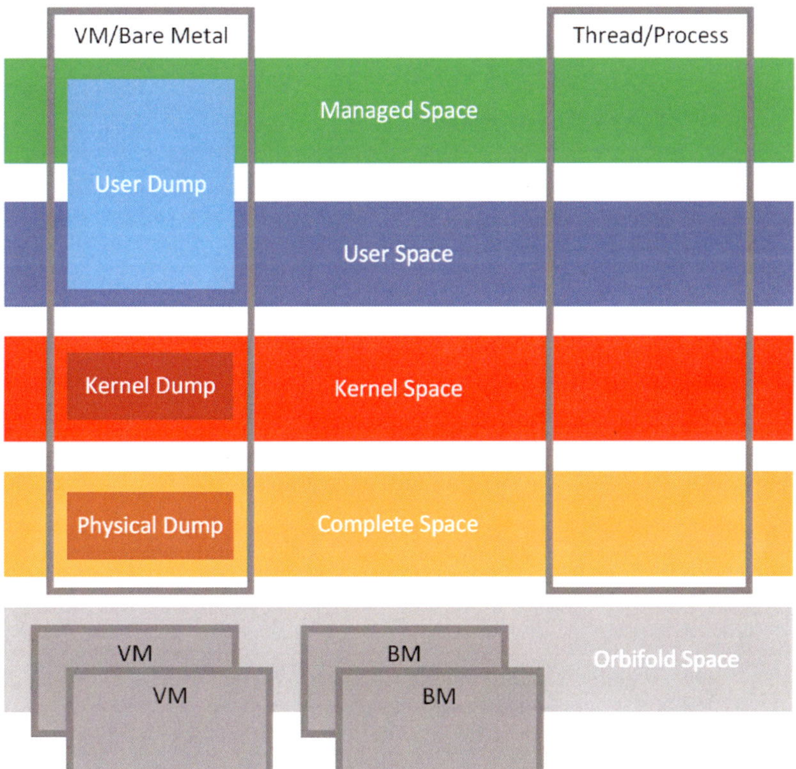

If we consider native cloud space as additional abstraction beyond the simple collection of memory spaces, we get the new native cloud memory space with corresponding cloud equivalents for traditional OS concepts:

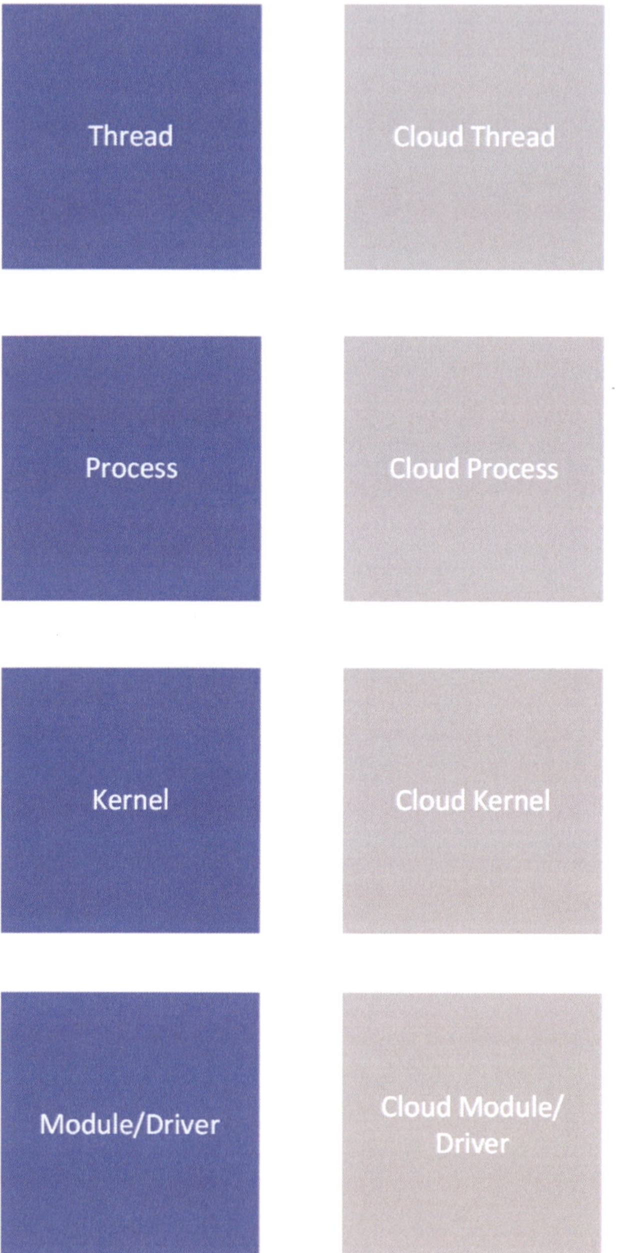

The advent of container orchestration platforms such as Kubernetes provides a similar hierarchy of concepts with containers corresponding to threads as units of execution, pods to processes as resource containers, kernel to control plane and kubelets, and operators to device drivers:

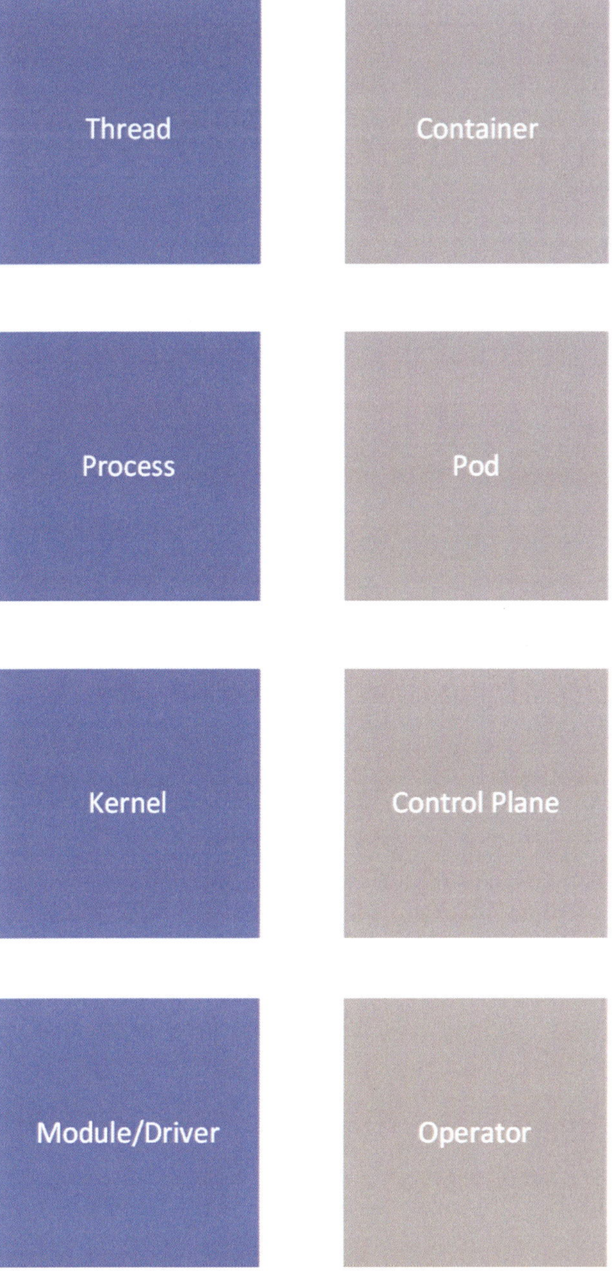

From the traditional memory perspective, Kubernetes concepts cut across the same spaces since they are implemented as collections of processes:

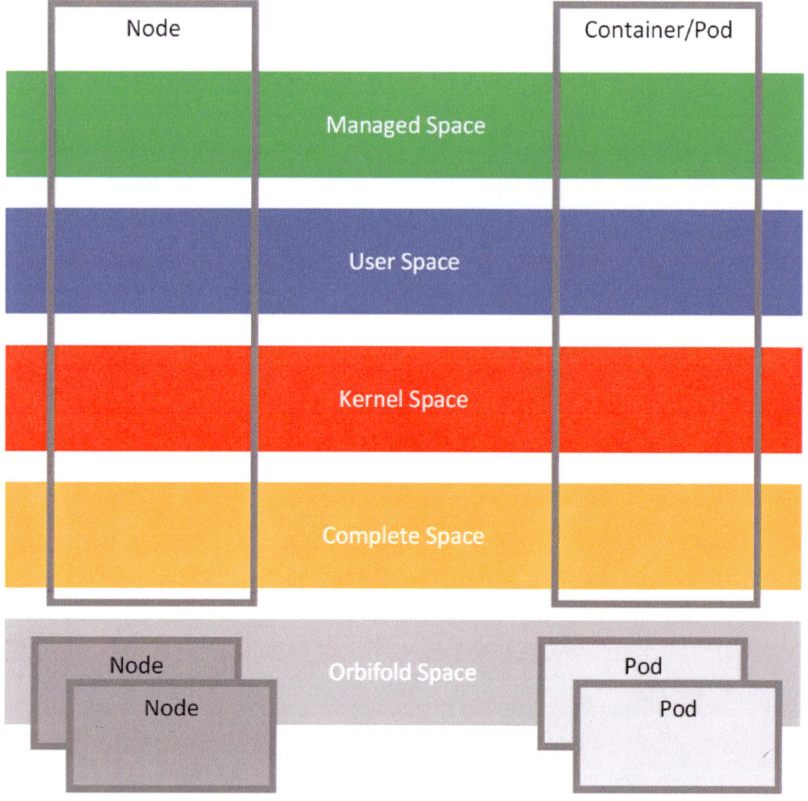

Our next step here is to adapt memory analysis pattern language to native cloud diagnostics and cloud problem analysis and provide analysis pattern specializations. The other part of software diagnostics, trace analysis pattern language, naturally extends to native cloud analysis, but from container environments, we recently discerned a few new log analysis patterns we plan to publish soon.

For the orchestration abstraction, we may add cluster space for nodes and pods in place of complete space and replace orbifold memory space with the native cloud space:

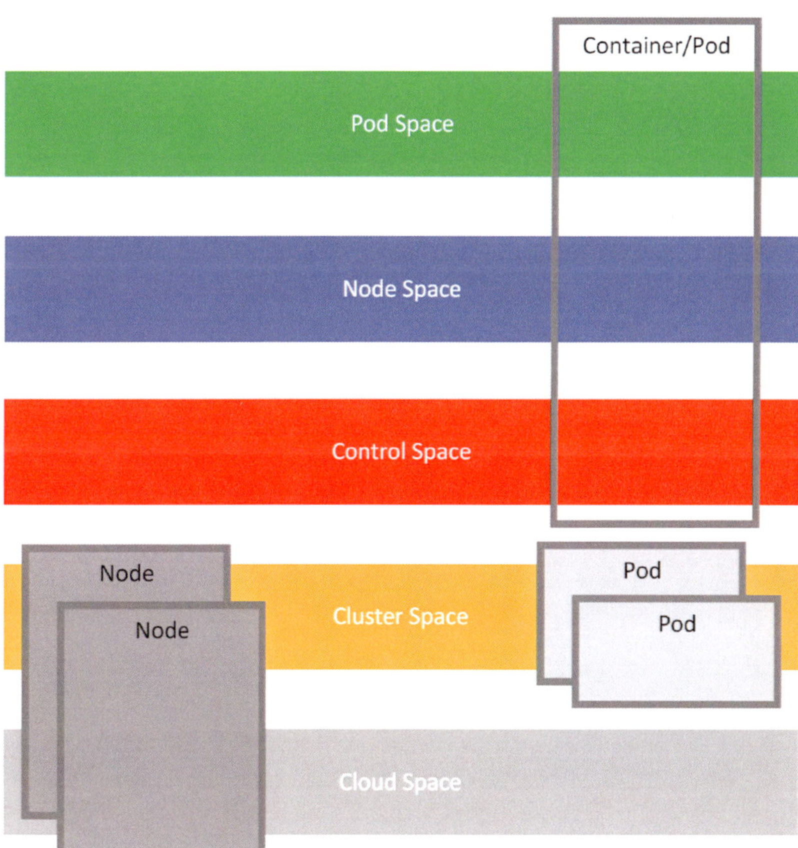

In the diagram above, nodes, containers, and pods have a different conceptual meaning instead of memory. They are more like spaces of relations between various objects/structures than spaces of objects/structures like memory spaces.

Now, having all these new abstract spaces, the next step is to consider this diagram where we replaced memory analysis patterns altogether with cloud analysis patterns:

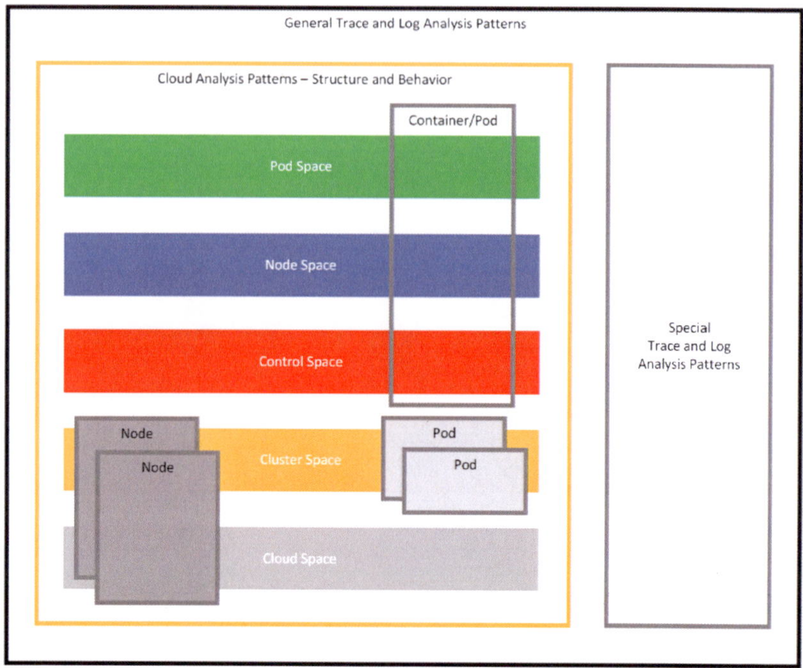

Memory analysis patterns are not gone but are at the lower level of abstraction, where individual spaces for cloud analysis patterns may require analysis of specific memory spaces if necessary. It is possible to represent both abstractions as **Trace Quilt**[513]:

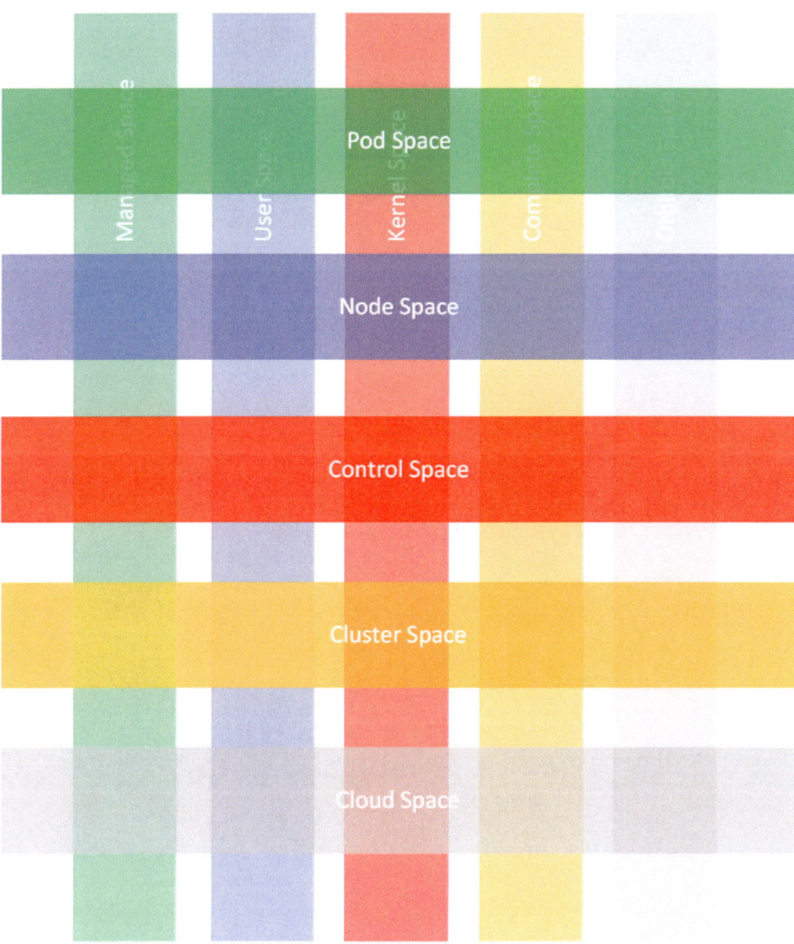

This description is preliminary and may have some modifications in the future. The corresponding analysis pattern language catalog is being developed now.

The Fractal Nature of Software Traces and Logs

Self-similarity of **Trace Shapes**[514] across sequences of trace runs, **Activity Regions**[515], trace messages, and parts of **Multidimensional Messages**[516] with the later adding fractional dimensions suggests analogies with fractals[517].

General Architecture of Analysis Pattern Networks

The system of diagnostic analysis patterns from Software Diagnostic Institute[518] was created for humans (page 316) and may appear too complicated for machines, although AI, machine learning, and data processing techniques may be used in individual computer-assisted pattern implementations. Fortunately, in theory, deep learning allows functional processing units of arbitrary complexity, and we can reuse its metaphors to propose a similar architecture but where all neurons in a layer perform different complex functions and use the same complex input. The output includes unmodified input plus the result of each neuron computation (enrichment). Some neurons may not produce any output given the set of data.

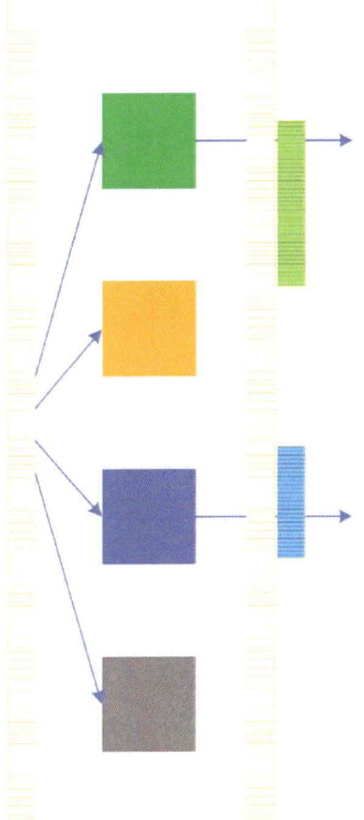

Concrete analysis patterns (page 216) as techniques (algorithms) to uncover diagnostic indicators can be represented as generalized complex data processing "neurons" interconnected like artificial neural networks.

Input data is a software execution artifact (or a set of them) such as a software trace and log, network trace, or memory snapshot. Each analysis pattern (AP) accesses the whole artifact data (no input neurons encoding data vector elements). Each AP processing enriches input data by adding another derivative artifact, artifact transformation, and the list of found diagnostic indicators (signs). Each AP from the next iteration processes the updated input data. Stateful AP may also store some other information for the next iterations (with or without data enrichment), and stateless AP may serve the role of pure transformation functions (operators). In summary, AP layers are identical but are fed with enriched artifacts for each iteration (backpropagation metaphor).

Links between AP from consecutive layers correspond to analysis and problem pattern sequences (schemas, page 81) known in advance (they may be the same between each consecutive pair of layers) and may also be built dynamically during iterations if correlations are discovered. Such links may also correspond to interfaces between AP components that query information from the previous iteration or ask for analysis services. The analysis report generator ("output neuron") may use the link "weight" matrix of discovered AP dependencies for further insight. Flagged AP "neurons" in the diagram below represent found diagnostic indicators and concrete problem patterns to be used either in subsequent iterations or during analysis report generation. We call this method and its corresponding architecture Analysis Pattern Network (APN).

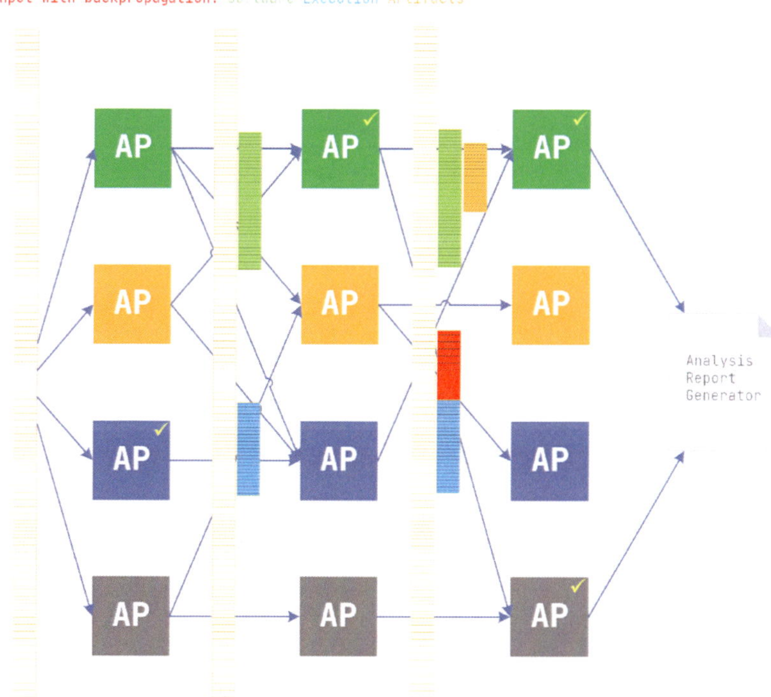

AP may be implemented using machine learning (ML), rule-based (RB), human-based (HB), and transformation-based (TB) techniques (page 275).

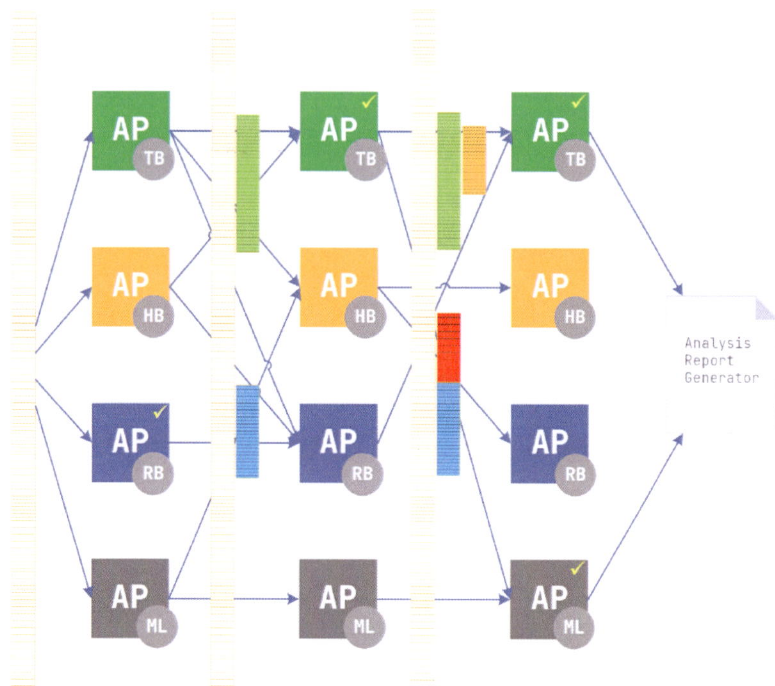

Different iterations may strategically use different implementation techniques based on pattern interconnections and enriched artifacts; for example, an AP during the first iteration used artifact transformation, during the second iteration used rule-based machine learning algorithm, and the third iteration required human introspection.

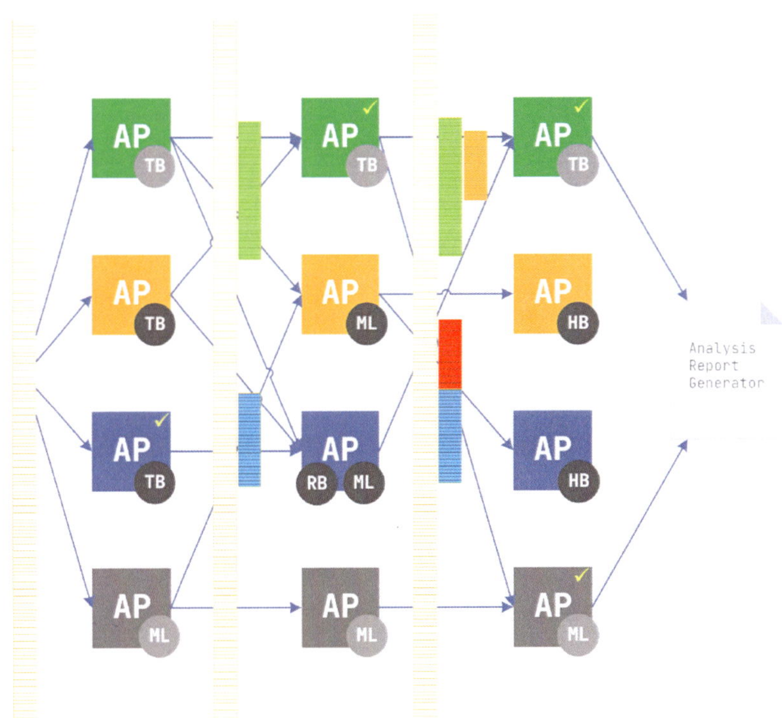

APN is an architectural pattern itself and is now added to our catalog of software diagnostics architecture patterns (page 178).

Software Narratives under Constraints

Software traces and logs are software narratives under constraints. As a metanarrative template, I chose a variation of narrative from "Exercises in Style" book[519] by Raymond Queneau:

> The software narrator "S" is a rule-based system tracing process, and it notices a long-running process that had loaded hat.dll and got into resource contention difficulties with another process. Two hours later, the software narrator notices the same process and a debugger process that gives some advice regarding the functionality of an extra GUI button.

Such constraints may be personal and organizational preferences and styles, programming language, execution environment, technology stack limitations, different coding phases (development, maintenance, early vs. mature code), external constraints such as source code scope, tracing and logging configuration, and rules, timing, the need for a quick debugging fix, or understanding program state and behavior.

Literary Theory Terms

The following are examples of mapping narratological and literary theory terminology to software narratology.

Ab ovo is a software story (for example, a trace or log, a problem description, see **Software Narratology Square**, page 147) that starts from the beginning of the use case events it narrates (see also **Use Case Trail** analysis pattern[520]) or the start of software execution (see also **Visibility Limit** analysis pattern[521]). Logging may start from some middle event of a use case, source code (see also **Declarative Trace** analysis pattern[522]), or a log may be a part of a larger full trace (see also a software narratological framework for **Presenting Software Stories**, page 121): **in medias res**. Such software stories may also have **flashbacks**, for example, stack traces, especially in software problem descriptions. Often, flashbacks are the only available software stories. Some tracing and logging sessions may be deliberately shortened to save space, communication throughput, or other reasons like security, similar to **abridged editions** of literary works (see also **Abridged Dump**[523] and **Missing Component**[524] analysis patterns). Such editions of software execution artifacts often hinder analysis (see **Lateral Damage** analysis pattern[525]).

Abstract is usually the summary of an artifact (see **Trace Summary** analysis pattern[526]) or not concrete description (see **Analysis Pattern Square** diagram, page 216).

Accent as stress in a line of verse has its correspondence to data in **Message Pattern**[527], which can be seen as a sequence of variables and **Message Invariants**[528].

Act as a play division corresponds to **Activity Regions**[529] (see also analysis patterns **Trace Partitioning**[530] and **Activity Theatre**[531]).

As the main story of a narrative artifact, **action** may involve a sequence of selected **Significant Events**[532], **Macrofunctions**[533], and **Activity Regions**[534] with **Motives**[535]. For example, in a software narratological framework for **Presenting Software Stories**, **action** is a sequence of selected messages that constitutes a software plot (an acquired software artifact that may not be complete/full due to **abridgment** like restricting tracing/logging to selected components).

Adaptation as interpreting an artifact as a different one (from one media to another, or a different structure) is similar to treating memory dumps as traces/logs or vice versa as in **Projective Debugging** (page 209).

Address as a story written for a specific group of people could be a software execution artifact explicitly acquired and adapted to some external users or **Declarative Trace**[536] messages crafted for a specific team in mind (see also **Embedded Comment**[537] analysis pattern).

Volume 15

The Dream of Quantum Software Diagnostics

We are adding quantum computing to our research agenda now by coining "Quantum Software Diagnostics" as a way to analyze different parts of very large software execution artifacts simultaneously, make sense of entire software traces and logs, and predict software behavior (software prognostics). It contains two adjoint phrases centered around Software: left adjoint Quantum Software Diagnostics and right adjoint Quantum Software Diagnostics. The former is about diagnosing quantum software, and the latter is about applying quantum methods to problems of software diagnostics.

In June 2009, we wrote about quantum memory dumps (page 71). Since then, we have added traces and logs, text, narrative, data to our pattern-oriented analysis approach. Now we broaden the application of quantum ideas and algorithms and add quantum information processing to our decades-long interest in contemporary mathematics, quantum theory foundations and applications to various domains, logic, semiotics, categories, and recently, in ML/AI, unconventional computing, conceptual mathematics, topos theory, and functional programming.

Systematic Software Diagnostics

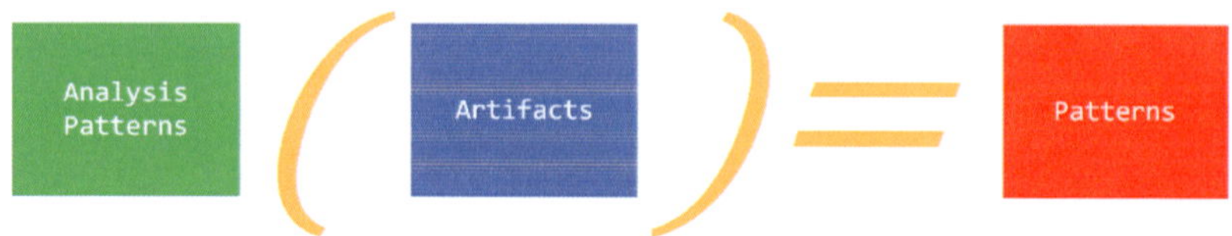

Systematic Software Diagnostics attempts to unify various disorganized and fragmentary individual software diagnostic approaches for software construction and post-construction phases.

Initially, when working on software diagnostics foundations, we recognized the need for systematicity by including some of our books and training courses in the Systematic Software Fault Analysis Series[538]. Over the following years, our many practical books became supplemented by theory and a series of seminars[539].

Now, after more than 15 years, coherent and complete theoretical, practical, and factual knowledge is systematically unified and ordered into pattern catalogs according to first principles after being integrated across individual observations as fully as possible at this time of the discipline development. In addition to systematicity, software diagnostics is also highly interdisciplinary and systemic, crossing boundaries of other disciplines. Its fundamental methodology is a pattern-oriented analysis of artifacts. Every artifact is considered a trace, log, text, and narrative[540]. Diagnostic analysis patterns, common recurrent analysis techniques and methods in specific contexts, organized into catalogs, are used to identify structural and behavioral patterns, common recurrent problems (sets of indicators, symptoms, signs) together with recommendations and possible solutions to apply in specific contexts.

Consider, for example, a typical diagnostic procedure called measurement. It is an analysis pattern[541] itself applied to artifacts or used to generate other artifacts to which analysis patterns are applied. Systematic Software Diagnostics is equally applicable to software development processes where the same analysis patterns are applied to development artifacts, repositories, documentation, management operations, monitoring, team structure, and dynamics. Even a diagnostic analysis is considered an artifact to apply analysis patterns (page 202). Where Systematic Software Diagnostic overlaps with other development and engineering activities, it offers additional pattern languages for software data analysis (page 265), troubleshooting (page 82), debugging[542], root cause analysis (page 239), performance analysis (page 195), writing tools (page 45), software[543] and memory forensics[544], memory dump analysis[545], network trace analysis[546], static[547] and dynamic malware analysis[548], reversing[549], vulnerability analysis (page 186), software internals (page 231), and cloud computing (page 333).

REPL Streaming (REPLS)

When we interact with a debugger, we use the so-called REPL, Read-Execute-Print-Loop (where we replace Eval in traditional REPL[550]). We type some command, it is executed by a debugger engine against a memory dump, the results are printed, and we repeat. However, the results can be streamed for further processing, for example, to automate certain analysis patterns, for example, **Structure Sheaves**[551] (as distributed logs), **Region Profiles**[552], and **Region Clusters**[553]. In the background, the stream processing results are provided back to the debugger Print phase (or in parallel as a further diagnostic aid).

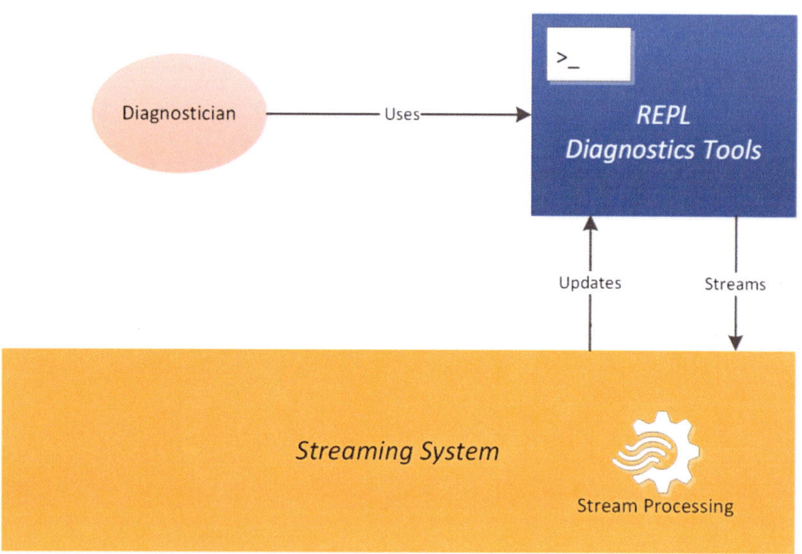

In the case of software traces and logs, streaming is a natural part of processing. But **CoTraces**[554] fit into REPLS (processed results can also form **Message Annotations**[555]) and, generally, **Diags** (page 331).

REPLS is an architectural pattern, and it is now added to our catalog of software diagnostics architecture patterns (page 178).

Dia|gram Language and Memory Dump Analysis Patterns

We illustrate trace and log analysis patterns using a graphical language named **Dia|gram** (page 251). When we analyze memory dumps, we get textual log output to which we can apply the same analysis patterns (page 206). Therefore, we can reuse the same **Dia|gram** language for memory dump analysis, for example, for analysis pattern illustrations. We start with the first memory dump analysis pattern, **Multiple Exceptions** (page 25). However, we now use some later analysis pattern names in the latter's description, for example, **Stack Trace Collection**[556] from multiple threads, which consists of **Stack Traces**[557] from individual threads.

Each individual thread stack trace can be illustrated using this trace diagram with an implicit time arrow but without time values:

If we knew individual stack trace frame timings, we could have assembled the normal trace diagram:

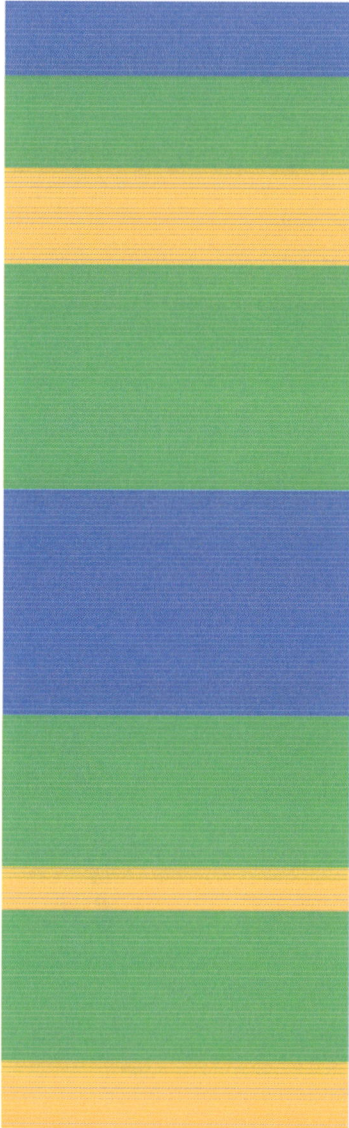

However, we can assemble the combined trace by gluing individual thread traces and sorting them by thread creation time (available in Windows memory dumps):

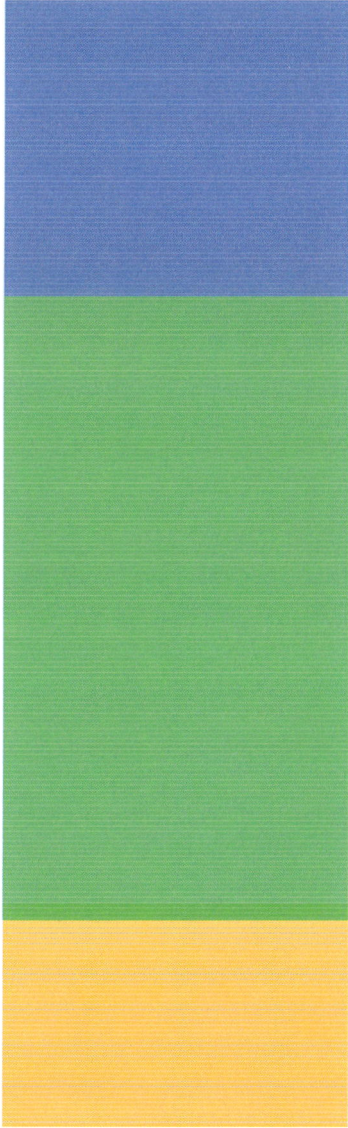

Additionally, we can impose sparse discrete time labels and structure via **Trace Schema**[558].

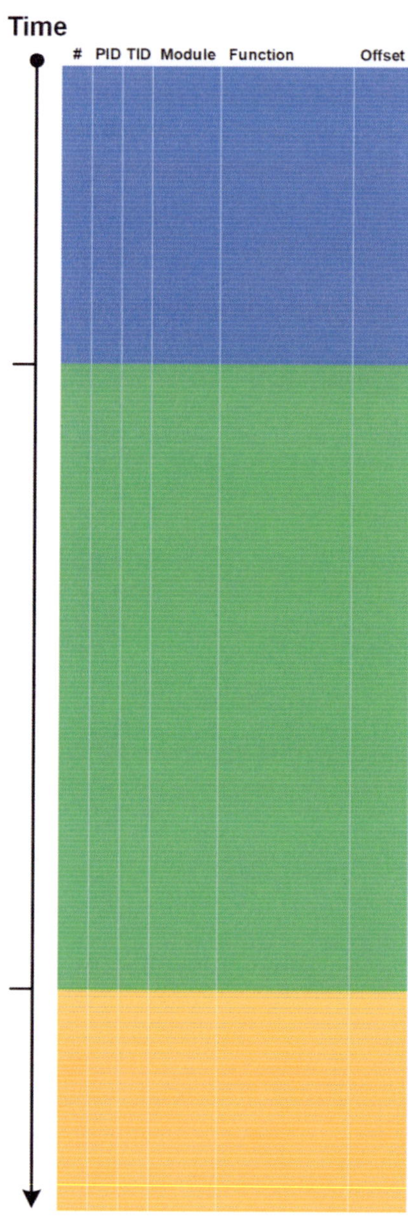

Having ATIDs, we can use the **Adjoint Thread of Activity** analysis pattern[559].

Since we know that top frames existed at the time of the memory snapshot, we can also group them at the end of the trace:

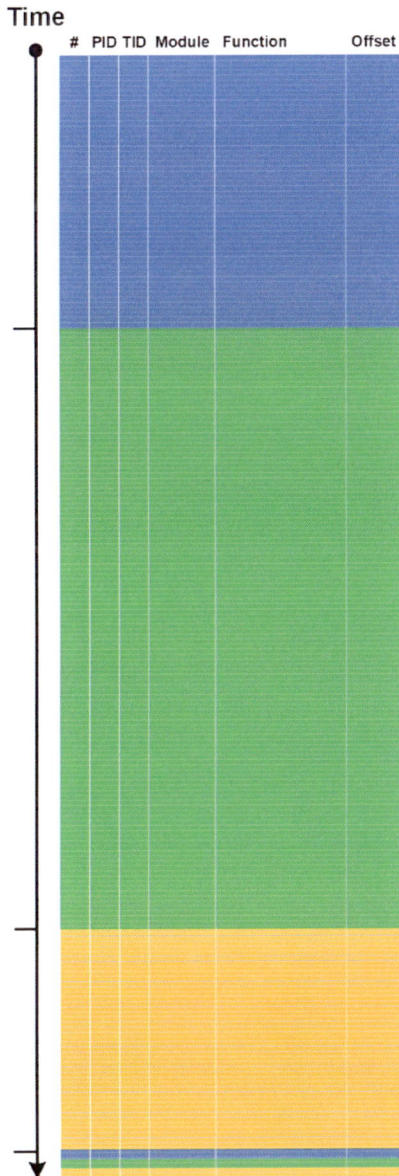

Exception indicators (like exception processing frames) can be highlighted as **Error Message**[560] and **Periodic Error**[561]. We can also use **Exception Stack Trace**[562]:

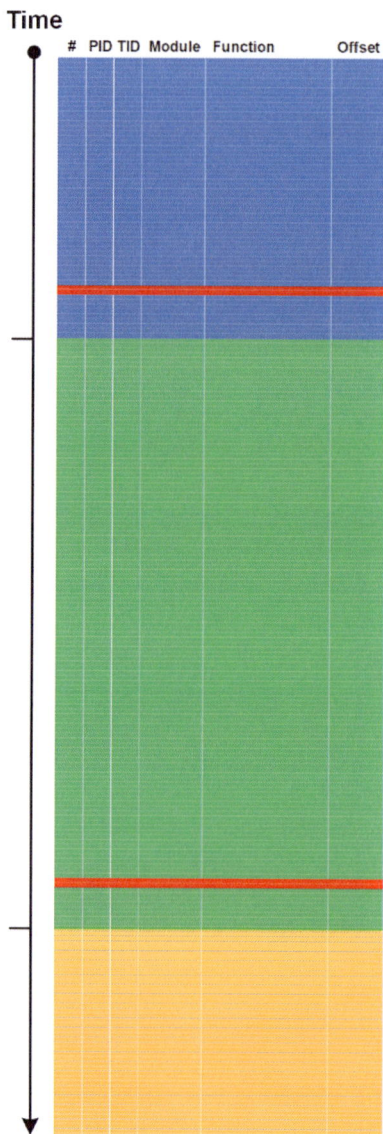

We can also add other debugger log output to such diagrams for **Intra-Correlation**[563].

Traces and Logs as 2-categories

In the past, we looked at software traces and logs as semigroups[564] or monoids[565] as a single object category. In the latter case, the monoid object is a trace or log, and arrows (morphisms) are trace messages.

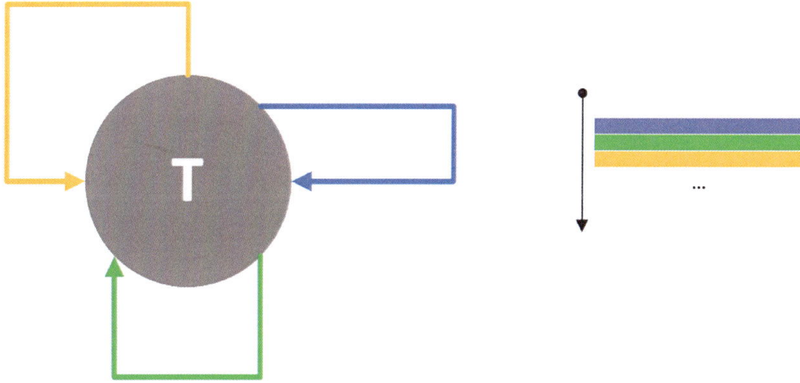

However, we can look at the traces and logs from another perspective. First, the monoid object is a system we trace, and messages are arrows. Then arrows between messages become arrows between arrows (2-morphisms[566]) in a 2-category[567].

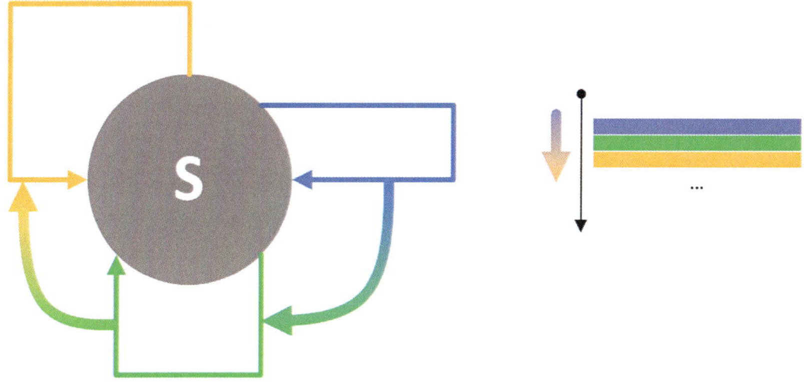

Therefore, we suggest looking at software traces and logs as 2-categories. Some forthcoming trace and log analysis patterns will use such a metaphor. For example, it provides some theoretical justification for the vertical and horizontal composition of traces and logs.

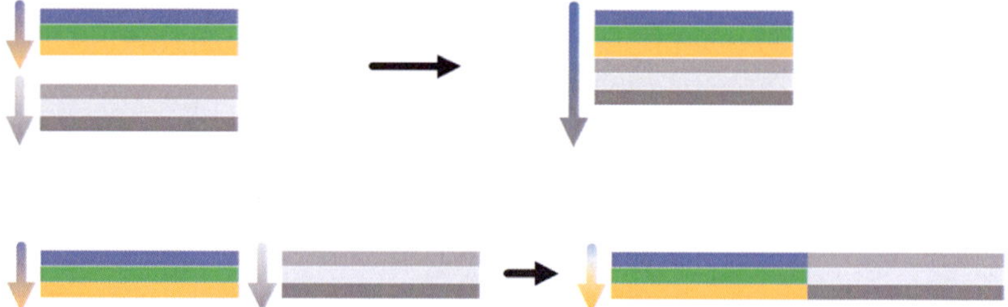

The horizontal composition type also allows the so-called whiskering[568].

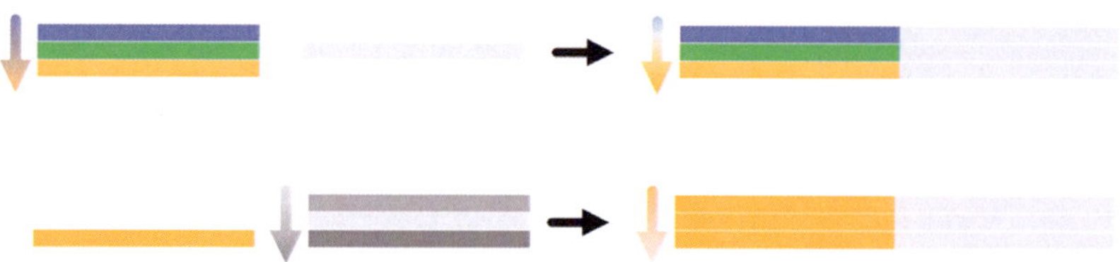

Diagnostics of Artificial Intelligence

DAIGNOSTICS

If wrong labels are ML bugs, then wrong answers are ML crashes.

We propose to define Diagnostics of AI as a combination of ideas and approaches from different disciplines such as software engineering, computer science, mathematics, physics, chemistry, biology, literary theory and criticism, narratology, semiotics, humanities, sociology, medicine, forensic science, psychology, psychiatry, and psychopathology with the following main directions of our research activities:

- Pattern-Oriented Software Diagnostics and Data Analysis (page 265)
- Systemic Software Diagnostics[569]
- Software Narratology[570]
- Software Pathology (page 305)

It is also important to differentiate diagnostics of artificial intelligence from diagnostics of artificial intelligence systems which is just software and hardware diagnostics, where diagnostics of AI may be just a part. Diagnostics of AI systems is metaphorically like medicine, whereas diagnostics of AI is like psychiatry and psychopathology.

Proof of Concept Engineering Patterns

Throughout my long software engineering career, I created countless PoCs, even during my 14-year technical support break. When you troubleshoot or debug a complex software post-construction problem, you may also need to do a quick PoC, for example, to create a simpler model of the problem case or write bad code[571]. This involves coding and, in general, software engineering practices. Of course, there were also many PoCs done from scratch to solve software construction problems, such as in software design and architecture. There are also security-related PoCs.

PoC engineering is very satisfying since you fully control all aspects of software construction and quickly get a working prototype.

When reflecting on and comparing all my PoCs, I see common recurrent problems solved by general solutions in specific contexts, and these observations prompted me to name these patterns and form a new pattern language. However, I avoid naming them PoC design patterns (or architectural patterns) since I believe normal architecture and design patterns should be used in PoC development.

Although PoC development goals may be similar to software project/product development goals, various constraints make PoC development a completely different process. Some PoC engineering principles would make a normal software engineering project a complete disaster but elevate PoC to success.

The first PoC engineering pattern I propose is called **In Vivo Development**. It is applicable when you need to use capabilities of some already existing project which can be your own or someone else's free one to extend. In such a case, instead of creating your own full-blown PoC project with a separate build system (or a new "make" file, for example) and files, you develop inside the already existing live project structure with little modifications, if all, to its structure (for example, file tree structure) and build system. You just do development inside the "live" system. By a living system, I mean not a running system but a project you can build and run. You immediately use new changes if the project is updated upstream while you develop your PoC. This in vivo style contrasts with a more detached in vitro development style where you create a new project structure with your PoC code and copy or reference required parts from a separate “living” project structure.

[This page is intentionally left blank]

Volume 16

Introducing Lov Language

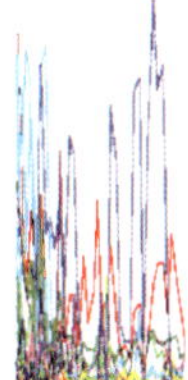

In the past, I paid little attention to traditional performance and system behavior visualizations, for example, for time series. My own visualizations included **Dia|gram** graphical language (page 251) for software narratives such as traces and logs[572] and, recently, memory snapshots (page 355). My latest exposure to open-source observability and visualization tools led me to think about how to describe patterns I see in a pattern language. It is easy to communicate what I see by just sending the picture, but often, we need to compare it to the previous observations or do some symbolic processing of such information.

I decided to tailor existing rich diagnostic analysis pattern languages I developed over the last +15 years into the **Language of visualizations** that I simply call the **Lov** language, my new old love of visualizations of software behavior (no pun intended). It is not a programming language but primarily a language for description and analysis; also, it can be used for hypothesis testing and simulation with the appropriate tool support. The initial inspiration for Lov comes from two dual activities: visualization synthesis for time series data and analysis of such visualizations. For a simple initial illustration, the visualization description above of CPU consumption for all processes in the system reuses the existing **Discontinuity**[573] for all PID **Adjoint Threads of Activity**[574] and **Blackout**[575] trace and log analysis patterns. We also see **Signals**[576] for **Counter Values**[577].

Carnot Cycle Metaphor for Trace and Log Analysis

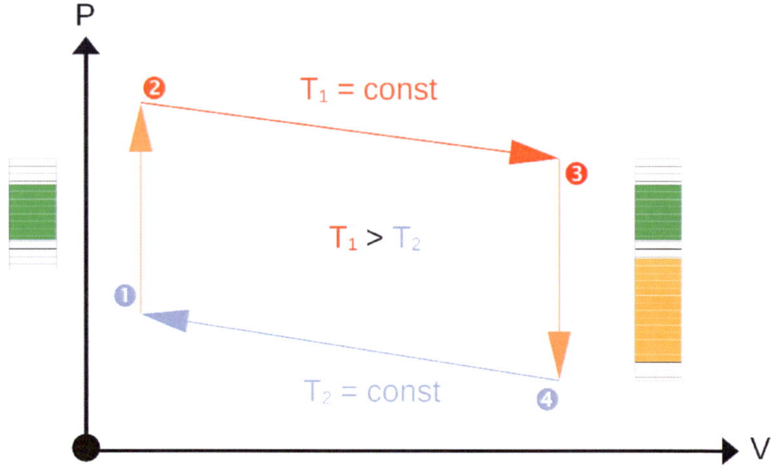

Recently, we added a few "thermodynamic" analysis patterns to our trace and log analysis pattern catalog, such as **Trace Volume**[578], **Trace Temperature**[579], and, finally, derived from an ideal gas equation metaphor, **Trace Pressure**[580]. These patterns allow us to employ a Carnot cycle[581] metaphor for a typical analysis cycle:

Initially, we have a low temperature (importance) for a low volume of traces.

1. During the incident, temperature (importance of traces) rises, triggering the rise in pressure.
2. The volume of collected traces increases during investigations, and the pressure may go up or down.
3. Once the problem is solved, the temperature comes down.
4. During this phase, we do a retrospective and gradually reduce the volume of traces necessary for continuous monitoring to their original volume.

Defect Mechanism Patterns (DMP)

In 2015, we introduced patterns-based root cause analysis methodology (page 239) by adding software problem mechanisms to accompany software diagnostic problems and their analysis patterns. We also planned to start populating the new pattern catalog at that time, but due to other developments and ideas, we have postponed it until now. We also plan to include a new pattern catalog and case studies in our modeling software defects course.

Usually, an identified software diagnostic problem may have several different mechanisms, and a mechanism may contribute to several diagnostic signs and symptoms. Knowing such mechanisms helps greatly in modeling a problem, devising a debugging strategy, and proposing a code fix.

We start with the **Spiking Thread**[582] memory analysis pattern, which has concrete analysis pattern variants for Windows, Linux, and macOS[583].

From its **Stack Trace**[584], we may identify the source code location. If the code uses some memory-intensive data structure, we may have an instance of **Inefficient Container Implementation**. Another mechanism to consider is **Partial Breaking Functionality**. The defect mechanism pattern names are provisional and may change as more patterns are added that require name revisions for generality, consistency, and perhaps just better names.

Inefficient Container Implementation is when a wrong container or flawed implementation is used for memory and CPU-bound code. For example, using a contiguous vector instead of a linked list may affect CPU resource consumption on insertions and deletions. Some containers, such as queues, may use underlying container implementations that can be replaced.

Partial Breaking Functionality is when we have a potentially infinite loop with checks for some conditions that prevent it from running forever. However, the list of such conditions is only partially implemented, leaving some conditions unchecked, which causes a real infinite loop with the detected CPU consumption.

Debugged! MZ/PE, Volume 2, Issue 1

Also available in print format in Debugged! MZ/PE: Multithreading, ISBN: 978-1906717834.

What is an Adjoint Thread?

Let's recall the definition of a thread from the Dictionary of Debugging[585]: A mapping T: t -> IP, where t is a discreet time arrow, and IP is a memory space (Instruction Pointer). The following diagram depicts a thread in an equi-bipartitional virtual memory space comprised of user and kernel spaces:

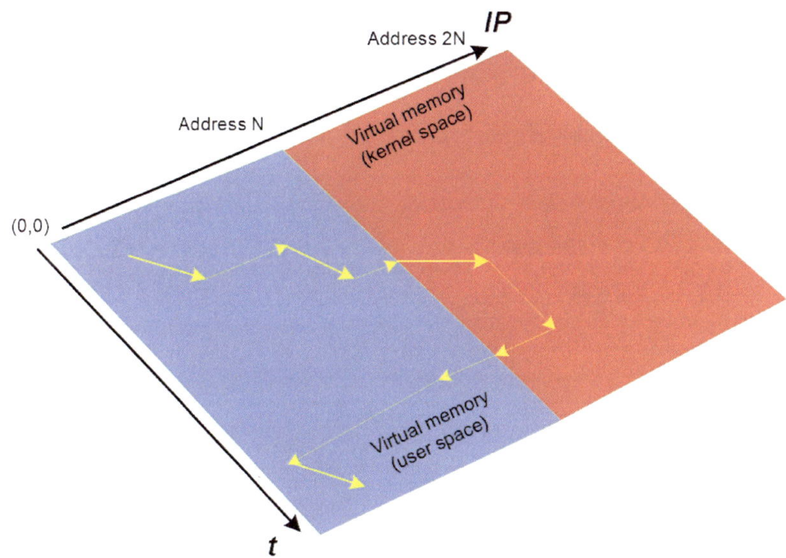

The following diagram depicts two threads running in parallel:

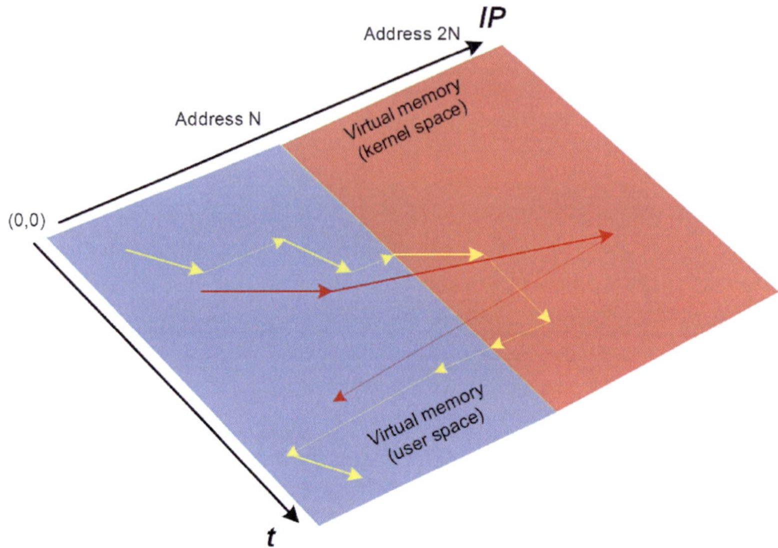

We select a certain module that has a fixed address range interval:

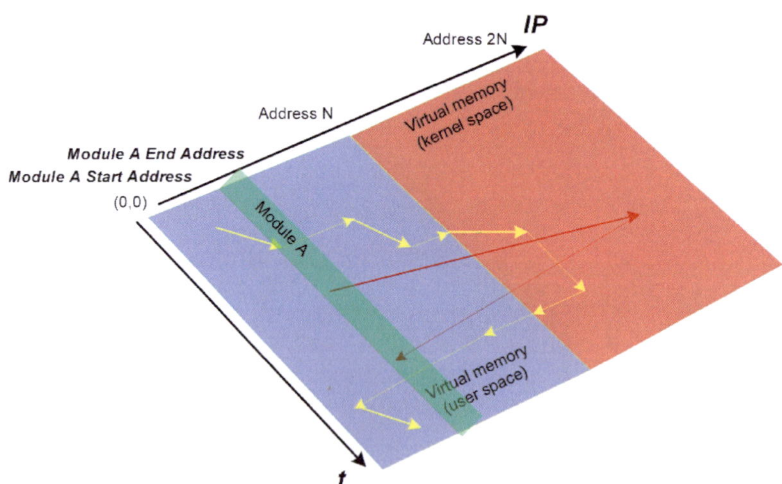

Now, suppose the source code corresponding to modules has trace statements that write trace messages whenever a thread passes through them. We put black dots in a diagram to show these trace points:

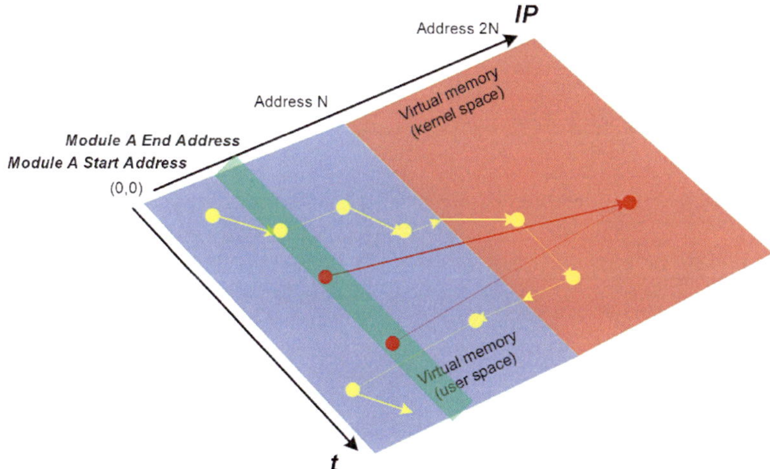

We also label these points according to the time and color where the latter corresponds to thread ID (TID):

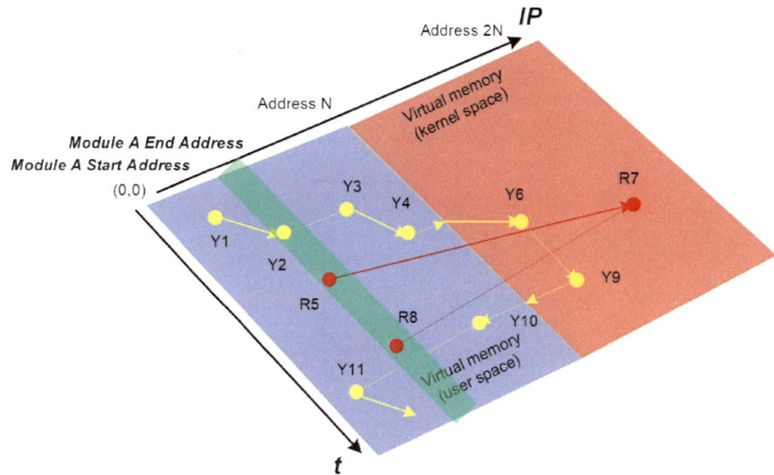

The full trace would look like this sequence of messages:

```
Y1
Y2
Y3
Y4 R5 Y6
R7
R8
Y9
Y10
Y11
```

If we restrict our messages to a particular thread, we get these thread sequences:

```
Y1
Y2
Y3
Y4
Y6
Y9
Y10
Y11
```

and

```
R5
R7
R8
```

However, if we restrict our space to only Module A, we get this sequence:

```
Y2
R5
R8
```

We call such restrictions (other than TID) adjoint threads. We can also restrict to a particular source code file, function, or even a trace message. Here is another illustration for a restriction by a process ID (PID) where black and red threads correspond to the same process:

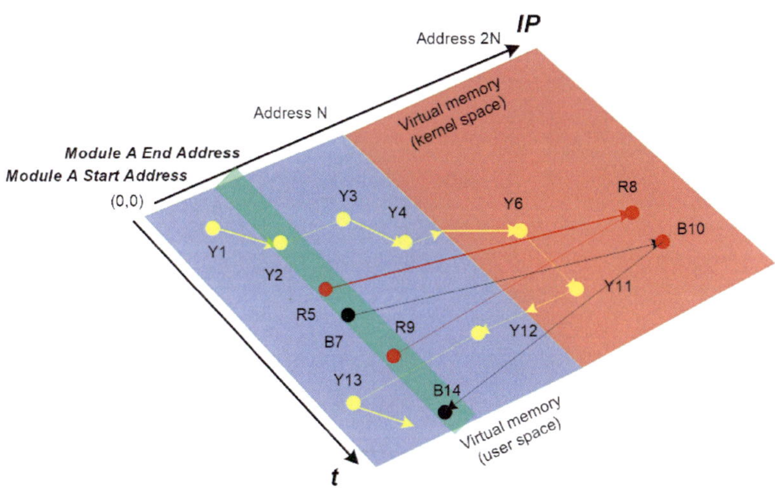

We get this adjoint thread:

```
R5
B7
R8
R9
B10
B14
```

Adjoint threads were introduced as an abstraction of particular software trace views. We can graphically view modules A and B as braid strings that "permeate the fabric of threads." We also call this multibraiding because by changing trace message filters, we can generate different adjoint threads:

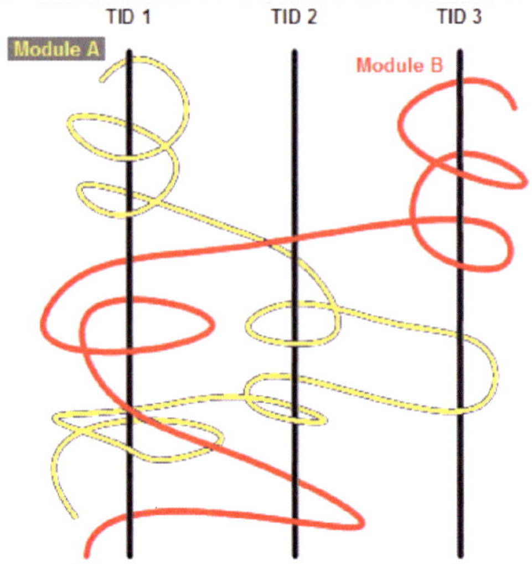
TID 1
TID 2
TID 3
Module A
Module B

Unpublished

Functionalist Trace Analysis

Based on the description of functional linguistics[586].

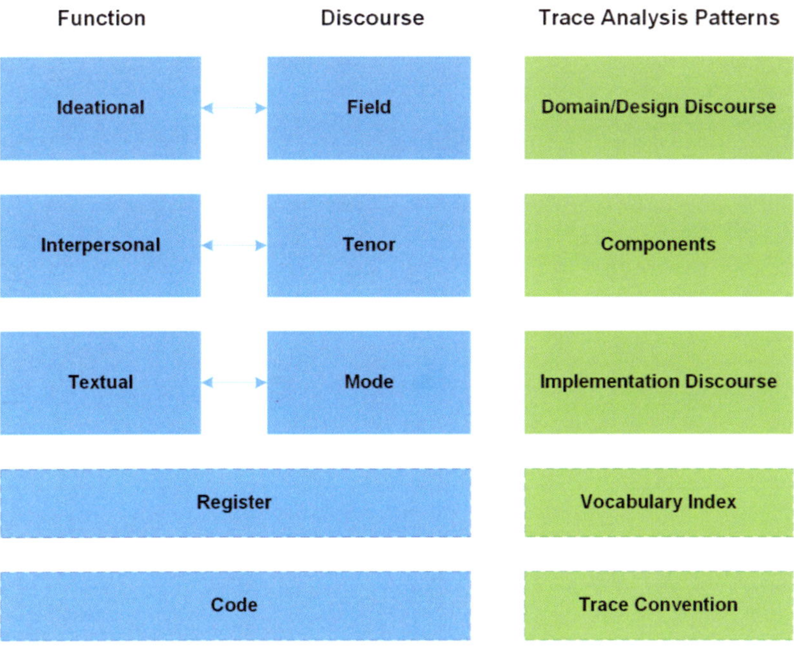

[This page is intentionally left blank]

Notes

MDAA – Memory Dump Analysis Anthology

---

[1] http://www.fallacyfiles.org/taxonomy.html

[2] Debugging by Thinking: A Multidisciplinary Approach (ISBN 978-1555583071)

[3] Why Programs Fail? (ISBN: 978-1558608665)

[4] MDAA, Volume 1, page 28

[5] Ibid., page 31

[6] Life Itself: A Comprehensive Inquiry into the Nature, Origin, and Fabrication of Life (ISBN: 978-0231075657)

[7] MDAA, Volume 1, page 269

[8] Ideas: A History of Thought and Invention, from Fire to Freud (ISBN: 978-0060935641)

[9] http://en.wikipedia.org/wiki/Delta_Debugging

[10] MDAA, Volume 2, page 440

[11] Component Software: Beyond Object-Oriented Programming, 2nd edition (ISBN: 978-0201745726)

[12] MDAA, Volume 1, page 395

[13] Ibid., page 409

[14] Ibid., page 457

[15] http://en.wikipedia.org/wiki/Narratology

[16] Software narratology should not be confused with computational narratology: http://www-cse.ucsd.edu/~goguen/projs/narr.html

[17] http://en.wikipedia.org/wiki/Bernhard_Riemann

[18] http://en.wikipedia.org/wiki/Multi-valued_function

[19] http://en.wikipedia.org/wiki/Riemann_surface

[20] http://www.dumpanalysis.org/windows-memory-analysis-checklist

[21] http://en.wikipedia.org/wiki/Iridium

[22] http://en.wikipedia.org/wiki/Quantum_computation

[23] http://en.wikipedia.org/wiki/Quantum_information

[24] http://en.wikipedia.org/wiki/No_cloning_theorem

[25] http://en.wikipedia.org/wiki/Ernst_W._Mayr

[26] MDAA, Volume 3, page 268

[27] MDAA, Volume 1, page 367

---

[28] MDAA, Volume 2, page 63

[29] The Variety of Software: The Richness of Computation (ISBN: 978-1906717544)

[30] The Road to Reality (ISBN: 978-0099440680)

[31] http://en.wikipedia.org/wiki/Feynman_diagram

[32] MDAA, Volume 3, page 381

[33] MDAA, Volume 4, page 169

[34] MDAA, Volume 1, page 257

[35] MDAA, Volume 3, page 236

[36] MDAA, Volume 2, page 177

[37] MDAA, Volume 1, page 490

[38] MDAA, Volume 2, page 184

[39] MDAA, Volume 1, page 419

[40] MDAA, Volume 3, page 97

[41] http://en.wikipedia.org/wiki/Workaround

[42] http://en.wikipedia.org/wiki/Injective_function

[43] MDAA, Volume 2, page 366

[44] http://en.wikipedia.org/wiki/Surjective_function

[45] http://en.wikipedia.org/wiki/Bijection

[46] http://en.wikipedia.org/wiki/Scientific_method

[47] Encyclopedia of Crash Dump Analysis Patterns: Detecting Abnormal Software Structure and Behavior in Computer Memory, Third Edition (ISBN: 978-1912636303)

[48] Trace, Log, Text, Narrative: An Analysis Pattern Reference for Data Mining, Diagnostics, Anomaly Detection, Fourth Edition (ISBN: 978-1912636327)

[49] MDAA, Volume 2, page 239

[50] http://en.wikipedia.org/wiki/Partially_ordered_set

[51] http://en.wikipedia.org/wiki/Category_theory

[52] Memory Evolutive Systems (ISBN: 978-0444522443)

[53] MDAA, Volume 4, page 46

[54] http://en.wikipedia.org/wiki/Fiber_bundle

[55] Trace, Log, Text, Narrative, Fourth Edition (ISBN: 978-1912636327)

[56] Looks like biology keeps giving insights into software, there is even a software phenotype[56] metaphor albeit a bit restricted to code and we need also an *Extended Software Phenotype*: http://en.wikipedia.org/wiki/The_Extended_Phenotype

[57] http://en.wikipedia.org/wiki/Adjoint

---

[58] MDAA, Volume 4, page 339

[59] http://www.dumpanalysis.org/care

[60] http://www.dumpanalysis.org/blog/index.php/2010/01/18/plans-for-the-year-of-dump-analysis/

[61] Encyclopedia of Crash Dump Analysis Patterns, Third Edition (ISBN: 978-1912636303)

[62] Trace, Log, Text, Narrative, Fourth Edition (ISBN: 978-1912636327)

[63] Encyclopedia of Crash Dump Analysis Patterns, Third Edition (ISBN: 978-1912636303)

[64] Trace, Log, Text, Narrative, Fourth Edition (ISBN: 978-1912636327)

[65] MDAA, Volume 3, page 387

[66] Ibid., page 388

[67] MDAA, Volume 6, page 311

[68] http://en.wikipedia.org/wiki/Category_theory

[69] Is There Any Life Inside Windows? MDAA, Volume 10, page 137

[70] MDAA, Volume 3, page 345

[71] Can be either a component-generated artifact or a component like a module or symbol file.

[72] Typical examples of memory system cultures are Windows, UNIX or even "Multiplatform".

[73] http://en.wikipedia.org/wiki/Chorography

[74] http://en.wikipedia.org/wiki/Chorology

[75] MDAA, Volume 1, page 409

[76] MDAA, Volume 2, page 239

[77] MDAA, Volume 5, page 235

[78] http://en.wikipedia.org/wiki/Literary_theory

[79] http://en.wikipedia.org/wiki/Plot_(narrative)

[80] http://en.wikipedia.org/wiki/Paratext

[81] http://en.wikipedia.org/wiki/Sujet

[82] Ibid.

[83] http://en.wikipedia.org/wiki/Discourse

[84] http://en.wikipedia.org/wiki/Intelligence_analysis

[85] Trace, Log, Text, Narrative, Fourth Edition (ISBN: 978-1912636327)

[86] MDAA, Volume 6, page 249

[87] http://www.PatternDiagnostics.com/files/Pattern-Driven-Software-Problem-Solving-Introduction.pdf

[88] http://www.PatternDiagnostics.com/files/FundamentalsCompleteDumpAnalysis.pdf (revised edition: http://www.PatternDiagnostics.com/files/Fundamentals-Physical-Memory-Analysis-Anniversary-Edition-Slides.pdf)

[89] http://www.patterndiagnostics.com/files/Software-Trace-and-Memory-Dump-Analysis.pdf

[90] http://en.wikipedia.org/wiki/Routine_activity_theory

[91] MDAA, Volume 5, page 120

[92] http://en.wikipedia.org/wiki/Principles_and_Parameters

[93] http://www.patterndiagnostics.com/files/Pattern-Driven-Software-Problem-Solving-Introduction.pdf

[94] http://en.wikipedia.org/wiki/Automatic_programming#Generative_programming

[95] http://en.wikipedia.org/wiki/Metaprogramming

[96] http://en.wikipedia.org/wiki/Orbifold

[97] http://en.wikipedia.org/wiki/Manifold

[98] The Old New Crash: Cloud Memory Dump Analysis (ISBN: 978-1908043283)

[99] MDAA, Volume 4, page 279

[100] Encyclopedia of Crash Dump Analysis Patterns, Third Edition (ISBN: 978-1912636303)

[101] Trace, Log, Text, Narrative, Fourth Edition (ISBN: 978-1912636327)

[102] MDAA, Volume 4, page 376

[103] http://en.wikipedia.org/wiki/Abduction_(logic)

[104] http://en.wikipedia.org/wiki/Philip_Marlowe

[105] Archaeology: The Basics (ISBN: 978-0415359757)

[106] http://www.dumpanalysis.org/Review+of+Debugging+by+Thinking

[107] http://www.PatternDiagnostics.com/files/Pattern-Driven-Software-Problem-Solving-Introduction.pdf

[108] MDAA, Volume 6, page 19

[109] Ibid., page 241

[110] MDAA, Volume 6, page 256

[111] Encyclopedia of Crash Dump Analysis Patterns, Third Edition (ISBN: 978-1912636303)

[112] Trace, Log, Text, Narrative, Fourth Edition (ISBN: 978-1912636327)

[113] MDAA, Volume 3, page 344

[114] MDAA, Volume 5, page 297

[115] Ibid., page 286

[116] MDAA, Volume 6, page 249

[117] http://en.wikipedia.org/wiki/Narreme

[118] MDAA, Volume 6, page 251

[119] MDAA, Volume 7, page 279

[120] MDAA, Volume 4, page 337

[121] Trace, Log, Text, Narrative, Fourth Edition (ISBN: 978-1912636327)

[122] http://www.patterndiagnostics.com/accelerated-windows-software-trace-analysis-book

[123] http://www.patterndiagnostics.com/accelerated-windows-memory-dump-analysis-book

[124] http://www.patterndiagnostics.com/accelerated-net-memory-dump-analysis-book

[125] http://en.wikipedia.org/wiki/Glossematics

[126] http://www.dumpanalysis.org/

[127] http://www.dumpanalysis.org/introduction-software-narratology

[128] http://www.dumpanalysis.org/STMDA-book

[129] http://www.dumpanalysis.org/pattern-driven-software-problem-solving

[130] Ibid.

[131] http://www.dumpanalysis.org/RADII+process

[132] http://www.dumpanalysis.org/introduction-pattern-driven-diagnostics

[133] Encyclopedia of Crash Dump Analysis Patterns, Third Edition (ISBN: 978-1912636303)

[134] Trace, Log, Text, Narrative, Fourth Edition (ISBN: 978-1912636327)

[135] First Fault Software Problem Solving: A Guide for Engineers, Managers and Users (ISBN: 978-1906717421)

[136] http://www.cs.utexas.edu/~witchel/pubs/pldi05ayers.pdf

[137] http://www.patterndiagnostics.com/debugging-diagnostics-revolution

[138] We could not find the valid article link at the time of this edition preparation.

[139] http://www.dumpanalysis.org/introduction-pattern-driven-diagnostics

[140] http://www.dumpanalysis.org/introduction-software-narratology

[141] www.dumpanalysis.org/pattern-oriented-network-trace-analysis

[142] MDAA, Volume 4, page 341

[143] MDAA, Volume 5, page 297

[144] Ibid., page 301

[145] Ibid., page 282

[146] Ibid., page 293

[147] Ibid., page 281

[148] MDAA, Volume 4, page 343

[149] MDAA, Volume 5, page 283

[150] http://www.dumpanalysis.org/pattern-driven-software-problem-solving

[151] http://www.dumpanalysis.org/introduction-pattern-driven-diagnostics

[152] http://www.dumpanalysis.org/introduction-systemic-software-diagnostics

[153] http://www.dumpanalysis.org/introduction-pattern-based-software-diagnostics

[154] http://en.wikipedia.org/wiki/Edmund_Husserl

[155] MDAA, Volume 5, page 301

[156] http://www.patterndiagnostics.com/

[157] http://www.patterndiagnostics.com/accelerated-windows-memory-dump-analysis-book

[158] http://www.patterndiagnostics.com/accelerated-net-memory-dump-analysis-book

[159] http://www.patterndiagnostics.com/accelerated-windows-software-trace-analysis-book

[160] http://www.dumpanalysis.org/introduction-software-narratology

[161] http://en.wikipedia.org/wiki/Static_program_analysis

[162] http://www.dumpanalysis.org/introduction-pattern-based-software-diagnostics

[163] MDAA, Volume 7, page 329

[164] http://www.patterndiagnostics.com/Training/Accelerated-Disassembly-Reconstruction-Reversing-Version2-Public.pdf

[165] http://www.debugging.tv/

[166] http://www.dumpanalysis.org/victimware-book

[167] http://www.dumpanalysis.org/introduction-pattern-driven-diagnostics

[168] http://www.dumpanalysis.org/pattern-oriented-memory-forensics

[169] http://www.dumpanalysis.org/introduction-pattern-based-software-diagnostics

[170] http://www.dumpanalysis.org/diagnostics-manual-software-problems

[171] MDAA, Volume 1, page 305

[172] http://www.dumpanalysis.org/victimware-book

[173] http://www.dumpanalysis.org/

[174] MDAA, Volume 4, page 343

[175] MDAA, Volume 7, page 288

[176] MDAA, Volume 5, page 283

[177] MDAA, Volume 6, page 243

[178] MDAA, Volume 4, page 345

[179] MDAA, Volume 4, page 348

[180] MDAA, Volume 5, page 281

[181] http://www.dumpanalysis.org/advanced-software-debugging-reference

[182] Accelerated Windows Debugging[3]: Training Course Transcript and WinDbg Practice Exercises, Second Edition (ISBN: 978-1908043894)

[183] Malware Narratives: An Introduction (ISBN: 978-1908043481)

[184] Pattern-Oriented Network Trace Analysis (ISBN: 978-1908043580)

[185] Software Trace and Memory Dump Analysis: Patterns, Tools, Processes and Best Practices (ISBN: 978-1908043238)

[186] Software Diagnostics: The Collected Seminars (ISBN: 978-1908043641)

[187] Pattern-Oriented Software Forensics: A Foundation of Memory Forensics and Forensics of Things (ISBN: 978-1908043696)

[188] Software Narratology: An Introduction to the Applied Science of Software Stories (ISBN: 978-1908043078)

[189] Software Diagnostics Institute: www.TraceAnalysis.org

[190] The Structure of Twitter Narrative: Applied Patterns from Software Narratology and Human-Computer Narratives (ISBN: 978-1908043610, not yet published)

[191] MDAA, Volume 4, page 341

[192] Ibid., page 348

[193] MDAA, Volume 5, page 281

[194] MDAA, Volume 7, page 283

[195] MDAA, Volume 8a, page 95

[196] MDAA, Volume 6, page 247

[197] MDAA, Volume 7, page 299

[198] MDAA, Volume 4, page 339

[199] MDAA, Volume 7, page 296

[200] http://www.dumpanalysis.org/introduction-software-narratology

[201] MDAA, Volume 4, page 341

[202] MDAA, Volume 5, page 282

[203] MDAA, Volume 6, page 244

[204] MDAA, Volume 7, page 296

[205] http://www.patterndiagnostics.com/Training/Accelerated-Software-Trace-Analysis-Part1-Public.pdf

[206] MDAA, Volume 8a, page 95

[207] MDAA, Volume 8b, page 61

[208] MDAA, Volume 8a, page 105

[209] Ibid., page 103

[210] MDAA, Volume 4, page 350

[211] MDAA, Volume 3, page 347

---

[212] MDAA, Volume 8a, page 37

[213] Ibid., page 39

[214] Ibid., page 43

[215] Encyclopedia of Crash Dump Analysis Patterns, Third Edition, page 1199 (ISBN: 978-1912636303)

[216] MDAA, Volume 1, page 343

[217] MDAA, Volume 2, page 319

[218] Trace, Log, Text, Narrative, Fourth Edition (ISBN: 978-1912636327)

[219] Accelerated Windows Debugging[3], Second Edition (ISBN: 978-1908043894)

[220] Encyclopedia of Crash Dump Analysis Patterns, Third Edition (ISBN: 978-1912636303)

[221] Software Narratology (ISBN: 978-1908043078)

[222] Pattern-Oriented Software Forensics, page 13 (ISBN: 978-1908043696)

[223] Ibid., page 14

[224] MDAA, Volume 4, page 337

[225] MDAA, Volume 1, page 267

[226] MDAA, Volume 8a, page 80

[227] MDAA, Volume 6, page 89

[228] MDAA, Volume 1, page 458

[229] MDAA, Volume 2, page 239

[230] MDAA, Volume 7, page 178

[231] MDAA, Volume 1, page 271

[232] Trace, Log, Text, Narrative, Fourth Edition (ISBN: 978-1912636327)

[233] Malware Narratives: An Introduction, page 14 (ISBN: 978-1908043481)

[234] MDAA, Volume 4, page 350

[235] MDAA, Volume 6, page 247

[236] MDAA, Volume 7, page 341

[237] http://www.DumpAnalysis.org + http://www.TraceAnalysis.org

[238] http://www.PatternDiagnostics.com

[239] http://www.DumpAnalysis.org + http://www.TraceAnalysis.org

[240] http://www.dumpanalysis.org/introduction-pattern-driven-diagnostics

[241] http://www.dumpanalysis.org/introduction-systemic-software-diagnostics

[242] http://www.dumpanalysis.org/introduction-pattern-based-software-diagnostics

[243] http://www.patterndiagnostics.com/training-courses

[244] http://en.wikipedia.org/wiki/Qualitative_research

---

[245] http://en.wikipedia.org/wiki/Qualitative_research#Coding

[246] Encyclopedia of Crash Dump Analysis Patterns, Third Edition (ISBN: 978-1912636303)

[247] Trace, Log, Text, Narrative, Fourth Edition (ISBN: 978-1912636327)

[248] http://www.dumpanalysis.org/blog/files/ArticodingExample.png

[249] MDAA, Volume 7, page 173

[250] Ibid., page 225

[251] Accelerated Mac OS X Core Dump Analysis, Second Edition: Training Course Transcript with GDB and LLDB Practice Exercises (ISBN: 978-1908043719)

[252] Pattern-Oriented Memory Forensics: A Pattern Language Approach (ISBN: 978-1908043764)

[253] Software Trace and Memory Dump Analysis (ISBN: 978-1908043238)

[254] Software Narratology (ISBN: 978-1908043078)

[255] Pattern-Oriented Network Trace Analysis (ISBN: 978-1908043580)

[256] Pattern-Based Software Diagnostics: An Introduction (ISBN: 978-1908043498)

[257] http://www.merriam-webster.com/dictionary/repertoire

[258] Introduction to Pattern-Driven Software Problem Solving (ISBN: 978-1908043177)

[259] Advanced Software Diagnostics and Debugging Reference http://www.dumpanalysis.org/advanced-software-debugging-reference

[260] Victimware: The Missing Part of the Equation (ISBN: 978-1908043634)

[261] Introduction to Pattern-Driven Software Problem Solving (ISBN: 978-1908043177)

[262] Pattern-Driven Software Diagnostics: An Introduction (ISBN: 978-1908043382)

[263] Pattern-Based Software Diagnostics: An Introduction (ISBN: 978-1908043498)

[264] Encyclopedia of Crash Dump Analysis Patterns, Third Edition (ISBN: 978-1912636303)

[265] Trace, Log, Text, Narrative, Fourth Edition (ISBN: 978-1912636327)

[266] http://www.dumpanalysis.org/files/SoftwareDiagnosticsCanvas.pdf

[267] Encyclopedia of Crash Dump Analysis Patterns, Third Edition (ISBN: 978-1912636303)

[268] Trace, Log, Text, Narrative, Fourth Edition (ISBN: 978-1912636327)

[269] http://en.wikipedia.org/wiki/Sequence_motif

[270] MDAA, Volume 7, page 329

[271] http://en.wikipedia.org/wiki/Motive_(algebraic_geometry)

[272] http://en.wikipedia.org/wiki/Structural_motif

[273] MDAA, Volume 4, page 345

[274] Ibid., page 348

[275] http://www.dumpanalysis.org/windows-memory-analysis-checklist

[276] MDAA, Volume 6, page 297

[277] Dynamic Memory Corruption, Encyclopedia of Crash Dump Analysis Patterns, Third Edition, page 315 (ISBN: 978-1912636303)

[278] MDAA, Volume 1, page 224

[279] Handbook of Technical Diagnostics: Fundamentals and Application to Structures and Systems, pp. 11 – 16 (ISBN: 978-3642258497)

[280] Introduction to Philosophy of Software Diagnostics, Part 1, page 7 (ISBN: 978-1908043571)

[281] Pattern-Oriented Software Forensics, page 18 (ISBN: 978-1908043696)

[282] A New History of the Humanities: The Search for Principles and Patterns from Antiquity to the Present (ISBN: 978-0199665211)

[283] Software Narratology (ISBN: 978-1908043078)

[284] Systemic Software Diagnostics: An Introduction (ISBN: 978-1908043399)

[285] Pattern-Oriented Network Trace Analysis (ISBN: 978-1908043580)

[286] http://3d-xplormath.org/

[287] MDAA, Volume 3, page 344

[288] Ibid., page 299

[289] MDAA, Volume 7, page 403

[290] The Riemann Programming Language (ISBN: 978-1906717605)

[291] http://mathworld.wolfram.com/RiemannSurface.html

[292] Pattern-Oriented Network Trace Analysis (ISBN: 978-1908043580)

[293] Trace, Log, Text, Narrative, Fourth Edition (ISBN: 978-1912636327)

[294] Encyclopedia of Crash Dump Analysis Patterns, Third Edition (ISBN: 978-1912636303)

[295] http://www.dumpanalysis.org, http://www.traceanalysis.org, http://www.patterndiagnosics.org

[296] http://riemann.io/

[297] http://www.dumpanalysis.org/diagnostics-scence

[298] Introduction to Pattern-Driven Software Problem Solving (ISBN: 978-1908043177)

[299] Introduction to Pattern-Driven Software Diagnostics (ISBN: 978-1908043382)

[300] Introduction to Pattern-Based Software Diagnostics (ISBN: 978-1908043498)

[301] Pattern-Oriented Software Forensics (ISBN: 978-1908043696)

[302] http://www.DiagWare.com

[303] http://www.PatternDiagnostics.org

[304] MDAA, Volume 4, pages 345 – 347

[305] Ibid., page 348

[306] http://www.patterndiagnostics.com/Training/Accelerated-Software-Trace-Analysis-Part1-Public.pdf

[307] Trace, Log, Text, Narrative, Fourth Edition (ISBN: 978-1912636327)

[308] MDAA, Volume 9b, page 11

[309] MDAA, Volume 8b, pages 132 – 134

[310] https://en.wikipedia.org/wiki/Profile_(UML)

[311] http://en.wikipedia.org/wiki/Theory

[312] http://en.wikipedia.org/wiki/Leo_Klejn#Theoretical_archaeology

[313] Software Diagnostics: The Collected Seminars (ISBN: 978-1908043641)

[314] Principles of Memory Dump Analysis: The Collected Seminars (ISBN: 978-1906717667)

[315] Extended Russian edition of Klejn L. S. Metaarchaeology (ISBN: 5-9259-0039-1) http://www.archaeology.ru/p15/t1503/l45/index.html

[316] Software Narratology (ISBN: 978-1908043078)

[317] https://en.wikipedia.org/wiki/Topology

[318] MDAA, Volume 9b, page 62

[319] MDAA, Volume 7, page 347

[320] Ibid., page 294

[321] Ibid., page 307

[322] MDAA, Volume 8b, page 67

[323] MDAA, Volume 5, page 347

[324] MDAA, Volume 9b, page 107

[325] Varieties of Graphs and Graph Models, Handbook if Discrete and Combinatorial Mathematics, pp. 509 – 512 (ISBN: 978-0849301490) See also https://en.wikipedia.org/wiki/Graph_(discrete_mathematics)

[326] MDAA, Volume 8b, page 78

[327] MDAA, Volume 1, page 419

[328] Trace, Log, Text, Narrative, Fourth Edition (ISBN: 978-1912636327)

[329] Encyclopedia of Crash Dump Analysis Patterns, Third Edition (ISBN: 978-1912636303)

[330] Pattern-Driven Software Problem Solving (ISBN: 978-1908043177)

[331] Software Diagnostics Institute, www.PatternDiagnostics.org (also www.DumpAnalysis.org + www.TraceAnalysis.org)

[332] Pattern-Based Software Diagnostics (ISBN: 978-1908043498)

[333] Pattern-Driven Software Diagnostics (ISBN: 978-1908043382)

[334] Systemic Software Diagnostics (ISBN: 978-190804339)

---

[335] Philosophy of Software Diagnostics, Part 1 (ISBN: 978-1908043573), pages 19 and 29

[336] B. Russo, The need for data analysis patterns (in software engineering), Perspectives on Data Science for Software Engineering (ISBN: 978-0128042069)

[337] WinDbg: A Reference Poster and Learning Cards (ISBN: 978-1906717292)

[338] MDAA, Volume 7, page 201

[339] http://en.wikipedia.org/wiki/Analog-to-digital_converter

[340] MDAA, Volume 2, page 457

[341] Debugged! Magazine, March, 2009 (ISBN: 978-1906717384)

[342] MDAA, Volume 5, page 296

[343] MDAA, Volume 7, page 294

[344] MDAA, Volume 8b, page 67

[345] MDAA, Volume 7, page 288

[346] MDAA, Volume 1, page 356

[347] MDAA, Volume 6, page 92

[348] Bart Jacobs, Introduction to Coalgebra: Towards Mathematics of States and Observation (ISBN: 978-1107177895)

[349] https://en.wikipedia.org/wiki/Category_theory

[350] MDAA, Volume 1, page 356

[351] https://en.wikipedia.org/wiki/2-category

[352] Pattern-Based Software Diagnostics (ISBN: 978-1908043498)

[353] https://en.wikipedia.org/wiki/Periodic_table

[354] Encyclopedia of Crash Dump Analysis Patterns, Third Edition (ISBN: 978-1912636303)

[355] http://www.dumpanalysis.org/ECDAP/Encyclopedia-Crash-Dump-Analysis-Patterns-Third-Edition-TOC.pdf

[356] MDAA, Volume 1, page 264

[357] MDAA, Volume 9a, page 130

[358] Trace, Log, Text, Narrative, Fourth Edition (ISBN: 978-1912636327)

[359] https://en.wikipedia.org/wiki/Dual_(category_theory)

[360] Communications of the ACM July 2005/Vol. 48. No. 7, pp. 87 – 92

[361] Common Mistakes, MDAA, Volumes 2 - 4, 6, 7

[362] Crash Dump Analysis AntiPatterns, MDAA, Volumes 1 – 4

[363] MDAA, Volume 1, p. 692

[364] Trace, Log, Text, Narrative, Fourth Edition (ISBN: 978-1912636327)

[365] https://en.wikipedia.org/wiki/Operad_theory

[366] Jean-Louis Loday, Bruno Vallette, Algebraic Operads, page vii (ISBN: 978-3642448355)

[367] Trace Analysis Patterns, Adjoint Message, MDAA, Volume 9a, page 90

[368] Trace Analysis Patterns, Braid Group, MDAA, Volume 10, page 57

[369] Trace Analysis Patterns, Braid of Activity, Ibid., page 69

[370] Trace Analysis Patterns, Cartesian Trace, MDAA, Volume 12, page 48

[371] Trace Analysis Patterns, Causal History, MDAA, Volume 13, page 53

[372] Trace Analysis Patterns, Causal Messages, Ibid., page 55

[373] Trace Analysis Patterns, Causal Chains, Ibid., page 56

[374] Crash Dump Analysis Patterns, Pointer Cone, Ibid., page 35

[375] Trace Analysis Patterns, Discontinuity, MDAA, Volume 4, page 341

[376] Trace Analysis Patterns, Message Cover, MDAA, Volume 7, page 347

[377] Trace Analysis Patterns, Critical Point, MDAA, Volume 12, page 37

[378] Trace Analysis Patterns, Shared Point, MDAA, Volume 7, page 341

[379] Trace Analysis Patterns, Defect Group, MDAA, Volume 13, page 49

[380] Trace Analysis Patterns, Trace Acceleration, MDAA, Volume 5, page 284

[381] Trace Analysis Patterns, Data Association, MDAA, Volume 7, page 344

[382] Trace Analysis Patterns, Trace D'Enfant, MDAA, Volume 13, page 58

[383] Trace Analysis Patterns, Activity Divergence, MDAA, Volume 7, page 352

[384] Trace Analysis Patterns, CoActivity, MDAA, Volume 15, page 70

[385] Trace Analysis Patterns, Collapsed Message, MDAA, Volume 15, page 58

[386] Trace Analysis Patterns, Equivalent Messages, MDAA, Volume 12, page 47

[387] Trace Analysis Patterns, Fiber Bundle, MDAA, Volume 7, page 294

[388] Crash Dump Analysis Patterns, Memory Fibration, MDAA, Volume 10, page 20

[389] Counterfactual Debugging, Dereference Fixpoints, MDAA, Volume 4, page 46

[390] Trace, Log, Text, Narrative: An Analysis Pattern Reference for Data Mining, Diagnostics, Anomaly Detection, Fourth Edition, page 122

[391] Trace Analysis Patterns, Trace Foliation, MDAA, Volume 13, page 67

[392] Trace Analysis Patterns, Fourier Activity, MDAA, Volume 9b, page 51

[393] Trace Analysis Patterns, Trace Field, MDAA, Volume 11, page 39

[394] Trace Analysis Patterns, Case Messages, MDAA, Volume 15, page 79

[395] Trace Analysis Patterns, Galois Trace, MDAA, Volume 10, page 66

[396] Trace Analysis Patterns, Causal History, MDAA, Volume 13, page 53

[397] Trace Analysis Patterns, Homotopy, MDAA, Volume 11

[398] Trace Analysis Patterns, Trace Path, MDAA, Volume 13, page 51

[399] Trace Analysis Patterns, Data Interval, MDAA, Volume 9a, page 99

[400] Trace Analysis Patterns, Trace Similarity, MDAA, Volume 12, page 57

[401] Trace Analysis Patterns, Glued Activity, MDAA, Volume 6, page 250

[402] Trace Analysis Patterns, Minimal Trace, MDAA, Volume 12, page 41

[403] Trace Analysis Patterns, Moduli Trace, Ibid., page 54

[404] Trace Analysis Patterns, Motif, MDAA, Volume 7, page 329

[405] Crash Dump Analysis Patterns, Stack Trace Motif, MDAA, Volume 10, page 42

[406] Trace Analysis Patterns, Motivic Trace, MDAA, Volume 11, page 48

[407] Trace Analysis Patterns, Trace Nerve, MDAA, Volume 15, page 75

[408] Structural Memory Patterns, Memory Region, MDAA, Volume 5, page 347

[409] Trace, Log, Text, Narrative: An Analysis Pattern Reference for Data Mining, Diagnostics, Anomaly Detection, Fourth Edition, Cord of Activity, page 70

[410] Trace Analysis Patterns, Event Sequence Phase, MDAA, Volume 8a, page 103

[411] Trace Analysis Patterns, Piecewise Activity, MDAA, Volume 7, page 333

[412] Trace Analysis Patterns, Poincaré Trace, MDAA, Volume 10, page 52

[413] Crash Dump Analysis Patterns, Thread Poset, MDAA, Volume 8b, page 43

[414] Trace Analysis Patterns, Error Powerset, MDAA, Volume 9a, page 94

[415] Trace Analysis Patterns, Trace Presheaf, MDAA, Volume 10, page 61

[416] Trace Analysis Patterns, Projective Space, Ibid., page 47

[417] Trace Analysis Patterns, Factor Group, MDAA, Volume 7, page 336

[418] Trace Analysis Patterns, Quotient Trace, MDAA, Volume 9b, page 62

[419] Trace Analysis Patterns, Trace Retract, MDAA, Volume 15, page 77

[420] Crash Dump Analysis Patterns, Rough Stack Trace, MDAA, Volume 8a, page 39

[421] Trace Analysis Patterns, Trace Field, MDAA, Volume 11, page 39

[422] Trace Analysis Patterns, Sheaf of Activities, MDAA, Volume 7, page 307

[423] Trace Analysis Patterns, Significant Interval, MDAA, Volume 11, page 50

[424] Trace Analysis Patterns, Message Complex, MDAA, Volume 15, page 65

[425] Crash Dump Analysis Patterns, Step Dumps, MDAA, Volume 7, page 173

[426] Trace Analysis Patterns, Structure Sheaf, MDAA, Volume 14, page 19

[427] Crash Dump Analysis Patterns, Stack Trace Surface, MDAA, Volume 9, page 22

[428] Trace Analysis Patterns, Tensor Trace, MDAA, Volume 10, page 70

[429] Trace Analysis Patterns, Ultrasimilar Messages, MDAA, Volume 11, page 35

[430] Trace Analysis Patterns, Hedges, Ibid., page 37

[431] Trace Analysis Patterns, Whisker Traces, MDAA, Volume 15, page 74

[432] Memory Dump Analysis Anthology Volume Set (http://www.dumpanalysis.org/advanced-software-debugging-reference)

[433] Pattern-Oriented Software Diagnostics Reference (http://www.dumpanalysis.org/pattern-oriented-software-diagnostics-reference)

[434] Pattern-Oriented Software Forensics (ISBN: 978-1908043696)

[435] Mobile Software Diagnostics (ISBN: 978-1908043658)

[436] The Old New Crash: Cloud Memory Dump Analysis (ISBN: 978-1908043283)

[437] Pattern-Oriented Memory Forensics, page 14 (ISBN: 978-1908043764)

[438] Systemic Software Diagnostics (ISBN: 978-1908043399)

[439] Introduction to Pattern-Driven Software Problem Solving (ISBN: 978-1908043177)

[440] Software Trace and Memory Dump Analysis (ISBN: 978-1908043238)

[441] Pattern-Oriented Network Trace Analysis (ISBN: 978-1908043580)

[442] Malware Narratives (ISBN: 978-1908043481)

[443] Pattern-Oriented Memory Forensics (ISBN: 978-1908043696)

[444] https://en.wikipedia.org/wiki/Blockchain

[445] Software Narratology (ISBN: 978-1908043078)

[446] https://en.wikipedia.org/wiki/Hash_chain

[447] MDAA, Volume 8b, page 87

[448] www.PatternDiagnostics.com

[449] MDAA, Volume 9b, page 49

[450] MDAA, Volume 5, page 281

[451] MDAA, Volume 6, page 244

[452] MDAA, Volume 7, page 296

[453] Ibid., page 346

[454] Ibid., page 288

[455] https://en.wikipedia.org/wiki/Category_theory

[456] Trace, Log, Text, Narrative, Fourth Edition (ISBN: 978-1912636327)

[457] Software Narratology (ISBN: 978-1908043078)

[458] http://www.DumpAnalysis.org + http://www.TraceAnalysis.org

[459] http://www.dumpanalysis.org/Software-Behavior-Patterns-Headline

[460] Jason McC. Smith, Elemental Design Patterns (ISBN: 978-0321711922)

[461] https://en.wikipedia.org/wiki/Dilemma

[462] MDAA, Volume 7, page 329.

[463] Ibid., page 299.

[464] MDAA, Volume 3, page 344.

[465] MDAA, Volume 7, page 290.

[466] Trace, Log, Text, Narrative, Fourth Edition (ISBN: 978-1912636327)

[467] Artificial Chemistries by Wolfgang Banzhaf and Lidia Yamamoto (ISBN: 978-0262029438). See also https://en.wikipedia.org/wiki/Artificial_chemistry for a very short introduction.

[468] https://en.wikipedia.org/wiki/Enzyme

[469] https://en.wikipedia.org/wiki/Law_of_mass_action

[470] MDAA, Volume 11, page 59.

[471] Malware Narratives: An Introduction (ISBN: 978-1908043481).

[472] Pattern-Oriented Network Trace Analysis (ISBN: 978-1908043580).

[473] https://en.wikipedia.org/wiki/Pathology

[474] Systemic Software Diagnostics: An Introduction (http://www.dumpanalysis.org/introduction-systemic-software-diagnostics)

[475] MDAA, Volume 8a, page 95

[476] https://en.wikipedia.org/wiki/Category_theory

[477] https://en.wikipedia.org/wiki/Olog

[478] Software Narratology: An Introduction to the Applied Science of Software Stories (http://www.dumpanalysis.org/introduction-software-narratology)

[479] Memory Dump and Live Memory Visualization and Picture Extraction (http://www.dumpanalysis.org/memory-dump-live-memory-visualization)

[480] https://en.wikipedia.org/wiki/Texel_(graphics)

[481] https://en.wikipedia.org/wiki/Voxel

[482] https://en.wikipedia.org/wiki/Pixel

[483] MDAA, Volume 7, page 339

[484] MDAA, Volume 6, page 251

[485] MDAA, Volume 12, page 66

[486] MDAA, Volume 7, page 288

[487] MDAA, Volume 11, page 52

[488] Process Monitor Log Visualized, MDAA, Volume 7, page 468

[489] MDAA, Volume 11, page 28

[490] MDAA, Volume 12, page 13

[491] https://en.wikipedia.org/wiki/Duality_(order_theory)

[492] MDAA, Volume 10, page 55

[493] MDAA, Volume 6, page 52

[494] MDAA, Volume 3, page 344

[495] MDAA, Volume 5, page 282

[496] MDAA, Volume 4, page 341

[497] Trace, Log, Text, Narrative, Fourth Edition (ISBN: 978-1912636327)

[498] Machine Learners: Archaeology of a Data Practice, by Adrian Mackenzie (ISBN: 978-0262036825)

[499] Visual Category Theory (https://www.dumpanalysis.org/visual-category-theory)

[500] Trace, Log, Text, Narrative, Fourth Edition (ISBN: 978-1912636327) (https://www.dumpanalysis.org/trace-log-analysis-pattern-reference)

[501] Visual Category Theory Brick by Brick, Part 3 (https://www.dumpanalysis.org/visual-category-theory)

[502] https://en.wikipedia.org/wiki/Musical_gesture

[503] The Topos of Music III: Gestures: Musical Multiverse Ontologies, Second Edition (https://www.springer.com/gp/book/9783319644790).

[504] Ibid.

[505] https://en.wikipedia.org/wiki/Langue_and_parole

[506] https://www.dumpanalysis.org/10-years-software-narratology

[507] Trace, Log, Text, Narrative, Fourth Edition (ISBN: 978-1912636327) (https://www.dumpanalysis.org/trace-log-analysis-pattern-reference)

[508] Dumps, Debuggers, and Virtualization, MDAA, Volume 1, page 516

[509] Encyclopedia of Crash Dump Analysis Patterns: Detecting Abnormal Software Structure and Behavior in Computer Memory, Third Edition (https://www.dumpanalysis.org/encyclopedia-crash-dump-analysis-patterns)

[510] The Old New Crash: Cloud Memory Dump Analysis (https://www.dumpanalysis.org/cloud-memory-dump-analysis)

[511] Hyperdump, MDAA, Volume 11, page 19

[512] Trace, Log, Text, Narrative: An Analysis Pattern Reference for Data Mining, Diagnostics, Anomaly Detection, Fourth Edition (https://www.dumpanalysis.org/trace-log-analysis-pattern-reference)

[513] Trace Quilt, MDAA, Volume 14, page 40

[514] Trace Shape, MDAA, Volume 13, page 61

[515] Activity Region, MDAA, Volume 4, page 348

[516] Multidimensional Message, Volume 14, page 37

[517] https://en.wikipedia.org/wiki/Fractal

[518] www.DumpAnalysis.org + www.TraceAnalysis.org

[519] https://en.wikipedia.org/wiki/Exercises_in_Style

[520] MDAA, Volume 8a, page 101

[521] MDAA, Volume 7, page 301

[522] MDAA, Volume 9b, page 49

[523] MDAA, Volume 5, page 88

[524] MDAA, Volume 2, page 233

[525] MDAA, Volume 1, page 264

[526] MDAA, Volume 13, page 52

[527] MDAA, Volume 9b, page 57

[528] MDAA, Volume 6, page 251

[529] MDAA, Volume 4, page 348

[530] MDAA, Volume 5, page 299

[531] MDAA, Volume 9b, page 58

[532] MDAA, Volume 5, page 281

[533] MDAA, Volume 7, page 283

[534] MDAA, Volume 4, page 348

[535] MDAA, Volume 7, page 329

[536] MDAA, Volume 9b, page 49

[537] MDAA, Volume 6, page 47

[538] https://www.opentask.com/systematic-software-fault-analysis

[539] Software Diagnostics: The Collected Seminars

[540] Trace, Log, Text, Narrative, Data: An Analysis Pattern Reference for Information Mining, Diagnostics, Anomaly Detection, Fifth Edition

[541] MDAA, Volume 15, page 56

[542] Accelerated Windows Debugging[4]: Training Course Transcript and WinDbg Practice Exercises, Third Edition

[543] Pattern-Oriented Software Forensics: A Foundation of Memory Forensics and Forensics of Things

[544] Pattern-Oriented Memory Forensics: A Pattern Language Approach

[545] Encyclopedia of Crash Dump Analysis Patterns: Detecting Abnormal Software Structure and Behavior in Computer Memory, Third Edition

[546] Pattern-Oriented Network Trace Analysis (ISBN: 978-1908043580)

[547] Accelerated Windows Malware Analysis with Memory Dumps: Training Course Transcript and WinDbg Practice Exercises, Third Edition

[548] Malware Narratives: An Introduction

[549] Accelerated Disassembly, Reconstruction and Reversing: Training Course Transcript and WinDbg Practice Exercises with Memory Cell Diagrams, Second Revised Edition

[550] https://en.wikipedia.org/wiki/Read%E2%80%93eval%E2%80%93print_loop

[551] MDAA, Volume 14, page 19

[552] MDAA, Volume 12, page 18

[553] Ibid., page 19

[554] Ibid., page 51

[555] Ibid., page 50

[556] Volume 1, page 409

[557] Ibid., page 395

[558] MDAA, Volume 14, page 50

[559] MDAA, Volume 5, page 283

[560] MDAA, Volume 7, page 299

[561] MDAA, Volume 3, page 344

[562] MDAA, Volume 4, page 337

[563] MDAA, Volume 3, page 347

[564] https://en.wikipedia.org/wiki/Semigroup

[565] https://en.wikipedia.org/wiki/Monoid

[566] https://ncatlab.org/nlab/show/2-morphism

[567] https://ncatlab.org/nlab/show/2-category or https://en.wikipedia.org/wiki/Strict_2-category

[568] https://ncatlab.org/nlab/show/whiskering

[569] https://patterndiagnostics.com/files/SystemicSoftwareDiagnostics.pdf

[570] 10 Years of Software Narratology, Volume 12, page 81

[571] https://www.dumpanalysis.org/writing-bad-code

[572] https://www.dumpanalysis.org/trace-log-analysis-pattern-reference

[573] MDAA, Volume 4, page 341

[574] MDAA, Volume 5, page 283

[575] MDAA, Volume 8a, page 97

[576] MDAA, Volume 11, page 45

[577] MDAA, Volume 7, page 288

---

[578] MDAA, Volume 16

[579] Ibid.

[580] Ibid.

[581] https://en.wikipedia.org/wiki/Carnot_cycle

[582] MDAA, Volume 1, page 305

[583] Encyclopedia of Crash Dump Analysis Patterns: Detecting Abnormal Software Structure and Behavior in Computer Memory, Third Edition (https://www.dumpanalysis.org/encyclopedia-crash-dump-analysis-patterns)

[584] MDAA, Volume 1, page 395

[585] Dictionary of Debugging, MDAA, Volume 11

[586] Functional Linguistics, The Routledge Linguistics Encyclopedia, 3rd edition, page 179 (ISBN: 978-0415421041)

www.ingramcontent.com/pod-product-compliance
Lightning Source LLC
Chambersburg PA
CBRC091941210326
41598CB00015B/877